FORT WORTH BETWEEN THE WORLD WARS

SUMMERFIELD G. ROBERTS TEXAS HISTORY SERIES

FORT WORTH BETWEEN THE WORLD WARS

Harold Rich

TEXAS A&M UNIVERSITY PRESS
COLLEGE STATION

First edition
This paper meets the requirements of ANSI/NISO Z39.48-1992 (Permanence of Paper).
Binding materials have been chosen for durability.
Manufactured in the United States of America

Library of Congress Control Number: 2020936948
ISBN-13: 978-1-62349-839-9 (printed case: alk. paper)
ISBN-13: 978-1-62349-840-5 (ebook)

It's in vain, Trot, to recall the past, unless it works some influence upon the present.

—Aunt Betsy Trotwood to David Copperfield
in *David Copperfield* by Charles Dickens

Contents

Preface

Fort Worth between the World Wars surveys Fort Worth's history from the close of World War I in 1918 to the start of World War II in 1939 using a topical format within a broad chronological division between the 1920s and 1930s. Readers of *Fort Worth: Outpost, Cowtown, Boomtown* will note that this begins when the earlier left off and uses similar resources and develops similar themes. Together, the two provide a broad study of the sixty years from 1880 to 1940 in which Fort Worth transitioned from a small town to an important city.

The twenty-plus years between the Versailles Conference in 1919 and the Japanese attack on Pearl Harbor in 1941 witnessed dramatic events with far-reaching consequences. Great issues such as Prohibition, the Great Depression, and rising world tensions reached every American city, but Fort Worth also faced unique regional and local trials. To the extent possible, a comprehensive approach was employed to present a broad-based discussion of most of the period's national issues as well as local topics and trends. Following World War I, Fort Worth dealt with exploding crime rates that abated but continued until the mid-1930s, presenting great challenges for local law enforcement at a time when the Fort Worth Police Department struggled with internal issues involving budget cuts, personnel upheavals, and technical innovations. Throughout the entire interwar period, Fort Worth also endured insidious racism, especially in the 1920s, when the Ku Klux Klan emerged as a blatant force exercising major political and social influence. Klan influence declined in the 1930s due to organized opposition as well as internal strife but still remained pervasive. In an environment of unrelenting racism, the ability of African Americans to survive and prosper represented a heroic display of strength and resilience. Fort Worth's city government fought to maintain services during lean budgets imposed by the dire economy of the 1930s but made an important advance by discarding the commission structure in favor of the city-manager form that continues to the present. Perhaps the biggest story of the era, the decline of Fort Worth's relative economic standing, remained largely hidden from view. Fort Worth entered the 1920s as the state's largest industrial producer but surrendered that position to Houston, which developed clear economic supremacy while Fort Worth experienced a clear economic downturn between 1920 and 1940. Throughout it all, Fort Worth's legendary vice culture continued unabated.

I owe gratitude and thanks to many educators, friends, and family who encouraged and supported me throughout. I most notably appreciate the efforts of Dr. Ben Procter and Dr. Todd Kerstetter of Texas Christian University. In *Fort Worth: Outpost, Cowtown, Boomtown,* I recognized my parents, Hugh and Edith Rich. I now acknowledge my son, Dr. Scott Rich, and my granddaughters, Aspen Elizabeth Rich and Emily Morgan Rich, in hopes they know what pride I have in them.

FORT WORTH BETWEEN THE WORLD WARS

PART ONE

From Versailles

Introduction

Fort Worth Enters the 1920s

Fort Worth entered the third decade of the twentieth century secure in its present and confident in its future. A severe cold front with subzero temperatures abbreviated celebrations on December 31, 1919—freezing Lake Worth so solidly that cars drove on its surface—but did little to dim expectations that the progress of the first two decades would continue. By 1920, Fort Worth had progressed from being an "also-ran" just twenty years earlier to having the largest economy of all Texas cities and to seeing its population grow from 26,668 in 1900 to 73,312 in 1910 and to 106,482 in 1920, a 400 percent increase that made Fort Worth the nation's sixty-fifth largest city and the fourth largest in Texas behind Houston (138,976), Dallas (158,976), and San Antonio (161,380). Tarrant County, Fort Worth's home, experienced similar growth, rising to become the state's third-largest county, trailing only Dallas County (home to Dallas City) and Bexar County (home to San Antonio) and becoming larger than Harris County (home to Houston). Over the next ten years, Fort Worth's population growth would slow but would still reach 163,447 by the 1930 Census, an increase of more than 53 percent. Statistics suggest that immigration rather than natural increases explained most of the added population. In December 1919, the Fort Worth Health Department reported 130 deaths and 162 births (5 classified as illegitimate), a small net increase of 32 persons that was consistent with the report for all of 1923, which showed 1,222 deaths versus 2,249 births—a gain of 1,027, or almost exactly 1 percent, and approximately one-fifth the average annual increase experienced in the 1910s. Most of the remaining

80 percent of new arrivals would have been native-born Americans. The 1920 Census listed only 7,359 foreign-born residents in Fort Worth, with Mexicans accounting for more than half (3,785) of these residents, followed by Russians (615) and Germans (459). Many of the internal immigrants would have come from approximately one hundred thousand soldiers who trained locally at Camp Bowie during World War I and the fifty-five thousand who mustered out there.[1]

Many of the pioneers most responsible for Fort Worth's remarkable growth would succumb to age and illness in the 1920s, creating a subtle changing-of-the-guard effect. William James was the first to go, dying on June 20, 1920. James became a major real estate developer of the east side after moving to Fort Worth following service in the Civil War with Quantrill's Raiders, where he fought alongside Jesse and Frank James and Cole Younger. He was dedicated to the lost cause, remaining an unreconstructed rebel who steadfastly refused to swear allegiance to the United States until the United States entered World War I, at which time James marched to the federal courthouse, swore an oath of allegiance, and then waved the flag in the streets (although even then he could not bring himself to abandon his hatred of Kansas). Ephraim M. Daggett, one of the earliest and most important settlers, followed on June 14, 1921, dying at home at 607 East Bluff Street. Daggett, who arrived in 1854, when the frontier lay just outside the meager settlement, helped drive out American Indians occupying much of the surrounding countryside and felled trees where the great packinghouses would open in 1903. Perhaps his most important contribution was the ninety-eight acres donated to help lure the Texas and Pacific Railway in 1876, Fort Worth's first railroad.[2]

One of the two men most responsible for Fort Worth's growth, Boardman Buckley Paddock (John Peter Smith was the other), died at home at 901 South Jennings Street on January 1, 1922, leaving behind his wife, Emily (who died on March 13, 1926), and a son, Will B. Paddock (who died in 1929 in Colorado Springs, where he had moved for health reasons). Paddock has often been cited as Buckley B. or Buckley Burton, but according to a family register printed in 1854 and a genealogical data study from 1944, he was born Boardman

Buckley Paddock, named for his father, Boardman, and his mother's maiden name, Buckley. For more than fifty years, Paddock served as mayor, newspaper publisher and editor, and state legislator, all the while tirelessly boosting Fort Worth to the extent that the *Fort Worth Press* recognized him as one of the six men who made Fort Worth a city (along with John Peter Smith, K. M. Van Zandt, Joseph H. Brown, B. C. Evans, and Walter Huffman). Paddock was born in 1844 in Cleveland, Ohio, but moved to Mississippi and served as an officer in the Confederate Army (his father served in the Union Army, dying from wounds received at the Battle of Vicksburg in 1863, a battle his son also fought). As the war neared its end, Paddock refused to accept defeat, proclaiming he would die before surrendering to the hated Yankees. He wrote his fiancée, Emily Harper, of plans to form a guerilla unit of eighty of the unit's bravest soldiers to continue the fight in Kentucky. Paddock's chain of command, reluctant to see their dwindling force further reduced, ordered him to cease preparations. Still, Paddock persisted, even after facing threats of a court-martial, writing Emily that he was certain his honor would be redeemed after a few daring exploits. Eventually, Paddock abandoned the plan and surrendered, returning to Mississippi to marry Emily.[3]

In 1872, Paddock left home and family to search for a likely spot to relocate. He traveled west, looking over Louisiana before moving on to Texas, which he described as rough but with land as rich as Louisiana. Paddock first visited McKinney and Dallas, describing the former as too slow and the latter as overgrown and so full of itself that it needed to come down, but he was charmed by Fort Worth. Exactly how he saw such promise in a small, raw village without a railroad is not clear, but he wrote glowingly of its potential, telling Emily that it was known to be a "coming place" destined to be a city. He may have been influenced by a director of the Texas and Pacific Railway named Throckmorton, who promised that the company would build machine shops that would turn Fort Worth into a major railroad center. Convinced of great potential, Paddock settled, taking over the *Democrat*, a local newspaper that became his principal organ in promoting Fort Worth. Things went so well at first that he soon expressed concerns that development had become too rapid, writing Emily (still back in Mississippi) in 1873 that demand had driven up the price of lumber so much that he would delay starting construction of their home until the railroad arrived, hoping that increased access would lower costs. Those hopes, along with hopes for a railhead, crashed in the Panic of 1873, a national depression that stifled the economy and left Fort Worth so dormant that a Baptist preacher named Fitzgerald living at Houston and Weatherford Streets reportedly found impressions of a panther's paw and body in the middle of Weatherford, then a dirt road. Fitzgerald showed the prints to Howard Peak and Bob Cowart, a lawyer who also wrote for the *Dallas Weekly Herald* and who used the report to illustrate Fort Worth's lack of activity, forever leaving Fort Worth with the nickname "Panther City." The local economy soon revived, bringing the railroad in 1876, and continued growing, with some stops and starts, while Paddock worked to make Fort Worth a great city.[4]

Other notable deaths included Captain Samuel Burk Burnet, who succumbed at his home, 1424 Summit Avenue, on June 27, 1922. Burnet, who was born in 1849 and arrived in Texas when he was eight, built a huge ranch, gathering thirty thousand acres by the time he was twenty-six and then buying the 6666 Ranch, a massive spread covering two hundred thousand acres in King County, and the Dixon Creek Ranch, with one hundred thousand acres in Carson County. Shortly before Burnet died, drillers found oil on the Dixon Creek property, adding to an already sizable estate. His widow, Mary Couts Burnet, inherited a fortune that included one-half the 6666 Ranch and one-fourth of twelve thousand acres in Wichita County, both with substantial oil production. Mrs. Burnet became an early and important benefactor to Texas Christian University (TCU), immediately gifting one-fourth of her estate, with the remainder transferred on her death (the TCU library is named for her). Captain Burnet disinherited his son, Tom, but left his daughter, Anna Burnet, nineteen, an annual stipend of $15,000 until she turned twenty-five, at which time she received the bulk of the estate, valued at $20 million. In September 1922 in New York City, Anna married Guy L. Waggoner, thirty-eight and the grandson of Dan Waggoner, who had settled in Wise County (thirty miles northeast of Fort Worth) in the 1850s and built a ranching empire that spanned six counties and eight hundred square miles, the largest ranch contained in one fence. Like much of West Texas, Waggoner's land was largely arid, offering insufficient surface water to sustain great herds of cattle, which forced him to dig wells. Water was such a critical commodity that Dan's son, William Thomas, or W. T., reportedly became annoyed when a drilling site struck oil instead and ordered the well capped, but W. T. changed his mind when oil profits began flowing. Guy and Anna began their life together in grand fashion, leaving for a European honeymoon on the *Majestic* of the White Star Shipping Lines (famed early aviator Eddie Rickenbacker was on the same voyage), but their marriage ended in divorce just six years later, with Anna receiving a $500,000 settlement, a small issue for Guy Waggoner, who had a net worth of $96 million.[5]

Two of Fort Worth's great men held on until the 1930s. K. M. Van Zandt, the founder of the Fort Worth National Bank, died on March 19, 1930. Van Zandt was so well respected that schools and many businesses closed for his funeral. Merida G. Ellis followed in 1932. Ellis, born in 1847 in nearby Denton County, moved to Fort Worth after serving in the Confederate Army (which he joined at age fifteen) and became a real estate developer, building a home at Lamar and Tenth Streets. Many old-timers referred to Ellis as the "Father of North Fort Worth" for his role in bringing packinghouses to the then separate city of North Fort Worth.[6]

Fort Worth was able to carry on thanks to new boosters, especially Amon Carter, who became Fort Worth's most ardent supporter after arriving in 1905. Carter, born in Wise County, northwest of Fort Worth, helped found the *Fort Worth Star* in 1906 and then bought the larger *Fort Worth Telegram*, combining the two to become the *Fort Worth Star Telegram* in 1909, where he served as both president and publisher. The *Star Telegram* served not only Fort Worth but West Texas, New Mexico, and parts of Oklahoma, giving it the largest circulation in the entire South from 1922 to the end of World War II. Its growth led to the opening of grand, new facilities at Seventh and

Taylor Streets in May 1921 and to the purchase of the rival *Fort Worth Record* from William Randolph Hearst in 1925, which was also merged with the *Star Telegram.* Carter expanded into the airwaves on September 17, 1922, when WBAP radio began broadcasting, a risky move into a new medium with no more than one thousand radio receivers in Texas and Oklahoma combined. WBAP was able to overcome scant regional numbers by employing a five-hundred-watt Western Electric transmitter costing $20,000 capable of reaching forty-one of the then forty-eight states (verified by listeners who mailed letters praising the broadcast). Carter remained in the news both locally and nationally and would continue as a major force in Fort Worth until his death in 1955 and afterward thanks to the Carter Foundation, which he established in 1945.[7]

J. Frank Norris, a fundamentalist Baptist preacher, attracted considerable attention in the 1920s, but not always and not solely for his theology. Norris, who attended Baylor University in Waco, Texas, and earned an advanced degree from Southern Baptist Theological Seminary in Louisville, Kentucky, became controversial soon after arriving in 1909 as pastor of Fort Worth's First Baptist Church. Initially, he drew considerable attention for his vocal and strident criticism of Fort Worth's lax to nonexistent vice enforcement, a problem made evident by the city's openly flourishing saloons, houses of prostitution, and gambling dens, especially in Hell's Half Acre, a legendary vice district south of Ninth Street. In 1912, it was Norris who faced accusations after being charged with arson and perjury related to a fire that destroyed First Baptist's sanctuary. The preacher won acquittal on those charges only to be implicated in a 1916 faked assassination plot in which a man shot himself in the hand during a church service. The woefully inept assailant claimed he had been sent to shoot at (but miss) Norris, but he fumbled the pistol and the shot. Somehow Norris not only survived one embarrassment after another but prospered, enjoying a successful career as a pastor; owner and editor of the *Baptist Standard,* a publication dedicated to the Baptist faith; operator of an early radio ministry; publisher of two newspapers, the *Searchlight* in Fort Worth and the *Fundamentalist* in Michigan (after becoming pastor of Temple Baptist Church in Detroit, Michigan, in 1935), both dedicated to promoting Norris's political, social, and religious views; and founder of the Fundamental Baptist Bible Institute in 1939, which would become Arlington Baptist College. All the while, Norris did well financially, moving in 1929 into a $20,000 home in the Kensington Addition, facing Worth Hills Golf Course.[8]

Most of Norris's notoriety came from secular incidents, but he was no stranger to disputes with other religious figures. He carried on a running feud with Dr. Lee R. Scarborough, president of Southwestern Baptist Theological Seminary, that began when Scarborough made disparaging remarks following Norris's arson indictment. He also feuded with Reverend Dr. Dan B. Brumitt, a leading Methodist minister who publicly ridiculed Norris's affinity for firearms, calling him "Two-Gun" Norris and saying he was a "gunman-pulpiteer" seeking notoriety. Perhaps even more controversial was Norris's open ties with the Ku Klux Klan, a clear connection displayed openly by Klansmen who often appeared in costume at church services and by praises heaped on the preacher by men like Lloyd P. Bloodworth, grand dragon of the Texas Klan, who publicly praised Norris for his years of service as a champion of Protestantism. Norris claimed his critics were mere pawns of a "liquor gang" out to get him because he attacked speakeasies and bootleggers. In January 1929, Norris blamed those unnamed opponents for a suspicious fire that destroyed the First Baptist Church (gasoline containers were found at the scene), saying he had received many threats from vice lords (this time Norris escaped suspicion because he was in Austin). Of course, Norris had supporters within the faith—men like J. T. Pemberton, a deacon at First Baptist and president of Farmers and Merchant Bank, and Dr. L. M. Aldridge, chairman of World Christian Fundamental Association. Aldridge and Norris shared a disdain for evolution, which they saw as a repudiation of fundamentalist faith and a threat to core Christian beliefs, all engineered as part of a grand scheme by the Modernist movement, funded by John D. Rockefeller Jr., bent on destroying Christianity. Norris gave no quarter in his attack, even criticizing a Baptist institution, Baylor University, after a faculty member dared to agree with Darwin's basic precepts. Aldridge was more strident, going so far as to predict a shooting war between fundamentalists and evolutionists.[9]

A quarrel in 1926 between Norris and Fort Worth city leaders over proposed taxes on some church property led to dire consequences. Relations between Norris and most of the city government were already strained, but the relationship between him and Mayor Henry C. Meacham reached a critical level when the mayor supported a proposed tax on revenue-producing properties owned by First Baptist. Incensed, Norris vehemently attacked Meacham in a July 26, 1926, speech at the local Klan Hall in which he suggested that the mayor's pro-Catholic position influenced the city's purchase of property from St. Ignatius Academy, a Roman Catholic school. Norris reported that D. E. Chipps, a Meacham supporter and wealthy lumberman who had lived in Fort Worth for only three years, telephoned him after the speech, threatening to settle matters, and then barged into the pastor's study without knocking. Norris, claiming he felt threatened by the abrupt entry and by Chipps reaching behind his back, drew a night watchman's pistol from his desk and shot, hitting Chipps several times and killing him. Police officers arrested Norris after determining that Chipps was unarmed, but the pastor was quickly released on a $10,000 bond. The only known witness at the time, L. N. Nutt, a bank auditor, corroborated Norris's account, but weeks later, Carl Gaze, a fourteen-year-old messenger boy, came forward to say that Chipps had been shot outside, not inside the study, suggesting that Norris had fired before facing a serious imminent threat. Glaze later recanted after being sequestered by friends and employees of First Baptist Church at the home of Bessie Williams, an employee of the church newsletter, the *Searchlight*. Ms. Williams also was a Methodist evangelist who had served as head of the local Women's Ku Klux Klan.[10]

Norris used his position as head of First Baptist to deny culpability and blame others, especially Mayor Meacham. The church announced a parade of ten thousand to demonstrate support but canceled it, blaming the mayor's obstructionism, but detractors suspected that the real cause was lack of support. Norris used his church offices and organs to promote his defense, arguing in sermons, radio broadcasts, and the *Searchlight* that Meacham and the Catholic Church had framed him. He also used the pulpit to solicit defense funds, placing a tub on stage during services for parishioners to fill with money. In the final weeks before trial, Norris held revivals in surrounding towns, a crafty move designed to create a favorable potential pool among county residents. That effort proved for naught after the court ordered a change of venue to Austin, citing a survey that showed most potential jurors already held strong opinions. Meacham became deeply involved in supporting the prosecution, spending $18,000 of his own money for special prosecutors to assist the state, stating he did so because Chipps had died defending him. After sixteen days of testimony, the jury took only two hours to find Norris not guilty.[11]

Again, infamy did not dim Norris's popularity. He remained somewhat low key afterward, at least by his standards, although in 1936, he sued his own church, First Baptist, for $85,200 plus interest due on a promissory note (all the while retaining the pulpit). Norris even expanded his domain, becoming pastor at Fundamental Baptist in Dallas as well as Temple Baptist in Detroit, Michigan, flying between two so often that he earned the nickname "The Flying Preacher." The three churches gave Norris a parsonage with more than $1 million in real estate holdings serving a flock of up to twenty thousand, but still, he reached out, becoming pastor in October 1939 of Fundamental Baptist of Shanghai, China. Age and overextended religious connections may have kept Norris out of outlandish stunts, but they did little to moderate his political views. Late in life, Norris campaigned to save the United States from what he saw as its two biggest threats, American Nazis and labor unions, especially John L. Lewis of the Congress of Industrial Organization, whom he personally abhorred.[12]

Fort Worth entered the 1920s as a growing city with a strong economy, having completed the transition from a Western cowtown to a medium-size city with all the issues and challenges that came with that status. The march of time wrought other changes as many figures critical to Fort Worth's early development succumbed to age and others arose, all the while facing broad currents sweeping the United States following World War I. But Fort Worth, flush with its own success, faced the future with a confident air born of success.

John Bostick Jr. and Brother Building, Seventh and Houston Streets, ca. 1930s. Courtesy Special Collections, the University of Texas at Arlington Libraries.

CHAPTER ONE

Politics and Other Entertainment

The 1920s began with a major political upheaval: in the 1921 election, only one Fort Worth city council incumbent won reelection. Such a radical makeover in personnel was especially critical because Fort Worth's government operated under the commission form, adopted in 1907, in which elected representatives oversaw municipal departments. For example, in April 1919, O. R. Montgomery was elected commissioner for fire and police, making him responsible for those departments, while fellow commissioners oversaw departmental operations for streets, water, and so on. Among the new commissioners taking office in 1921 was John Alderman, a deputy US marshal who defeated five opponents, including three policemen, to replace Montgomery as commissioner of fire and police. E. R. Cockrell, who had run against and defeated Mayor W. D. Davis for a commission seat, became mayor (commissioners selected the mayor from among their membership). Cockrell defeated Davis again in 1923 but resigned on October 8, 1924, after accepting the presidency of William Woods College in Fulton, Missouri, leaving Willard Burton, a lumber millionaire, to serve out Cockrell's second term.[1]

The electoral housecleaning may have been a reflection of growing discontent with the commission format. Complaints had arisen about the influence of powerful political machines aligned with elected officials who, blessed with hiring authority by virtue of their administrative office, packed city payrolls with supporters committed to maintaining their public offices. By 1924, even staunch civic boosters such as the chamber of commerce and the Federation of

Women's Clubs argued that identity politics had become a serious problem—the latter formally proposing a change to a city council government with an appointed city manager holding operational responsibility, an early example of women exercising political clout just a few years after winning the right to vote in 1920. Their petition was adopted, leading to a plebiscite in December 1924 that narrowly approved (6,946 to 5,559) a charter amendment for a nine-member council elected at large with a mayor selected among the council (Fort Worth has the same number of councilors in 2017 but has changed to eight single-member districts with the mayor elected at large). On April 7, 1925, voters elected all nine candidates endorsed by the Citizen's Association, a political group dominated by local businessmen. The new council named a retailer, Henry C. Meacham, as mayor and offered the city manager job to A. Cobden, a fuel dealer who lived at 1416 Hemphill Street, but Cobden declined the position, leading to a broad search that hired Ossian E. Carr, the city manager of Dubuque, Iowa. Carr took office June 1, 1924, with a $13,500 annual salary. In 1927, the council reappointed Meacham, but citing poor health, he resigned before his term expired and was replaced by William Bryce, a building contractor from Scotland who had been in Fort Worth since 1883. Bryce proved durable, serving three terms from 1927 to 1933.[2]

The switch in political structure was a major part of several changes that helped bring a more modern urban government. The charter revision of 1925 also placed police officers and teachers under civil service protection—joining firefighters, who had been covered for years—and established a three-person civil service board empowered to hear appeals from all municipal employees except those in the law department and library. In 1929, the council established a zoning commission after south-side residents sought a ban on businesses in their residential neighborhood. The board of nine unpaid members developed governing ordinances that worked so well that Dallas scheduled its own plebiscite, a move the *New York Times* applauded, noting that zoning had "done wonders" for Fort Worth.[3]

Annexation was probably the biggest story dominating local politics in the 1920s. The push for geographic expansion was a

Fort Worth City Council, 1925. *Back row*: L. P. Card, Mayor H. C. Meacham, William Bryce, G. T. Renfro, W. E. Austin, W. Monnig Sr. *Front row*: Willard Burton, A. E. Thomas, T. B. Hoffer. Courtesy Special Collections, the University of Texas at Arlington Libraries.

direct outgrowth of Fort Worth's competition with Texas' other large cities—most notably Dallas, Houston, and San Antonio—that had all pulled substantially ahead in population, thanks, at least in part, to annexation. Of the four, Fort Worth, which had not taken new territory since 1910, encompassed the smallest land area, covering only 16.8 square miles compared to 23 for Dallas and 36 for both Houston and San Antonio. Concerned about falling further behind the growth curve, Fort Worth looked to its suburbs, where it saw 50,000 bodies ripe for the taking. Poly, with around 10,000 residents, garnered the most attention, but lustful eyes also fell on Riverside's 5,000 and the 2,000 who lived around the south end of Hemphill Street near the Bolt Works. In addition, annexation offered the potential for significant tax revenue gains with little risk. Niles City's mere 650 residents were insignificant in absolute numbers, but its tax base was a huge prize thanks to the packinghouses, stockyards, and 7 millionaires counted among the 650. The Fort Worth School District, then aligned with the city government, also supported annexation, seeing it as a means to add valuable property tax income without incurring significant increases in liabilities (debt) or costs (students). The district calculated that Poly, Niles City, Arlington Heights, Diamond Hill, Washington Heights, Van Zandt, Riverside, South Fort Worth, and Rosen Heights would add $34,934,000 to the tax rolls but only 5,630 students and just $1,067,000 in debt—an excellent trade-off. Poly, the largest in population, offered the poorest pupils versus income return due to its large student body of 1,498, the most of any proposed section, and its small tax base, but Poly's cost would be more than offset by Diamond Hill, the richest plum with a $9,026,000 tax valuation and only 509 students.[4]

Poly, as well as many other targeted areas, opposed annexation and put up strong fights in opposition. But this opposition was not unanimous. In August 1920, a group of Poly residents circulated supporting petitions, but most of its city's leadership, including Poly Mayor C. E. Baker, stood steadfastly opposed, arguing that Poly could succeed on its own and did not need to become part of Fort Worth. Mayor Baker was especially proud of Texas Women's College's eight buildings and thirty-six professors, which he claimed constituted the finest college anywhere, offering a truly liberal education instead of vocational training to its 538 women students. The mayor's argument evidently prevailed, leading Poly residents to vote seventy-five to zero against annexation, a lopsided tally that suggested the earlier supportive petition may have been the work of outside (Fort Worth) influences. Alas, the vote meant nothing, since Fort Worth had engineered a state constitutional amendment that allowed annexation without consent, an option it exercised on January 31, 1922, taking in Poly, Sycamore Heights, Tandy, White Lake Dairy, Nona, and Oakland—a grand seizure that added eleven thousand to Fort Worth's population.[5]

Niles City, which had been created to avoid Fort Worth incorporation and taxes, united early and vocally in opposition. Fort Worth attempted to sidestep those efforts in March 1921 by pushing a bill through the Texas legislature that authorized a city of more than 100,000 to annex a town of fewer than 2,000 without the smaller entity's consent. Niles City countered by annexing an adjoining square mile of Washington Heights and Diamond Hill, thereby increasing its population from 700 to 2,500, but Fort Worth countered by pressuring state legislators to rush through an amendment raising the population threshold to 5,000, putting Niles City back in jeopardy. Niles City Mayor Mrs. E. P. Croarkin then gave up the legislative battle and turned to the courts, where she vowed to fight all the way to the Supreme Court. Riverside, Rosen Heights, and Mistletoe Heights joined in the court fight, helping win an injunction halting the annexations, but only temporarily; the Sixth Court of Appeals disallowed the injunction and upheld annexation in 1923. Still, Niles City persisted, filing a new lawsuit before finally conceding on August 1, 1923, after a twenty-three-month struggle. Fort Worth's hard-fought victories were well worth the effort, allowing it to add $30 million in taxable assets and several thousand to its population.[6]

Other annexations went off without opposition or were actually initiated by the affected residents. In July 1922, Fort Worth voters overwhelmingly approved (7,892 to 1,010) a plebiscite to take in Arlington Heights, Diamond Hill, Washington Heights, Van Zandt, Riverside, South Fort Worth, Rosen Heights, Mistletoe Heights, and Texas Christian University (TCU). The formal takeover was set for September 7, 1922, but Fort Worth began extending city services immediately, a rather involved process that involved several challenges, including changing 275 street names to avoid duplications. In 1923, a proposal to add Sagamore Hills, an area east of downtown running along both sides of the interurban line to Dallas, failed by a mere twenty-eight votes, a loss blamed on the opposition of black residents, although it seems strange that many African Americans would have voted in the solidly Jim Crow era of the 1920s. Once again, the setback proved to be only a minor speed bump. In 1924, Sagamore Hills was divided into north and south sections, allowing the white section north of the interurban to fast-track annexation, while the largely black southern half waited until most African American residents were disenfranchised.

Mayor Cockrell welcomed northern Sagamore Hills, boasting that its many fine homes would boost tax revenue, but he had problems convincing others of the viability of extending the eastern city limits to the area south of the Texas and Pacific Railroad tracks, where property values were considerably lower. The total area taken in was so huge, it virtually doubled Fort Worth's area to thirty-two square miles, raised the tax rolls to $175 million from just $127 million in 1920, and increased the population by fifty thousand, a figure that accounted for almost all of Fort Worth's recorded population growth in the 1920s.[7]

Fort Worth undertook annexation while dealing with several other issues, especially finances. In the 1920–21 fiscal year, the city's tax rate remained unchanged at $2.17 per $100 valuation, but valuations increased to 100 percent of actual worth, driving a rise in taxable property to $127 million that increased tax revenues more than 46 percent—from $1,845,733 to $2,704,000. However, the 1923–24 budget year brought a severe crunch as estimated tax income fell to $1,352,000, a sparse figure. With property valuations already at 100 percent and tax rates hovering near state-mandated maximums, Fort Worth was left with no other option than to institute major cutbacks, a move that unleashed complaints about poor or nonexistent city services. The cuts were felt particularly hard because the city's infrastructure already suffered from neglect; Fort Worth counted only 72 miles of paved streets in 1920 (398 miles of streets total) and spent only $0.80 per capita on street maintenance, considerably less than Dallas ($2.40), Houston ($3.30), or San Antonio ($2.37). City administrators opted to borrow their way out of the crisis, proposing a large bond package covering streets, parks, and the water and sewer systems and adding an annex to the City-County Hospital. Voters approved the package, but bond sales stagnated in large part because the state of New York, the center of investment capital, had prohibited trade in Fort Worth bonds after the city had technically defaulted on interest payments in 1904. Mayor Meacham somehow managed to get the New York statutes modified, freeing financing.[8]

The fire department took the biggest slice of the budget, accounting for 30 percent of total expenditures, or $395,062 in 1924. Firefighters stayed busy in 1925, the department's busiest year to date, answering 1,830 fire alarms and dealing with $1,427,011 in fire losses. Fire Chief Standifer Ferguson blamed increased demand on carelessness created by liberal insurance coverage, but lack of professionalism also may have contributed. As late as 1926, the department offered no formalized training, requiring only that recruits pass a written examination before going to work as substitutes, where they learned the ropes while waiting for a position to open that would give them full-time status, leading to a ninety-day probationary period before becoming permanent employees.[9]

The school system, then part of the city budget, remained critically underfunded and in debt. By 1921, the Fort Worth district had developed urban dimensions, with sixteen schools serving 13,478 "white" students and two "colored" schools for 1,909 African American students, but all schools continuously struggled with poor funding that budgeted only $45.40 per student, the least of sixteen cities analyzed in one survey. The great wave of annexation in 1924 and natural increase more than doubled the district's schools to fifty-one and the student body to 30,000, all taught by 800 faculty, but the rapid expansion had little effect on per-capita funding, which rose to $50.31 (suggesting an annual budget of $1,509,300)—still the least of all large Texas cities and far less than Dallas's $58.41. Poor funding created large, unwieldy classes (average class size was 39 students) held in buildings so deteriorated that an auditor described many as "disgraceful." Remedies seemed remote given that the estimated cost of bringing facilities and classrooms to par totaled $646,000, almost half the total annual budget. By the end of the decade, class crowding eased somewhat as the student population stabilized, climbing only marginally to 33,946, while the number of faculty reached 1,014, suggesting a decrease in average class size to 34. Without money to repair or build, the district simply closed some schools, consolidating to forty-seven, including ten black grade schools and one black high school.[10]

Public health was a persistently troublesome issue, but the 1920s saw some helpful advances. The municipal water supply, which had plagued Fort Worth for most of its first forty years, was now so safe that health officials credited its clean water, which they called the "basis of health," for a comparatively low mortality rate. Other factors also contributed, including institutions serving the Hispanic community, such as the Methodist Church's Wesley House on the north side and a health center south of the Trinity River run by women of the First Christian Church. In addition, Fort Worth and Tarrant County united in 1923 to build a joint hospital west of St. Joseph's Infirmary on five acres donated years earlier by John Peter Smith. The new joint operation replaced the city hospital located downtown at Jones and Third Streets, which had become so overcrowded that staff could not isolate contagious diseases, admit the mentally ill, or provide beds for African American men, whom they shuttled off to the basement of the Free Clinic. Despite the hospital's serious shortcomings, opponents successfully blocked a construction bond election until the public uproar that followed the death of a young boy with an infectious disease who was refused admittance. Infections were a serious health threat for Fort Worthians in the 1920s; pneumonia was the leading cause of natural death in 1923.[11]

Many health problems, including infections, stemmed from or were related to unsanitary conditions found throughout the city. A visitor in 1920 complained that pools of stagnant water, loose papers, and banana peels made crossing at Tenth and Commerce Streets an extended chore. Most collected garbage was burned, but the lack of adequate incinerators left piles of waste lying for days in huge, odorous mounds, creating stenches that plagued adjoining neighborhoods. Ben M. Terrell, a district court judge with a home at 1001 Samuels Avenue, sued the city over the smell emanating from the Cold Springs Dump located one mile away, and residents of Mistletoe Heights threatened legal action unless improvements were made to a dump located just north of their neighborhood. The city tried to alleviate the problem by banning perishables and adding a second incinerator shift while waiting for the installation of four Stokes incinerators, purchased at a cost of $57,200. Still, C. E. Mead, superintendent of garbage collection, argued that Fort Worth was cleaner than Houston and just as clean as Galveston despite their advantages—namely, that

Houston had the Buffalo Bayou and Galveston the Gulf of Mexico, both large waterways where the two cities dumped waste, while Fort Worth was forced to burn its trash. Dumping into waterways remained a common practice for many cities, including Fort Worth, but the city lost the cheap alternative after complaints from downstream neighbors on the Trinity River forced the state to act.[12]

While the city of Fort Worth stopped dumping into the Trinity River years earlier, the waters running through the middle of downtown still suffered from past and continued abuse. Many businesses and individuals continued dumping unabated into the river itself and upstream tributaries such as Marine Creek, which ran along the packinghouses and fed into the Trinity. The sad state of the water leaving Fort Worth brought so many complaints from downstream cities (such as Dallas) that the state forced adoption of ambitious plans to reduce the flow of pollutants, a move that carried the unintended benefit of improving the area's quality of life and property values. In 1920, the council proposed relocating Fort Worth's sewage treatment plant from the adjacent downtown area to a thirty-three-acre site downstream on the West Fork of the Trinity River (near the current Beach Street Bridge), removing an unpleasant operation from the city center and enabling the construction of a much larger facility that could handle all the city's waste as well as that of the packinghouses, stockyards, and Belt Railway—all three were outside Fort Worth city limits at the time but were major sources of contamination, since much of their sewage, inadequately treated at their private facilities, went into the Trinity via Marine Creek. The companies contributed to the plant's construction cost, estimated at $475,000 (but actually costing $871,384), and installed onsite screening devices and retention basins that reduced pollutant flow. Construction drew a scathing report from the district court grand jury, charging that Fort Worth, due to noncompetitive bidding, had overpaid for land and materials, charges city administrators tacitly admitted by requiring bidding procedures for future purchases. The new plant began operation in May 1924, providing an eight-million-gallon daily capacity—the most complete and efficient in the nation—that made Fort Worth one of few major cities able to eliminate raw sewage dumping completely. The facility worked well except for a period in 1925 when an explosion put the plant offline for a month and effluent back into the water.[13]

City services also faced a major challenge when eleven inches of rain fell in just two days—April 22–23, 1922. The downfall resulted in seventeen breaks in Trinity River levees, flooding much of Arlington Heights and the north side, including the Power and Light Company boilers, leaving the city without power and stranding a train with two hundred passengers for days near Aledo, Texas, fifteen miles west of Fort Worth. Regular police officers worked twenty-four hours straight before being relieved by volunteers from the American Legion, Reserve Officers Training Corps, Army and National Guard, Red Cross, and dozens of regular citizens. Initial exaggerated reports claimed the flood had covered three thousand acres, caused $8 million in property damages, and killed sixty-two persons, although the number of fatalities was quickly revised downward to thirty-seven. Subsequent reports gave less severe but still significant estimates of ten deaths and $2 million in property damages.[14] In the aftermath, a few concerned citizens, convinced the levees would not have failed unless sabotaged, offered a reward for information confirming they had been dynamited (no suggestions provided about suspects). None was forthcoming. A more likely explanation held that the massive rainfall aggravated an already precarious balance created by siltation that by 1925 had reduced Lake Worth's capacity 40 percent and would, by some estimates, consume the lake by 1940. To forestall a repeat, the 1925 bond package funded raising the dam's height ten feet, which so increased the water level that the municipal beach and two hundred camps were closed. The bond package was grand in scope, providing initial funding for construction of Lake Bridgeport and Eagle Mountain Lake, both northwest of Fort Worth, which would greatly expand the city's water supply.[15]

In the autumn of 1923, Fort Worth celebrated a Diamond Jubilee commemorating seventy-five years since the fort's establishment in 1848. The event began with a historical context presented through a series of interviews with local pioneers running in the *Star Telegram* beginning on September 28, 1923, and plaques marking historically significant locations, Fort Worth's first church, school, and store. Most of the other activities focused on entertainment, including an official birthday song—"I've Got a Date with Jub E Lee," written by J. M. Petrilli, secretary of foreign trade for the chamber of commerce—and several dramatic theatrical productions, including a historical pageant written and directed by Mrs. Elizabeth Hanley of New York that featured a "Negro chorus" singing "I've Been Working on the Railroad" as actors portrayed the laying of track for Fort Worth's first railroad in 1876. The finale included a week-long series of band concerts, theatrical productions, and carnival rides, all capped off on November 15 with a downtown parade and street dance highlighted by flyovers of one hundred army and civilian aircraft, including bombers and observation balloons. The downtown party experienced one negative incident when fireworks started fires that caused $150,000 in damages, leading to the banishment of pyrotechnics, enforced by one thousand citizens deputized to act as "plainclothes officers." Texas Governor Pat Neff along with two hundred Texas mayors attended many of the events.[16]

Fort Worth took significant steps to expand outdoor recreation, especially through the ambitious development of its park system. Forest Park Pool, Fort Worth's first municipal swimming pool, opened on June 17, 1922, charging $0.20 entrance fees for adults and a dime for children. Marine Park Pool on the north side began four years later, opening despite opposition from M. A. Peck of 1503 North Houston Street, who thought that "mixed bathing" (male-female) was inappropriate in an area with seven churches within three blocks. In 1926, the city paid $10,000 for 140 acres stretching along the Trinity River, somewhat parallel to Grand Avenue, which included "Old Rocky," a longtime favorite swimming hole on the Trinity River northeast of downtown. The city assigned lifeguards to the pool, including sixteen-year-old Mary Dillard, the first Fort Worth girl to hold the position. Most of the land was sold by Sam Rosen, a merchant who developed much of Fort Worth's north side, including Rosen Heights, a 320-acre residential addition located north of the stockyards around Gould and Hanna Avenues. Eventually, Rosen expanded that development, adding another 1,171 acres as well as an electric plant, the Rosen Heights Railway to downtown, and a White City recreation area.[17]

Some city parks offered varied entertainment options. In June 1923, Tourist Park, a campground near Trinity Park, began renting overnight campsites for $0.50 per carload, drawing some ten thousand patrons with an average of four persons per car in its first five months. To accommodate golf's growing popularity, Fort Worth in 1922 spent $84,000 for ninety-six acres southwest of TCU for Worth Hills Golf Course, projecting the course would be self-supporting through $0.25 green fees. The council followed up in 1928, spending $30,000 to build Boaz Golf Course on three hundred acres off Weatherford Road donated by the Boaz family. Fort Worth so aggressively added parkland that in 1926, its park system boasted of 3,496 acres, the nation's seventh largest—an impressive statistic tempered somewhat by noting that Lake Worth, the third-largest municipal park in the United States, accounted for 2,779 acres, almost 80 percent of the total.[18]

Lake Worth had provided camping, swimming, boating, and general outdoor recreation since its construction in the 1910s, but in 1927, work began on what would be, for a time, Fort Worth's grandest entertainment center. The Casino at Lake Worth, or Casino Beach as it was commonly known, sat on the lake's western shore just off the main highway to Jacksboro, Texas. Billed as the Atlantic City of the South, Casino Beach was a $1 million amusement park with a 1,500-foot boardwalk that featured carnival games and rides, including a state-of-the-art roller coaster rising 72 feet as well as a large pavilion offering nightly music (church pressure soon brought an end to Sunday dances). The opening in June 1927 brought a first-day crowd of fifteen thousand, and the amusement center continued to do well, drawing an estimated one million its first year. In the off-season, the owners spent another $75,000 on more rides and attractions, including a $35,000 "Blue Beard's Castle" fun house copied from Coney Island. The opening of the second summer season on April 11, 1928, featured a grand pavilion dance with an eleven-piece orchestra, the music relayed by loudspeakers to every section of the dance floor, another second-year addition. The upgrades, especially the improved amplification, helped bring the Miss Texas Beauty Pageant of 1928, won by Jewell Dodson of Cleburne, who defeated forty women for the crown. Lake Worth had drawn other large entertainment operations such as the Moslah Mosque of the Shriners, opened July 4, 1919, which had the largest ballroom in the Southwest, capable of accommodating one thousand couples. The mosque was eventually sold to the First Methodist Church and renamed the Epworth Center before being destroyed by fire in January 1927. Nearby, Amon Carter hosted lavish parties, entertaining celebrities from around the world at his Shady Oaks Farm, and in the 1930s, Whiting Castle, made to resemble Macbeth's home, opened across the lake from Casino Beach, replacing an 1860s farmhouse.[19]

Fort Worth also supported various art forms, both high and low. The 1920s marked the beginning of the great radio age, a period when

Aerial of Casino Beach, ca. late 1920s–1930s. Courtesy Special Collections, the University of Texas at Arlington Libraries.

ownership spread rapidly, bringing a receiver to one out of three American homes by 1930. The first radio station, WBAP, began broadcasting in 1921, with few programs and few local listeners, but programming expanded quickly, filling the airwaves both day and night, although broadcasts varied greatly in type and quality while coverage also increased thanks to more powerful transmitters. For example, in 1925, WBAP aired a local church revival from midnight to 4:00 a.m. On January 4, 1923, WBAP became one of the first radio stations to offer country music when it began broadcasting ninety minutes of square-dance music directed by Captain M. J. Bonner, a Confederate veteran. Country music proved so successful that WBAP inaugurated a hillbilly barn dance that reached listeners as far away as Canada. Radio was the most important new entertainment medium, but the decade was also known for marathon dances in which partners danced for days to win prizes. In 1923, Fort Worth police stopped a marathon dance after thirteen hours, saying they did so to protect the dancers.[20]

Higher art gained a real foothold in 1922, when the Comité de Diffusion de l'Art Francais Moderne dans les Musées des États-Unis donated three paintings to the Fort Worth Art Association. The association was already well established and recognized as an art outpost by the *New York Times* thanks to an impressive thirty-eight paintings in its portfolio and its annual exhibition at the local Carnegie Library. In addition, Kay Kimbell, owner of Kimbell Mills, began building a collection that would become the Kimbell Art Museum, a world-class exhibition. Fort Worth had a long history of supporting dramatic arts popular with the masses, but it had struggled to offer legitimate theater. R. C. Evans opened the first theater, Evans Hall, in 1870 on the northwest corner of Houston and First Streets years before municipal incorporation and the arrival of the first locomotive. Captain George Bird Holland's My Theater, the first variety theater, a forerunner of vaudeville, opened in 1881, two years before the Greenwall Opera House, owned by a group headed by Walter Huffman, began operation at Rusk and Third Streets. In the 1920s, local theater had ties to Broadway through William R. Edrington of Fort Worth's Trader's National Bank. Edrington lived in Fort Worth but maintained a second home at 830 Park Avenue in New York, where he backed many productions, most notably those of producer Earl Carroll, for whom Edrington named a theater at Fiftieth Street and Seventh Avenue. Edrington also dabbled in other projects, including helping build parts of Texas Agricultural and Mechanical College in College Station, Texas, but all his enterprises crashed at the start of the Depression, leaving him to declare bankruptcy shortly before dying in Fort Worth in 1932.[21]

In the 1920s, several theaters opened, and many existing cinemas adapted to technology by adding sound. The Worth Theater, billed as Texas' finest and largest with seating for three thousand, opened in November 1927 at 312 West Seventh Street. Its first feature, *She's a Sheik*, was a Hollywood movie, but the Worth also presented stage shows featuring top vaudeville entertainers, one of only fourteen theaters in Texas at the time to offer both filmed and live performances. In 1929, the New Opera House at 113 East Seventh Street became

Hippodrome Theater looking north on Main Street, ca. 1928. Courtesy Special Collections, the University of Texas at Arlington Libraries.

the Palace, the second of three grand cinemas on Seventh (the Hollywood would come later). In 1927, Fort Worth was one of thirty-five cities to have Vitaphone equipment, an early attempt to add sound by synchronizing images on the screen with a phonographic record. The Rialto Theater premiered the system to a select audience for *Don Juan*, starring John Barrymore, but the experience was less than stunning; the press reported that the audience gasped at the marvel but that coordination was less than perfect. Actual "talkies" arrived in 1929 and quickly spread out from downtown to reach the recently opened Tivoli Theater at 808 West Magnolia Avenue.[22]

The Majestic Theater was the great venue for vaudeville, drawing many big names. A typical show featured a name act supported by several lesser-known performers and a film. A run in 1925 featured the Four Foys, a family vaudeville act that began in 1910 as Eddie Foy and the Seven Foys. The bill included performances by the Kate and Wiley

Majestic Vaudeville Theater banner stretched across Main Street, 1928–30. Courtesy Special Collections, the University of Texas at Arlington Libraries.

balancing act; Billy Taylor's musical comedy, featuring the Lemarr Sisters; the Stuart and Lash dancing team; a burlesque act featuring a skit, "Queer Folks," with comedian Irene Trevette, known as "The French Girl with Dancing Eyes"; and a movie feature, *Everyman's Wife*, accompanied by short features and a newsreel. While waiting in the alley between performances, the Foys met a young aspiring dancer, Ginger Rogers, who was attending the show with her mother, a theatrical reporter for the *Fort Worth Record*. Obviously taken with the young girl, they taught her the Charleston, a popular dance, and later had her fill in for an ill sibling. Rogers used her dance skill a few months later, on November 6, 1925, to win a local Charleston contest, sending her to the state competition, where she also won, earning a month's contract with the Interstate-Keith Orpheum circuit for appearances in several cities, including St. Louis, Missouri; Chicago, Illinois; and Los Angeles, California (the contest's runner-up was future Broadway star Mary Martin). Afterward, Rogers built on her dancing skills and added runners-up from the state competition to form "Ginger Rogers and the Dancing Red Heads." The group opened in Waco and then won acclaim on the vaudeville circuit, propelling Rogers to Hollywood stardom and fame as Fred Astaire's partner in several Hollywood movies.[23]

Several nationally known celebrities visited Fort Worth. In 1920, hundreds were left without hotel rooms when Enrico Caruso drew eight thousand to concerts at the North Side Coliseum in Niles City. Caruso at first balked at performing in what he called a cattle barn but relented after testing the acoustics. In November 1923, Harry Houdini promoted an upcoming appearance at the Klan Hall by escaping from a straitjacket while hanging upside down from the *Star Telegram* building. In 1924, William Jennings Bryan spoke on politics and evolution at TCU and the First Baptist Church. Two years later, boxer Jack Dempsey signed a contract at the *Star Telegram* office with promoter Tex Rickard for a September title defense in New York or New Jersey against an unnamed opponent thought to be either Gene Tunney or Harry Will. The agreement guaranteed Dempsey $450,000 and part of the gate.[24]

Commercial air traffic led to the development of a municipal airport, later named Meacham Field, facilitating air travel as well as visits from notables. In 1926, Will Rogers flew in from Vinita, Oklahoma, to meet Amon G. Carter and H. L. Mencken, a renowned journalist and cultural critic who was Carter's frequent guest. Rogers spent the night before flying on to Houston the next morning to attend the Democratic Convention. On September 26, 1927, Charles Lindbergh landed in the *Spirit of St. Louis* just a few months after his historic solo flight across the Atlantic. Lindbergh was paraded down Main Street to Panther Park, where he spoke before spending the night at a downtown hotel and then left the next day for Dallas. Over a decade later, in September 1938, thousands greeted Douglas "Wrong Way" Corrigan two months after his infamous flight. Corrigan received the nickname after filing a flight plan from Brooklyn, New York, to California but landing in Dublin, Ireland—the result, he claimed, of confusion but more likely due to his intentional misdirection after authorities denied official approval for the overseas flight. The city airport also witnessed a well-publicized stunt by Reginald Robbins and James Kelly to set a new endurance record. The two landed May 27, 1929, after remaining aloft more than 172 hours (more than seven days) in their Ryan monoplane, a feat made possible by in-flight refueling and provisioning. A crowd of seventy-five thousand lined the streets for eight miles to cheer as they were taken away to rest.[25]

Baseball was a popular diversion in the 1920s. In the 1920s, the local minor league team, the Cats, won the league championship six years straight while playing to large home crowds and being followed by avid fans who gathered outside the *Star Telegram* for updates on away games. In addition, many major league teams played exhibition games in Fort Worth. In a 1923 match between the New York Yankees and the Brooklyn Robins at Panther Park (two blocks west of North Main Street on Northwest Seventh Street), Babe Ruth homered over the right-field bleachers, only the second player to do so. Legend claims that the ball struck and killed a steer grazing in a nearby field. In 1925, President Paul LaGrave of the Fort Worth Baseball Association announced plans for a new stadium east of Main Street on eight acres near Jones, Calhoun, and Pecan Streets between Northeast Sixth and Northeast Seventh Streets. The new arena carried on as Panther Park until LaGrave's death in 1929, when it was renamed in his honor.[26]

Baseball and other entertainments had to contend with a rather stringent moral code that banned most Sunday diversions. Blue laws prohibited a long list of activities, including baseball or movies, although the statutes had been suspended during World War I so that soldiers, many off only on Sundays, could attend cinemas and other diversions. After the war's end in November 1918, many groups, led by the Ministers Association, began calling for reinstatement, and some, such as the Pastors Alliance, went further, proposing an expansion of prohibited activities to cover gasoline stations, Lake Worth beaches, stores, and even elevators. Resistance developed in many quarters, including Seventh Day Adventists, who supported the concept but wanted Saturday as the Sabbath, while others, including District Attorney Jesse Brown, opposed blue laws on secular grounds, arguing that denying people benign Sunday recreations would simply drive them to take their entertainment dollars to Dallas. Brown added that the better moral battle would be to concentrate on closing the gambling houses and houses of prostitution running full tilt, all hours, all days. The city council not only reinstated the codes but expanded them to cover most businesses, a decision that the Dallas Booster Club celebrated with full-page "Welcome to Dallas Sunday" advertisements in Fort Worth papers, touting their open theaters and shops. In response, many local merchants chose to ignore the law, leading Sheriff Sterling Clark to file complaints against sixteen theaters, warning that actions against other businesses would follow. Some theaters closed under the threat, but so many continued operating that local courts soon faced a logjam of more than one thousand pending "blue law" cases. In February 1920, the local business community united in opposition, exerting enough pressure that the court dismissed the existing cases, and Sheriff Clark agreed to defer further enforcements as long as Dallas remained open. Ironically, supply problems kept some cinemas closed that first Sunday, but operators assured the public they would open the next.[27]

Theaters and cinemas still faced heavy censorship. In 1924, Police Commissioner John Alderman ordered the "purity squad" to step up arrests after hearing reports of girls smoking and "petting" while sitting on men's laps in theater balconies. In 1928, the local board of censors banned the movie *Is Your Daughter Safe?* showing at the Rialto Theater at Fifth and Main Streets. The Pantages Theater had run the same film earlier but avoided censure by segregating audiences by gender and by coupling showings with an educational film and lecture. The Rialto did neither and, even more egregiously, admitted children under eighteen. Censors also objected to a dance during a live show, *Padlocks of 1929*, at the Plaza Theater but allowed it after the woman performer donned a "more elaborate costume."[28]

Crusaders also focused considerable attention on dance halls, especially low-rent operations known as "taxi dance" clubs, where men paid a nickel or a dime to dance with a woman of their choice. The women working such clubs generally worked only for tips, which often came with strings attached or expected. In 1920, the opening of a large taxi dance club at Seventh and Main Streets stirred cries for a citywide ban, a move supported by County Judge Small, who argued that such operations ruined young girls by convincing them that they could earn an easy living. In 1921, faced with a public outcry, Police Chief Harry Hamilton ordered all dance halls closed pending investigations, but in October, Doc Otto, who ran the 1920 Social Club, sought an injunction against police interference, charging that the police action constituted selective enforcement, targeting only dance halls catering to lower-income crowds while ignoring dances at upscale places such as the roof of the Texas Hotel. Local musicians supported Otto, noting that public halls were the only places working people could afford entertainment. In November, a county court judge also agreed, ruling the ordinance invalid and unenforceable, paving the way for reopening. In response, the police tightened scrutiny, vowing to arrest any woman with a record found on the premises. To make good on that pledge, they began making timely inspections, making twelve arrests during one raid in April 1923. For many, strict enforcement of sexual mores was required to defend a society beset by corruption on all sides. As proof, they pointed to statistics showing that in 1924, Tarrant County issued 2,586 marriage licenses and granted 1,008 divorces (649 divorces granted to wives and 359 to husbands), a divorce rate of almost 40 percent.[29]

The heart of most morality issues focused on sex outside of marriage, a touchy issue at the time that carried severe moral liabilities (in some quarters) as well as the risk of unwanted pregnancies and venereal disease. A common response to an unmarried woman's pregnancy was a rushed marriage, often accompanied by extreme encouragement. In 1922, C. B. Sharp, returning home from oil field work, found his seventeen-year-old daughter pregnant. Shotgun in hand, Sharp wasted no time in confronting the surprised father, I. Turpin, asking if he preferred attending a wedding at Sharp's home or a funeral at Turpin's. When Turpin opted for the former, Sharp marched the prospective bride and groom to the courthouse, but the wedding was stymied. It seems Turpin confessed he had married another woman in Weatherford the previous week. Luckily, police rescued Mr. Turpin by arresting him—certainly a better outcome than Mr. Sharp would have offered. Nonmonogamous sex of all forms also carried significantly increased risks for venereal diseases, an important medical hazard that, according to a Fort Worth health report, was responsible for 90 percent of all insanity cases (the rest were attributed to a poor diet, "transition" [menopause], hereditary, grief, and old age). In 1926, Fort Worth and Tarrant County considered creating a joint treatment center for social diseases at the City-County Hospital, but the plan ran into considerable opposition from many who feared the ward would expose other patients. A counterproposal suggested adopting the practice of Dallas, Houston, and San Antonio of housing venereal disease patients at the county jail, a proposal Sheriff Carl Smith rejected, noting that the jail lacked sufficient space, that it would be unfair to expose other prisoners, and that he could not jail anyone without charges.[30]

Despite the liabilities, prostitution was rampant. In 1919, District Attorney Jesse Brown claimed that gambling and prostitution were more prevalent than in any other time in history, a very bold statement given Fort Worth's history of prolific vice. Still, even allowing for the possibility of exaggeration, Brown's point was well made and supported by others. A letter to the *Star Telegram* in 1922 complained that Main and Houston Streets were cluttered nightly with "coupe lizzards [*sic*]." In response, the police arrested fifteen women for vagrancy (the common charge for prostitution), making for good press but little else. Prostitution survived and thrived because many considered it, like gambling, a harmless vice. Evidence of that perspective can be seen not only in prostitution's relatively open existence but also in the number of stalwart citizens involved in the trade. A private detective hired by the Ministers Association at J. Frank Norris's urging identified eighty houses of prostitution in Fort Worth, many owned by prominent men, including one owned by a church deacon. During a subsequent church service, Norris named at least eight church members involved in the promotion of prostitution (unfortunately, the names were not recorded).[31]

Moral crusaders might well have also turned their attention to city hall, where several officials faced accusations of shady financial dealings. In 1922 and 1923, reports surfaced that in 1921, numerous city officials or former officials, including former mayor W. D. Davis and former police chief O. R. Montgomery, had bought land owned by the city around Lake Worth under questionable circumstances and had not made required payments. Some of the information came from C. A. Burton and Margaret McLean of the park board, who charged that Mayor Davis bought land just two days before leaving office in 1921 but had failed to make the $200 annual payment. Once the story broke, all the accused paid the back rents except Montgomery, who relinquished his claim, and Davis, who said he would only surrender the land if the city paid him for his cattle kept there. A group of local Methodists bought Davis's property, thereby removing him from the matter and saving the city considerable embarrassment. Other incidents involved Dan H. Hedge, who resigned in 1924 as superintendent of streets just days before he was charged with defrauding the city of $670, and Albert Tankersley, city tax assessor-collector, who in 1926 received a two-year sentence for each of four fraud charges involving the misappropriation of almost $4,000 in city funds.[32]

High-ranking city officials and notable citizens engaged publicly in a variety of inappropriate behaviors. In 1922, Dr. E. H. Boaz, the son of a Fort Worth pioneer, was sentenced to five years in prison in Dallas for killing a Dallas barber, George McDowell, in a dispute involving Boaz's wife. William P. McLean Jr., son of the Fort Worth lawyer who represented notable clients such as Texas Senator Earle Bradford Mayfield, was one of three men and one woman told not to return to the University of Michigan for violations of the morality code. Unfortunately, the school omitted details, saying they would only serve prurient interests. In 1926, violence intruded into the city council chambers when City Manager Carr and a police officer had to separate City Councilman A. E. Thomas and James Ellis, secretary of the city planning board, after Thomas accused Ellis of profiting from city contracts to pave Lubbock Avenue and extend sewer lines around West Seventh Street. Ellis admitted receiving a $4,500 commission when the city bought land from Max Bergman to extend West Seventh Street but denied other charges. Police arrested Ellis for affray, releasing him on a $10 bond. That same year, another incident at city hall had roots in the murder of D. E. Chipps by Pastor J. Frank Norris. City Manager Carr gave a deposition in a $150,000 civil suit brought by Chipps's son in which he charged that Marvin Simpson, a lawyer representing the son, was responsible for sending hoods to Mayor Meacham with offers to kill Norris for $5,000, a crude effort to frame the mayor. After the deposition ended, Simpson knocked Carr down before being subdued by several bystanders.[33]

In the decade, Fort Worth refined much of its political, environmental, social, and cultural infrastructure, bringing much of it to grander scales more appropriate for its urban standing. Many of those changes are still evident in the current city political structure, in the city's expanded geographic limits, and in its park development, but under the physical surface, many rough edges remained of its frontier past.

CHAPTER TWO

Good Guys and Bad Guys

Fort Worth entered 1920 with an upward crime trend that continued for several years before abating. Police Chief R. R. Porter blamed the increase on World War I, a charge supported by Pastor Charles Chapter of Saint Paul's Methodist Church, who said the war unleashed "savage instincts." Whatever the cause, statistics showed that Fort Worth's postwar crime problem was worse than other large Texas cities. From November 1920 to February 1921, seven persons were murdered in Fort Worth, equal to Houston and more than San Antonio, both considerably larger cities. In addition, Fort Worth led in thefts from persons, robbery by firearms, and car thefts and ranked second in assaults and burglary, falling to third only in thefts of more than $50. The trend continued into 1923, when Fort Worth recorded seventeen murders (and sixteen suicides), a homicide rate of more than sixteen per one hundred thousand, unusually high. Laxity of punishment did not seem to be a contributing factor, as Tarrant County courts tended to deal harshly with major crimes, assessing an average term of thirty-three years for criminal homicide. Lesser crimes, especially property theft, also rose precipitously, largely because of a marked uptick in automobile thefts. In 1919, Fort Worth reported 401 cars stolen, the most ever to that date, and only 317 recovered. The surge continued unabated in 1920, forcing some insurance companies to withdraw coverage and the rest to increase premiums dramatically. In contrast to the rise in murder, lax prosecution may well have played a role in soaring thefts. In 1919, Tarrant County criminal courts adjudicated 214 cases, rendering 6 mistrials, 15 acquittals, and 192 convictions (1 case unaccounted), a respectable conviction rate of almost 90 percent, but judges suspended the sentence in 42 cases, almost 22 percent of the 192 convictions. No record indicates the specific charges involved, but the Fort Worth Police Department's sponsorship of legislation mandating a two-year minimum sentence for first-offense automobile theft suggests they were concerned about judicial leniency in that area. It is possible that prosecution fatigue and jail crowding played roles in fostering leniency. In December 1920, the Tarrant County grand jury returned 176 indictments, but 140 were for chiropractors charged with practicing medicine without a license. Fortunately, automobile thefts declined dramatically in 1921 and continued to fall the rest of the decade.[1]

The crime wave may have motivated Fort Worth police to institute some rather innovative reforms. The department created a "Flying Squad" to combat robberies and burglaries, selecting ten officers from several who volunteered to work nights, some even donating the use of their own cars for patrol. In 1921, Police Commissioner John Pendleton reinstated the disbanded bicycle squad, assigning twelve officers in two-man teams to patrol the south side, the largest residential district. The twelve bicycle officers, riding new bicycles equipped with coaster brakes and lights, joined fifteen motorcycle officers (each motorcycle cost $600) and the city's four mounted (horseback) officers assigned to high-risk Irishtown and the flats around the Trinity River. Police Lieutenant J. A. Olson tried to go even further, proposing an "aerial squad" to patrol country lanes and assist in vehicle pursuits, an idea supported by Assistant Chief Henry Lee, who suggested that pilots could use "grabhooks" to "fish" crooks out of moving cars. The city commission rejected the air force but granted Commissioner Pendleton's request for a new regulation uniform introduced in June 1921. That November, the full squad paraded in review before the chief and mayor as well as many onlookers, starting an annual tradition. Yet innovation only went so far; the jail remained, in the words of a 1928 grand jury report, "deplorable" and a "disgrace" threatening the health of prisoners.[2]

Most patrol officers still walked assigned beats on foot. The most active police areas were the following: Irishtown, an area east of Jones

Street originally settled by the Irish that became largely African American with a reputation as the bloodiest district and the only one assigned two officers; lower Calhoun and Jones Streets, known as Little Mexico; Little Africa along East Ninth Street; the vegetable market along Front Street, known initially as the Cabbage Patch before switching to the League of Nations after European immigrants moved in following World War I; Battercake Flats west of the courthouse between Weatherford and Belknap Streets; Brown's Mule Square around the Tarrant County Courthouse; Hogan's Alley on Thirteenth Street; Bum's Bowery north of the west yard of the Texas and Pacific Railroad, a nationally known refuge for traveling types (hoboes), which accounted for the most arrests, largely for minor charges such as vagrancy; and Quality Grove, a black section of the north side. Ritzy sections with little criminal activity included the Gold Coast, the grand homes around Summit and Pennsylvania Avenues, and the exclusive shops of the Silk Stocking District along Main and Houston between Fourth and Eighth Streets. Foot patrols worked out of various neighborhood patrol stations, including the Northside Station with ten officers commanded by Captain Tom McClure. McClure, known as "Sixshooterless Tom" because of his preference for a shotgun or Winchester over a pistol, came to Fort Worth after serving as a deputy US marshal in Fort Smith, Arkansas, where he dealt with Belle Starr and the Pickens Gang.[3]

Professionalization took some important steps in the 1920s. In 1924, Commissioner John Alderman banned officers from working off duty in the employ of private concerns, a common practice for events like dances, and in 1926, the department standardized firearms, buying two hundred .38 caliber pistols for patrolmen and twenty-five smaller-frame weapons for detectives. In 1927, the department made several major reforms: issuing written guidelines limiting officers to a top speed of thirty miles per hour, requiring a written exam for promotion to sergeant, and setting standards for police applicants that required they be between twenty-one and forty years of age and not lighter than 170 pounds nor shorter than five feet ten inches. In 1928, applicants were required to take a physical exam, with a written "mental exam" covering grammar and basic arithmetic as well as city laws and ordinances added in 1929. The physical exam had a noticeable impact, eliminating 42 percent of applicants, but the academic "mental" test was truly exclusionary, dismissing 90 percent of all applicants. One standard did not change in that the department remained solely a male preserve. In 1927, the police chief granted that women could be valuable assets but that he would never hire one as a "patrolman" because he could never send her out to make an arrest.[4]

Two of the most important developments in professionalization came through the formalization of training and implementation of retirement benefits. In 1924, Lieutenant Claud Green and Captain William E. Wyatt became directors of the Fort Worth Police Academy after attending the New York City Police Academy. On October 4, 1924, the academy they developed began offering classes at the YMCA for both recruit and in-service training. In-service training, conducted weekly in four-hour classes on officers' days off, focused on physical exercises during the first year before turning to instruction in laws and ordinances as well as evidence collection, including fingerprinting. In 1929, the city adopted a pension plan for officers and firefighters who had reached the age of sixty-two or had thirty years of service or were disabled on the job after at least five years of employment as well as for widows of officers killed in the line of duty. A three-person oversight committee set pensions at one-half the officer's wage at retirement, to a maximum of $75 monthly, while widows received one-fourth pay, and children younger than sixteen received $18 monthly each—in all cases not to exceed the $75 limit. The pensions were not exorbitant but also not unreasonable in the context of the period, when patrolmen earned $140 monthly ($1,680 annually) and the chief $320 ($3,840 annually).[5]

Fort Worth officers also organized outside the municipal structure. In a May 1919 meeting at the Labor Temple, more than 60 percent of Fort Worth officers, assisted by representatives from the carpenters' and waiters and waitress' unions, endorsed an application for a union charter with the American Federation of Labor (AFL), a first step for unionization. In the aftermath of World War I, police unionization enjoyed some success but was rare in the South. Fort Worth; Tulsa, Oklahoma; and Oklahoma City, Oklahoma, were the only southwestern cities of thirty-seven city police departments affiliated with the AFL. The national police labor drive suffered a crippling blow after the 1919 Boston Police Strike turned public opinion against police unions, effectively killing the movement. Shortly thereafter, Fort Worth's police commissioner announced that the local organization had withered and its charter had been revoked. In 1921, Fort Worth officers successfully formed a police benevolent association that continues to this day.[6]

Traffic enforcement became a major police issue in the 1920s. A big part of that job involved citing violators, prompting an unofficial nickname for traffic officers as the "Ten a Day Squad," a reference to the goal of ten traffic and parking citation daily for each officer. In the early days, traffic violators were not simply issued citations and released but were required to drive to the nearest police station, often with the issuing officer riding along on the car's running boards, where violators would either pay a fine or furnish a bond. In July 1920, traffic control entered a new era with the installation of a stop/go signal (borrowed from the San Antonio police for testing) at Tenth and Main Streets. The first permanent traffic signal light system began operation on May 7, 1924, controlling traffic on Main Street from Third to Thirteenth, with similar lights planned for Commerce and Throckmorton Streets.[7]

Most police officers conscientiously did their best at a dangerous job. In the 1920s, Fort Worth police foiled two train robberies. On September 15, 1921, officers lay in wait at a water tank near Camp Bowie pursuant to an informant's tip that the Texas and Pacific train would be robbed while stopped to take on water. The information proved correct, but the operation turned into a shootout that claimed the lives of the train engineer, Billy Edwards, and a second man, J. L. Morris. In 1928, the lone mail car attendant of an arriving Texas and Pacific train was found bound and $53,000 missing. Police retracing the train's route discovered a woman loitering east of the terminal under the Summit Avenue Bridge. The woman claimed to be waiting for a date but later confessed to being sent to collect the robbery loot stashed nearby by T. H. "Blackie" Wilson. Wilson had jumped from the train after robbing the mail car but left the money to avoid the risk of

Main Street, 1925. Courtesy of the Genealogy, History and Archives Unit, Fort Worth Library (Historic Photograph Collection, box A, folder A004).

being caught with the incriminating "goods" on him. Both incidents made national news, including the *New York Times*.[8]

Some officers made the ultimate sacrifice in the line of duty. In April 1920, Officer George Gresham was killed at Terry and Eighteen Streets by a deranged man who had just accosted an African American woman, accusing her of stealing his money. Gresham, on the force for sixteen years, was on his way home when the suspect jumped from behind a utility pole and shot him several times. Only eight months later, in December 1920, Officer Jeff Couch was shot and killed by Tom Vickery, a chauffeur, at the Dollar Dodge Service Company, where Couch had been dispatched on a disturbance call. Vickery was arrested but never made it to trial; twenty masked men took him from the Tarrant County Jail, lynching him from a hackberry tree near Samuels Avenue and Twelfth Street, where officers found him still hanging after anonymous callers telephoned Chief R. R. Porter and

Tarrant County Sheriff Carl Smith with the location. A subsequent grand jury probe returned no indictments, but suspicions of official involvement thickened when Judge George Hosey reported that witnesses had seen uniform pants under robes worn by some of the lynch mob. Motorcycle Officer J. D. Bell, only on the force four months, was killed on August 12, 1921, in a crash at Fourth and Commerce Streets, and in 1926, Bicycle Officer Frank Maco succumbed to injuries incurred when he was thrown from a car's running board. Maco, directing traffic on West Seventh Street, jumped onto the car when it failed to stop on command, but the vehicle accelerated, causing Maco to fall and strike the pavement. The car's driver, W. E. Ponder, claimed that he thought the officer was a hijacker, although both Maco and the other officer wore uniforms. Afterward, the department banned officers from boarding moving vehicles, which had been a common practice.[9]

Bicycle Officer George Turner of 1409 Fifth Avenue was shot and killed on May 20, 1928, during a vehicle stop at Louisiana and Rosedale Streets in which one of two men ordered out of the car drew a pistol and fired. The second man, who remained at the scene, identified the assailant as Tenola "Snappy" Moore, a twenty-three-year-old African American who had worked at a tire shop and for the Texas Christian University (TCU) football team as a "rubdown" man and water carrier. An intense search continued for several days, spreading into adjacent Wise County, where officers used dogs and airplanes to scour the countryside. The dragnet failed, but a year later, Moore was arrested in Chicago after George Carlis, described as a Fort Worth Greek who knew Moore from the tire shop, saw him working as a dishwasher in a Chicago restaurant. Moore admitted to the shooting but claimed he acted in self-defense after the officers threatened to beat him.[10]

Assaults on police officers did not end when they went off duty. In November 1920, Bessie King shot Motorcycle Captain Quincy Burnett twice in the chest while the two sat at LaBeaume and Terrell Drug Store at Eleventh Street and Jennings Avenue. Ms. King, twenty-three, was a telephone operator at the Westbrook Hotel who, according to her sister, had been engaged to Burnett for four years but had recently discovered that he married another woman five weeks earlier.

Immediately after the shooting, King swallowed poison, but both she and Burnett were still clinging to life the next day. King left a note in her purse stating she hoped she had killed Burnett because he had "done me wrong," asking that someone finish the job if she failed. In October 1920, Special Officer J. B. Loper of the Frisco Railroad was killed when he resisted a robbery at the Texas and Pacific Railroad grounds. Ernest Vickers confessed to the crime, saying he did not mean to kill anyone but had done so when Loper fought back. The court sentenced Vickers to death, but the sentence was later commuted to life imprisonment.[11]

The Fort Worth Police Department dealt with considerable internal strife in the 1920s, much of which was its own making. The decade began with a new chief of police who would become the catalyst for a major internal dispute. The election of April 1919 returned Mayor W. D. Davis and Police and Fire Commissioner O. R. Montgomery, but in April 1921, John Pendleton succeeded Montgomery. Pendleton appointed Harry Hamilton chief of police, a controversial move due to Hamilton's youth—he was only twenty-nine—and his lack of experience, having served as a peace officer for only six years, the previous two as a Tarrant County Sheriff's Office detective. In office barely a year, Chief Hamilton was charged in July 1922 with assaulting S. J. Brogdon in the chief's office. Brogdon, the editor of the Texas School News and a member of the Liberty League, an anti-Klan organization, was at odds over the chief's refusal to name private citizens holding police commissions to carry firearms, a group Brogdon alleged were mostly Klansmen. Both men admitted fighting but differed over who instigated the exchange, Hamilton claiming Brogdon threatened him while Brogdon charging the affray began after Hamilton accused him of printing anti-Klan literature, which he certainly did.[12]

Hamilton survived that incident only to face corruption allegations a few months later. In November 1922, Commissioner John Alderman suspended the chief for insubordination, stating that he lost faith in Hamilton following complaints of officers breaking into hotel rooms, a rather nebulous explanation. The more likely cause lay in whispered rumors of selective enforcement of vice laws tied to corruption and police payoffs. Alderman appointed Deputy Chief Henry Lee as acting chief, but things got complicated when the commission board rejected a supporting resolution, leaving the department confused for several days as both men claimed the chief's office before Lee emerged as the sole department head. A petition demanding an investigation into corruption charges led to formal hearings held over the course of several days that heard from citizens and police officers, both current and former. J. Frank Norris, supported by several former officers, including former Captain Joe Cornett, charged that Alderman dismissed Hamilton because the chief refused to obey Alderman's orders to ignore gambling and bootlegging at certain businesses, most notably the Metropolitan and Siebold Hotels. Officer Lawler supported Norris's testimony, reporting that Alderman chastised him directly after he arrested twenty-two gamblers at the Siebold at Seventh and Commerce Streets, a charge affirmed by Chief Hamilton, who added that two of twenty-four gamblers arrested at the Metropolitan Hotel, 111 East Ninth Street (two blocks from city hall), became indignant, saying they would take the matter of their arrests directly to Alderman. It was after those arrests that Alderman ordered Hamilton to leave the Metropolitan Hotel alone and fired him when he refused. Alderman, represented by lawyer W. P. McLean, denied the allegations, and the investigative committee agreed—at least to the extent that they ruled the evidence did not establish the existence of corruption. The city commission still decided not to reinstate Hamilton, opting instead to make Lee permanent chief on January 2, 1923, at an annual salary of $2,500. Ironically, Joe Cornett was later arrested for bootlegging from his drink stand at 123 Northeast Twenty-Third Street.[13]

Rank-and-file officers also received negative scrutiny, revealing a pattern of petty bribes and indiscretions. One such incident occurred in 1922, when Chief Harry Hamilton, making an unannounced night visit to headquarters, found several officers sleeping soundly, some on the bedding they brought with them. The practice of rank-and-file officers receiving small favors from local businesses was so common that when Chief Henry Lee fired a patrolman for buying a pint of liquor, the *Star Telegram* expressed surprise not that an officer of the law had violated of the Volstead Act (Prohibition) but that he had paid for the liquor. More serious graft, the kind that came with expectations of favors in return, also existed but was infrequently reported or subjected to recorded discipline. In 1920, a grand jury probed charges by carnival operators that police officers demanded under-the-table payments to forestall being shut down; regrettably, the investigation was interrupted by the end of the term without a report being filed. In another case, a robbed woman charged that detectives offered the return of her jewelry contingent on a "consideration" of $100. Again, no published account of investigations or reprisals appeared in the local press, perhaps because the press routinely censored reports of malfeasance in office. An example occurred in 1922, when vice officers raided 810 Calhoun Street, arresting and naming three women—Clara Russell, Mrs. Adams, and Louise Smith—for vagrancy (the common charge for prostitution) and the property owner, Kate Dobbs, for running a disorderly house, but not identifying an arrested man from Dallas or three other men, including one described as having statewide prominence, who were released.[14]

A few police officers were involved in questionable incidents involving serious injuries and death. In 1925, Motorcycle Officer Alexander Farrar was charged with murder and several other police officers faced improper-use-of-force allegations after Farrar fired at a fleeing automobile, killing a John Oscar Bond. Farrar was terminated but escaped adjudication when Luther Herring killed him shortly afterward for "wronging" Herring's eighteen-year-old daughter. The same year, Officer C. P. Cronkite faced murder charges in the death of W. V. Rumph, and Motorcycle Officer Harvey Olman was suspended after witnesses reported that the officer struck Ira Burton with a blackjack despite the suspect's compliance. In 1926, Officer Tom Poe, dispatched on a report of an armed man at Fourteenth and North Houston Streets, shot a man he found holding a gun on a couple in the middle of Fourteenth Street. After the smoke cleared, Poe learned that the wounded suspect, J. W. Kimbrell, had confronted his wife and a man he found kissing her. Also in 1926, Officer Clarence Leslie went berserk, running into the Commercial Hotel and adjacent businesses, waving his pistol and firing at the first responding officer before others arrived and subdued him without injury. One of the more interesting police-related shootings occurred in 1924, when former Tarrant County Sheriff John T. Honea killed John Estes, an ex-deputy who had become a lawyer. The shooting occurred in the lobby of the Westbrook Hotel after Estes accused Honea of lying about witnessing the marriage of John L. Jackson (deceased) and Sarah Vestal Jackson. Estes had represented Jackson's family in a suit by a woman who claimed to be his widow (despite not having a marriage license), seeking all or a share of John Jackson's $500,000 estate. A jury convicted Honea, earning him a seven-year prison sentence.[15]

Part of the reason police work seemed more controversial in the 1920s may have been due to Prohibition, the decade's great social experiment. The Eighteenth Amendment banning the transportation, production, and sale of alcoholic beverages took effect on January 16, 1920, but enforcement proved problematic from the very start. Many within the government opposed Prohibition but were unwilling to say so publicly. One example was Joseph W. Bailey, a Texas politician who served as a congressman and senator but lost the 1920 Democratic primary race for governor to Pat M. Neff. Bailey, a staunch conservative, sued the *Fort Worth Record* for $100,000 over its reports tying him to antiprohibitionists. In contrast, many rank-and-file Americans had no qualms voicing their reluctance to comply with the law. In 1920, twelve of sixty-four members in a Fort Worth jury pool were dismissed after refusing to swear that they would uphold and enforce Prohibition laws.[16] The most common form of opposition came in widespread disobedience—the use of various means, legal and illegal, to circumvent the law and obtain alcohol. The Eighteenth Amendment did not outlaw possession and consumption, allowing the financially able to simply stock up before the effective date. Amon Carter took full advantage, buying a complete liquor warehouse that became his personal supply, but the less wealthy stockpiled what they could at home, a practice that fostered a marked increase in home burglaries, including one in which thieves made off with three hundred quarts of liquor valued at $10,000. Other imbibers got doctors to prescribe alcohol as a treatment for various ailments, a ruse that permitted "patients" to buy liquor from pharmacies like E. T. Renfro's shop at 315 Main Street. While legal, prescriptions proved both costly and limited, allowing only one pint every ten days—not enough to satisfy serious drinkers. Some made their own supply or drank substitutes, both of which carried serious risks. Fort Worth City Physician Dr. Webb Walker reported that in Prohibition's first year, approximately twenty persons died and many others went blind after drinking homemade hooch or "denatured" alcohol such as perfume and hair tonic. The threat posed by tainted spirits was widespread and sustained, taking the lives of two thousand persons in the United States in 1926, the same year that federal officers seized five thousand gallons of potentially lethal liquor in North Texas.[17]

Most simply bought from bootleggers, who seemed to be everywhere and well supplied. The economically advantaged paid premium prices for name-brand products supplied by rum runners moving liquor from Mexico across the Rio Grande River, a lucrative trade in which known brands like Johnnie Walker Scotch brought as much as $20 a bottle. The less well-heeled drank locally distilled corn whiskey selling for $3 a pint or $0.50 a shot at soft drink stands (which sprung up everywhere) and pressing stands or from service cars that delivered. By whatever means, liquor flowed freely. In 1921, the *Fort Worth Press* called Fort Worth the most wide-open town in Texas, stating that liquor was readily available. A 1925 article in *Tom Hickey's Magazine* said the same for the whole state, reporting that a simple phone call in any Texas town would bring alcohol in fifteen minutes.[18]

Federal Prohibition agents did what they could to stem the flow but faced many obstacles. Combating a commodity that many honest citizens deemed innocuous made their job difficult if not impossible, especially with the huge profits associated with such a huge demand. A case of liquor costing $40 in Mexico sold for three times as much in the United States, a profit margin that attracted suppliers willing to use extreme measures, including violence, as evidenced by the deaths of several federal agents and smugglers in Texas alone. Enforcing an unpopular law involving serious money was difficult enough, but it was made impossible by a serious lack of staffing. Initially, no more than one hundred federal agents covered the entire Southwest, an impossibly large swath of territory for such a tiny force. The Fort Worth office alone covered more than 115 counties that stretched from Oklahoma to West Texas. Still, federal agents did their best, seizing forty-six stills and 2,280 gallons of liquor and destroying 26,000 gallons of mash in the nine-month period ending January 31, 1921. Given their limited resources, federal agents concentrated on large operators like Fort Worth's Calloway brothers. In 1921, agents raided their home at 819 Bryan Street and three of their other locations, destroying several stills and making five arrests, a sizable haul that did little considering the very next month, another 2,700 gallons of whiskey mash were seized from a warehouse at 101 Boaz Street.[19] Occasionally, federal officers would hit suppliers at the final stage, raiding local joints like the Tenth Street Buffet and the Meadowmere Country Club, a jazz club and dance hall, but more often they concentrated on larger operations, like a sixty-gallon still on West Bluff Street and a brewery running behind a laundry at 2800 Northwest Street. For all their efforts, the supply flowed with little interruption. In the twelve months ending June 3, 1926, Federal Courts in North Texas recorded a total of 437 convictions (only 9 acquittals), including 262 for liquor violations, a respectable average of 5 convictions per week that spoke well of federal efforts, but the presence of so many liquor cases clogging courts six years into Prohibition indicated that enforcement had done little to slow production. To be fair, some disagreed. Henry Zweifel, US district attorney for the Northern District of Texas from 1921 to 1927, claimed that the ninety-nine counties he oversaw were the nation's driest, a comparative statement that would have been impossible to prove or disprove but one that was more likely an expression of Zweifel's own hubris. Such an inflated view of the effectiveness of law enforcement was especially interesting in view of Zweifel's membership in the University Club, a private club in the Metropolitan Hotel notorious for illegal gambling (see above).[20]

Local police were less effective and often complicit in the illegal trade. Many police officers shared in the thirst for alcohol, and a few were fired for liquor violations, but the more serious problem lay in tolerance or feigned ignorance of illegal alcohol operations, both often bought and paid for by bootleggers. Captain Joe Cornett, already under investigation for his ties to bootleggers, tried to minimize his culpability by claiming that one hundred stills at Lake Worth operated with the compliance of authorities, a charge Chief Hamilton and local prohibition agents denied. Their denial was suspect, since Lake Worth was a known haven for stills, thanks to having twenty-four wooded acres (providing seclusion) adjacent both to water and to a large population but patrolled by only three park policemen. Publicity over Cornett's charges brought state agents who found and closed a few small operations but reported nothing close to the quantity alleged. To appease critics, Mayor Cockrell increased the number of park officers to five—hardly enough to make much difference. Some crooks took advantage of the lack of police presence to steal from illicit operators. In July 1922, four men, including a former police officer and a former prohibition agent, were arrested after a series of raids on liquor "resorts" in which they, pretending to be cops, confiscated alcohol only to resell it. Of course, no one had to travel as far as Lake Worth to find illegal liquor; the Gem Restaurant at 808 Throckmorton Street, one block from police headquarters, was well known for its fifty-cent shots. The corrupting influence of Prohibition upon police was not just a Fort Worth issue; in 1921, Chicago Chief of Police Charles Fitzmorris admitted that half his department was involved in transporting liquor.[21]

Officers on the street and the command staff seemed blind to the obvious, or at least they claimed to be. In 1925, Mayor Henry Meacham professed ignorance of any illegal alcohol operations in Fort Worth, leading the Anti-Saloon League to offer the services of one thousand "investigators" able to point out bootleggers for him. The issue was not that police were unable to find bootleggers but that, for one reason or another, they chose not to do so, and when they did make arrests, the charges were usually downgraded to divert fine income into city coffers rather than the county. Police Chief Lee, under some pressure to increase revenue, made that policy official, ordering that bootleggers be charged with disturbing the peace, a city court case, rather than with higher offenses that went to county courts. The first person arrested under the new policy, the operator of a cold drink stand at Magnolia and

Jennings Avenues who was charged with selling beer and whiskey, was taken downtown and released on a $25 bond, which was forfeited—the same procedure used with prostitutes charged with vagrancy.[22]

Gambling, like alcohol, was common in Fort Worth and faced few threats from law enforcement. Sometimes the higher arms of law enforcement would close a casino or prosecute larger operations, such as in 1920, when District Attorney Brown obtained a court injunction restraining the Texas Athletic Club at 1205½ Throckmorton Street from operating gambling devices, or in July 1921, when the Tarrant County grand jury returned twenty-two true bills against gamblers (out of thirty-nine total indictments). More often, enforcement action focused on the lowest levels, with the cop on the beat arresting low-level violators who forfeited $10 bonds taken at the scene or upon arrival at police headquarters. There certainly was no shortage of gambling operations or participants. In 1926, police raided five upstairs casinos just on Main Street, making seventy-two arrests—mostly patrons who were released immediately on bonds. Occasionally, more noteworthy clients faced arrest, such as in 1923, when Hugh Jamieson, a former police commissioner known for his concern for the welfare of prostitutes, was charged with running a casino at 1312½ Houston Street, or in 1924, when Fred Wheat and his wife, owners of the Jefferson Hotel at 1007½ Houston Street, were arrested for running a gambling house.[23]

One of the area's most notorious and popular gambling joints got its start in the 1920s. Beulah Marshall opened Top O' Hill Terrace as a fine-dining establishment complete with a tea room, but the format and clientele changed in 1926, when Fred Browning, a local plumber, club owner, and gambler, bought the property and set about adding a basement twice as large as the superstructure where he built a lounge, brothel, and casino. The operation thrived and persisted thanks in no small part to impediments that made it virtually raid-proof. The building stood alone in a field removed from the roadway, forcing entry via a guarded gate that opened to a nine-hundred-foot driveway to the front, where everyone had to pass through five secured doors before reaching the center of the action—all designed to provide ample time for patrons and staff to hide themselves and the equipment or to make surreptitious exits through a fifty-foot escape tunnel ten feet tall and four feet wide. The club's reputation grew and spread after Benny Binion, a Dallas bootlegger and gambler who later opened a Las Vegas casino, became a partner, attracting celebrities such as Howard Hughes, Clark Gable, Gene Autry, Lana Turner, and John Wayne as well as musicians and bandleaders Benny Goodman and Tommy Dorsey.[24]

Prostitution had long been a staple of Fort Worth life, and it remained widespread, especially in the Acre and around poorer areas, although a few operated in finer neighborhoods. Like alcohol and gambling, the presence of sex for hire was too obvious not to have come to the notice of the police. A grand jury report in 1920 described gambling and prostitution as blatant, asserting that lewd women (as well as pickpockets) plied their trade openly in Little Mexico and Irishtown, sections the report called "disgraceful." The jurors excoriated city and county officers for routinely fining and releasing gamblers and prostitutes on the scene, but prostitutes liked the system; several testified that it allowed them to work unobstructed as long as they paid periodic fines. Occasionally, officers would make a few arrests, usually after complaints reached a critical mass of intensity, but things quickly returned to business as usual. In 1923, reports of mixed-race orgies in "Little Mexico" brought police raids on drink stands and other prostitution fronts around Calhoun, Jones, and Fourteenth Streets as well as five-day suspensions for four beat officers for their failure to deal with the flagrant operations. Prostitution, along with gambling and liquor, was common in Fort Worth's blighted sections, but some houses carried finer addresses. In 1923, Mrs. Minnie Miller was charged for running a disorderly house (house of prostitution) at 1704 Summit Avenue, called by the *Star Telegram* a "highly respectable neighborhood." Miller's husband, A. T., was also arrested for Prohibition violations, and three men and one woman on the premises were arrested for vagrancy, the common charge for prostitution.[25]

Fort Worth became known in the 1920s as a national center for illegal narcotics. J. A. Riley, head of Fort Worth police's narcotics section, spent time with New York City's narcotics squad, who told him that Fort Worth was well known as a major point on the drug pipeline due to the ease of transit provided by its seventeen railroads and its proximity to the Mexican border, where many drugs originated, and to West Texas' large transient population of oil field workers prone to drug use. A federal officer seconded those remarks, saying that more drug transactions occurred in Fort Worth than in any city south of Chicago. Riley himself claimed that Fort Worth had one thousand addicts and dealers, including one hundred minors, about 1 percent of the city's population, adding that 85 percent of all criminals were addicts and that drug use was responsible for half of all crime. Others thought Riley's estimates were high—that the actual total was six hundred dealers and addicts involved in a daily drug trade worth $4,800, still rather high figures for a city only slightly above one hundred thousand in population. Tangible evidence of illegal narcotics activity appeared in the number of cases prosecuted in the court system. Several known "dope fiends" were identified as part of twenty-eight persons convicted in Fort Worth's district court between January 1 and February 15, 1921. By 1922, the problem was large enough that Fort Worth considered building a drug treatment hospital, although the idea never progressed very far due to other "pressing problems."[26]

In contrast to vice and alcohol offenses, police at every level tended to prosecute narcotics cases vigorously, although they were never able to eliminate the problem. In 1915, Fort Worth police started a crackdown on morphine, the most commonly abused drug, but their efforts did little except drive the price from $35 to $180 an ounce and cause many users to stop carrying syringes, which marked them for prosecution as addicts, in favor of injecting using safety pins and eye droppers. The effort was laudable, but arrests kept coming, indicating that the impact was limited. A 1922 raid at a house on Congress Avenue found two women and an eighteen-month-old infant under the influence of morphine, the adults having injected the child to keep her from crying. Not only did morphine not disappear, but the size of seizures increased dramatically. Officers arrested Ed Wilson of 1300 Holman Avenue with thirty ounces and charged C. Dollihite and Ruth Harris with possessing a "sizeable quantity," but the largest bust came in 1924, when federal agents raided the Cary Hotel, 1501½ Houston

Street, seizing morphine valued at $50,000, the largest quantity in the entire Southwest to that point. The hotel owners, A. D. Cary and his wife, were known suppliers for a vast region that stretched from Wichita Falls (125 miles northwest) to Waco (90 miles south). The amount of money involved was a corrupting force driving risky behavior, including one couple caught brazenly supplying prisoners at the Tarrant County Jail. It also drew in some unlikely operators such as Dr. G. A. Hamlett, who was arrested for distributing morphine from his home at 856 Grove Street.[27]

Morphine dominated the illegal trade, but drugs such as cocaine, opium, and marijuana were available. In 1920, J. B. Davis, a druggist on Boaz Street, was charged with selling twenty ounces of paregoric, an opium-based liquid, to one person, and in 1922, officers raiding the home of W. A. Master, a former policeman, at 717 Davis Avenue, found both liquor and cocaine. Master, working as a night watchman around Forest Park Boulevard and Rosedale Street, learned of the seizure when he telephoned his wife, then fatally shot himself as police approached. Marijuana did not get as much notice as other narcotics probably because it was associated largely with Hispanics, although it was considered a dangerous drug capable of causing psychotic reactions; a 1928 Fort Worth health report listed three men adjudicated insane due to marijuana use. While drugs tended to receive more press coverage, court prosecutions indicate that alcohol was much more widespread. In 1926, Fort Worth's federal court reported 262 Prohibition convictions compared to only 21 for drugs.[28]

Like the city in general, the Fort Worth police adopted new techniques and procedures, including some that endured to the current era. The changes made police officers more professional by providing standards for recruits, establishing training, and broadening patrol modes. Officers also confronted new challenges in modern traffic control and in the growth of illegal drug use, both becoming major law enforcement issues. Prohibition brought widespread disobedience and aggravated corrupting influences. However, much remained the same concerning prostitution and gambling, both of which remained widely available in Fort Worth.

CHAPTER THREE

Racism and the Ku Klux Klan

In the 1920s, Fort Worth touted its lack of diversity as an attribute. Following the 1920 Census, the *Star Telegram* boasted that only 7,359 foreign-born persons called Fort Worth home, fewer than Dallas (8,730), Houston (12,012), or San Antonio (36,846), and a 1924 chamber of commerce pamphlet bragged, "With a smaller percentage of Negro and foreign-born population than any other city . . . Fort Worth is enabled to add the real pleasures of life to her business and commercial advantages." Fort Worth city officials accepted without question the superiority of native-born Anglos and inferiority of both dark-skinned Americans and immigrants, including ancillary assumptions concerning their cleanliness and honesty. In 1922, city health officials blamed cramped conditions among foreigners living in crowded tenements for spawning diseases spreading to the rest of the population. In the mind-set of the period, foreigners were not only unsanitary but rude and venal. In 1924, C. A. Burton of the board of parks moved to ban Greek drink stands from city parks, saying the operators were known for rudeness and for charging patrons a dime for items meant to sell for a nickel.[1]

The span of acceptable ethnicity was narrow, excluding not only foreign-born people but also most nonwhites as well as non-Protestants and non-Christians. Fort Worth's Jewish population in the 1920s was small but known as far away as New York City, where it received recognition for its generosity after contributing $10,000 to the Palestine Fund. None of that mattered to the local Ku Klux Klan, who disdained Jews. Klan members beat Morris Strauss, the owner of a local plumbing supply, for taking business away from white Protestant businessmen. Few Mormons, members of the Church of Jesus Christ of Latter-Day Saints, called Texas home; the only significantly large population, approximately one thousand, lived in Upshur County of northeast Texas. Fort Worth Mormons numbered no more than one hundred but, led by A. F. Kutler, were one of the first organized Mormon groups in the state, an achievement that brought the North Texas Conference of the Church of Jesus Christ of Latter-Day Saints to Fort Worth in November 1926. The conference, held at 311½ Main Street, heard from George Richard, one of the church's twelve apostles.[2]

Hispanics were part of Fort Worth's history from its beginning, and their presence grew over the years. The 7,359 foreign-born residents identified in the 1920 Census included 3,785 persons born in Mexico, but the actual Hispanic population, including Mexican nationals and their descendants, was considerably larger. Hispanics, whether born in the United States or not, were considered outsiders and subjected to crude racial assumptions but were valued for their labor. In 1928, Dayton Moses, a Fort Worth lawyer representing the Texas and Southwestern Cattle Raisers Association, testified before a committee of the US House of Representatives on proposed immigration legislation. Moses opposed the bill because it set immigration quotas on countries of the Western Hemisphere, a critical issue for cattle raisers who, Moses argued, could not find anyone else to do ranch work.[3]

Shunned by mainstream white society, Mexicans and their descendants united around their common culture. Those shared qualities were proudly displayed during a Mexican Independence Day celebration in September 1924 that drew six hundred to the Presbyterian Mexican Mission, 214 East Twelfth Street. The program, led by Reverend A. B. Arrreo, included music, dancing, food, and speeches from five leaders of the local Hispanic community, described by the *Fort Worth Press* as "diminutive brown senors." Such events helped Mexican immigrants and native-born Mexican Americans, known as Chicanos, endure life in the United States while facing many of the same cultural and social prejudices experienced by African Americans. In 1923, Fort Worth police officers lectured a white couple from

New Jersey found in a Mexican dance hall, telling them "that people in the South associate with their own race." Racial divides extended into charity and welfare, separating Hispanics from the services of most relief agencies or institutions, with the significant exception of the Catholic Church, which provided religious as well as secular support. Most of the church's work never made the news, but an exception came in 1928, when seven women from the San Jose Mission were lauded as the first Hispanic graduates of the nursing service of Fort Worth's Department of Public Health and Welfare. They were, the newspaper reported, slated to work caring for "their people."[4]

African Americans faced the most widespread, blatant, and severe discrimination of all, a pervasive part of their everyday lives that required adaptation and endurance to survive. Segregation was not only de facto but de jure, enforced through local ordinances and state legal codes mandating separate accommodations in public transportation and education. In that environment, blatant and crass racial epithets were so common that they often appeared without comment in the local press. Anyone picking up a daily newspaper could read that "Nigger Creek Pool" just outside Mexia, Texas, produced eleven thousand barrels of oil daily; see advertisements for a residential addition off Azle Road with lots for "colored people" at $1 down and $1 weekly; or gaze upon captioned photographs of large white families proclaiming "THEY DON'T BELIEVE 'RACE SUICIDE' IN ERATH COUNTY." In the few instances when journalists praised blacks, their efforts tended more to display existing racist attitudes than enlightened viewpoints. An example appeared in 1920, when an article described William Madison "Gooseneck Bill" McDonald as having abilities "far above the average negro [*sic*]." McDonald, an extraordinary man born the son of a slave, achieved remarkable success after moving to Fort Worth in 1906, including opening the Fraternal Bank and Trust to serve African Americans, the bank becoming the anchor of a flourishing black business district around Jones and Ninth Streets. Gooseneck Bill's many commercial successes helped make him Texas' first African American millionaire, while his political involvement made him a force in the Republican Party.[5]

Juneteenth at Stovall Drug Store at East Eighth Street in the African American business district, year unknown. Courtesy of the Genealogy, History and Archives Unit, Fort Worth Library (Tarrant County Black Historical Genealogy Society, series 8, box 5, folder 16).

Racial ideology permeated into everything, in all facets of society, even into otherwise benevolent organizations and certainly into the economic realm. Alarmed over a movie scene in which three black men danced in a chorus of white women, the Fort Worth League of Women Voters, led by Mrs. F. N. Graves, organized a letter-writing campaign demanding that Hollywood producers ban blacks from appearing onscreen with whites. While cultural and social discrimination carried serious consequences, the bias in the economic sphere proved especially harmful, impacting core quality-of-life issues such as wages and employment opportunities. In 1922, the average Fort Worth teacher earned $3.11 daily, but rates ranged from $5.03 for white men and $3.94 for white women down to $2.91 for "colored males" and an abysmal $2.12 for "colored women" (not to mention the gender disparity that was almost as significant as race). Race played a big role in who got hired and at what job. In 1921, a protest at the Methodist

Church on Weatherford Street by white construction workers upset over having to work alongside blacks became a near-riot after rumors spread that a black man had been made foreman.[6]

Some of the strictest color lines defined neighborhoods, and threats to the existing racial boundaries brought serious reactions. In 1922, some three hundred white residents of the Seventh Ward, a neighborhood southeast of downtown and east of the railroad tracks around East Myrtle Street and East Maddox Avenue, met at the fire hall at Maddox and New York Avenues. The group adopted a resolution agreeing to accept blacks already living in the neighborhood but demanding that the city stop the "invasion" of others. Fort Worth officials offered understanding but regretted they could not limit a person's right to live where they chose. A second meeting in January 1923 at the Church of Christ at 1501 East Hattie Street, a few blocks north, threatened a lawsuit to stop construction of a Negro Amusement Park planned for the area. In 1924, police officers removed six staked placards placed at each corner of East Myrtle Street and Louisiana Avenue, each featuring a skull and crossbones and signed "100 per cent [*sic*] Americans" and warning, "Mr. Negro, don't you move south of East Myrtle Street if you want to live and prosper! Be wise Negro!" The signs were a reaction to the recent arrival of eight African American families, leaving only nine white residences in the 900 to 1400 blocks of Louisiana and the 700 to 1500 blocks of East Myrtle Street. When intimidation, appeals to city authorities, and warning signs failed, neighborhood whites attempted to buy out black residents. One hundred fifty whites meeting at the neighborhood fire hall formed a finance committee charged with selling sufficient shares to raise $7,000 needed to purchase ten black-owned homes located from 1100 Maddox Avenue, west to Evans Avenue, north to Magnolia Avenue, and west to Missouri Avenue, then turning south to Myrtle Street before returning to Maddox Avenue. The group reported they had sales agreements from all but one family.[7]

If all else failed, racists turned to intimidation and threats, then violence. The escalation began with warnings to black residents living as far south as Allen Avenue to either move or face dire consequences, the threats delivered anonymously and, in one case, by a brick thrown into the yard with a note attached instructing the family to move within a week or be "blown sky high." When threats failed, violence followed. In January 1925, explosions damaged a black-occupied home at 942 East Maddox Avenue, followed in March with blasts at 937 and 941 East Maddox Avenue. After a year's lull, the mayhem resumed in March 1926, with dynamite damaging homes on East Leuda Street belonging to A. L. Hunter and C. Daniels and two homes on East Cannon Avenue hit in April. The first explosion that April came at 1125 East Cannon Avenue; the second moments later next door at 1129. Two weeks before the dynamiting, Dan Hill and his wife, the residents at 1125 East Cannon, had found two dynamite sticks under their home. Hill, a porter at the Fort Worth Club, disavowed knowledge of any personal issues that could have been responsible. The next month, May 1926, a black-owned home on East Maddox and two vacant houses at 1013 and 1015 East Leuda Street were bombed.[8]

African Americans victimized by violence found little relief from law enforcement officials more concerned with maintaining racial divisions and prosecuting African Americans, especially for alleged offenses involving white women. Even minor transgressions to the existing racial mores brought legal sanctions; a black man was arrested in June 1920 for simply winking at a white woman, while more serious incidents brought severe reactions. In 1920, Fort Worth officers twice rescued Robert Lowe, a black man accused of assaulting a ten-year-old girl, from lynch mobs bent on quick and lethal revenge. Lowe's escape was uncommon but paled in comparison to his acquittal at trial, an event so rare as to earn notice from the *New York Times*. The rushed drive for informal resolutions seemed hardly necessary given the speed at which the wheels of formal justice turned. For example, in February 1921, Charles Moden was arrested for an attempted assault on Mrs. C. W. Bishop at her home on Tremont Avenue. The alleged incident and arrest occurred on a Wednesday, and the grand jury returned an indictment the next day, with the trial set for that Saturday, but Mrs. Bishop's condition forced a postponement, resulting in Moden being sent to the Dallas Jail for safekeeping, a common practice to thwart lynchings. A few days later, the two Tarrant County officers returning him for trial shot and killed the accused when he, despite being handcuffed, jumped from the car and ran. Apparently, black prisoners made a habit of attempting to escape while handcuffed. Only months later, David Bunn, arrested after a crime spree involving several robberies and "outrages" against two white women, was also moved to Dallas. After the transfer, a lynch mob estimated at one thousand sought Bunn at both the Fort Worth and Tarrant County Jails, leaving the latter only after being allowed inside to verify the prisoner was not present (part of the group showed up at the Dallas Jail but left without causing much disturbance). Once again, deputies returning Bunn shot and killed the accused, claiming he, also wearing handcuffs, jumped from the car. From today's perspective, it seems strange that no one questioned the necessity of two armed law enforcement officers shooting a running, unarmed, handcuffed prisoner.[9]

Lynchings were a real threat for criminally accused African Americans and even some whites. The two most common and distinguishing characteristics surrounding lynchings were geographic (most occurred in the South) and racial (most victims were black). Studies estimated that 2,843 people were lynched between 1885 and 1920, an average of more than 80 per year. Georgia led all states with 427 persons dying by lynching, or more than 15 percent of the total, followed by Mississippi with 400 (those two states accounting for 29 percent the total), but Texas, with 304, ranked among the leaders. Statistics vary in degree, but all agree that blacks constituted the great majority of victims; for example, only 8 whites were counted out of 65 lynched in 1920. Indeed, the lynching of a white person was enough of an aberration to receive widespread notice. In 1920, the lynching of Tom Vickery, a white man taken by a mob after he killed a Fort Worth police officer, was reported by the *New York Times* under the headline "Texans Lynch a White Man."[10]

Perhaps the most infamous Fort Worth lynching occurred in 1921. Fred Rouse, an African American man in his thirties and a father of three, came to Fort Worth from East Texas seeking comparatively high wages at the local packinghouses. Rouse found work during the meatpacking strike of 1921, forcing him to cross picket lines, a dangerous endeavor given the harsh economic realities workers faced. Rouse, with a family to feed, endured the verbal assaults and name-calling without complaint, but as the stoppage wore on, striking workers—left without a paycheck—grew more desperate, leading to a vicious attack as Rouse left work. During the melee, Rouse pulled a pistol and shot brothers Tom and Tracy Maclin, wounding one and killing the other before being subdued and beaten severely, saved only by the intervention of Niles City police, who sent him to the City-County Hospital at Jones and Third Streets. Some days later, thirty masked men wearing dusters took Rouse from his hospital bed and left him hanging from a hackberry tree off Samuels Avenue and Twelfth Street, the same tree from which Tom Vickery had been lynched (three days later, someone chopped the tree down). Robert Maclin, Tom and Tracy's younger brother, was brought to the scene in time to see Rouse, barefooted and wearing only a hospital gown, still hanging with his neck grotesquely bent and the crowd firing shots into his dead body. Witnesses reported seeing uniform pants under the dusters worn by some of the mob, stoking suspicions that police officers made up part of the lynch mob. In February 1922, two Niles City officers, W. H. Atherton and G. H. Tiller, as well as Tom Howell, a railroad switchman and a former police officer, were charged with Rouse's murder. In April, the grand jury no-billed all three, but a subsequent jury indicted them as well as three others.[11]

Violence toward blacks often involved the Ku Klux Klan, a potent force throughout most of the 1920s. The Klan formed after the Civil War but declined following the end of Reconstruction, only to revive around 1915 and become a major political force in most southern states and parts of the Midwest as well as wield a significant national presence. Klan official Joe Camp, speaking in Fort Worth in 1922, claimed that six thousand national leaders were dues-paying members and that many other high-ranking members of government, including President Warren Harding and Attorney General Harry M. Daughtery, were sympathizers. President Harding voiced Klan-like racial views, saying in a speech at Birmingham, Alabama, that differences between the races were "fundamental, eternal, and inescapable" and that World War I had demonstrated that race problems (buzz words for "black problems") were national and not sectional. Klan influence was displayed in Texas politics as early as 1921, when the statehouse defeated a resolution declaring the Klan an illegal organization. The Texas Klan grew rapidly throughout the first half of the 1920s, enrolling twenty thousand dues-paying members by 1923 and counting on thousands more who supported their agenda, the numbers forming a formidable political base.[12]

In 1922, the Klan solidified and demonstrated its political position in Texas, winning enough state offices to have clear political dominance. In the Democratic primary, Pat Neff, a supporter of the Klan but not an official Klansman, won the nomination for governor, and Earle Mayfield, a secret Klansmen, was named a candidate for the US Senate. The Democratic Party nomination essentially assured election in the post-Reconstruction era, when the party dominated southern politics. In 1922, Klan-favored candidates running as Democrats won most state offices, including majorities in both houses of the legislature, the governorship, and the senate seat up for election—such a complete victory that the *New York Times* conceded that the Klan controlled the Texas state government. The only real challenge to Democrats in the 1922 general election came in the senate race, where the party's candidate, Mayfield, ran without a Republican opponent but faced a write-in campaign from George E. B. Peddy that garnered one-third of the vote—very substantial for a write-in candidacy. Peddy lost but contested the election before the US Senate, charging that Klan influence and voter irregularities tainted the vote. Mayfield, defended by W. P. McLean of Fort Worth, denied intimidation had played a role or that the Klan had spent $150,000 on his campaign. Peddy fought hard, but Mayfield prevailed, keeping his senate seat.[13]

In some cases, the Klan's political influence allowed it to ignore or challenge law enforcement at the local level and even higher. In 1921, District Judge James Hamilton of Austin claimed Klansmen had whipped or tarred and feathered at least fifty persons during the previous six months without suffering consequences in law or reprisals.

When the McLennan County sheriff tried to stop a Klan parade in Lorena, Texas (eighty miles south of Fort Worth), the marchers fought back, sparking a bloody battle that left four persons critically wounded. In 1923, local authorities in Burleson County, east of Austin, refused to indict a known Klansmen who killed Otto Lange, shot Lange's twelve-year-old daughter, and pistol-whipped his seventy-year-old mother. Lieutenant Governor T. W. Davidson, acting governor while Neff was out of state, ordered the Texas Rangers in, but Neff recalled them on his return. Davidson did not give up, sending the rangers back when he again assumed the governorship, this time with orders to prepare cases for the grand jury. The Klan's ability to circumvent officials was not unique to Texas. In November 1923, Oklahoma Governor J. C. Dalton was impeached and removed from office after he called out the National Guard to combat a Klan "insurrection."[14]

Klan political dominance extended to local governments. The extensive electoral success in 1922 carried over into precinct and county offices in most of Texas' large cities, including Fort Worth, Dallas, Houston, and Waco. The Klan was large, but its political power transcended its membership thanks to outside support and because they demanded that members support all Klan candidates without exception. In Harris County, Houston Mayor Oscar F. Holcombe, Justice of the Peace Campbell Overstreet, and Baptist Pastor E. P. West were expelled after they criticized Klan leadership and refused to vote the straight Klan ticket. Little dissension or opposition existed in Dallas, the city called the "Star City of Klandom" by the *New York Times*. In 1921, before the landslide of 1922, dues-paying Klansmen already dominated the public payroll, including leading figures such as Dallas County Sheriff Dan Harston, Dallas Chief of Police Elmo Straight, two-thirds of the entire police force, Dallas Commissioner Louis Turley, and many other civic leaders who were open Klansmen. In the infamous election of 1922, the Klan extended its power base, winning every office and challenging the Citizens' League, Dallas's established political power center. Many public officials who refrained from joining the Klan still shared and supported its ideology. For example, Dallas Federal Judge James C. Wilson praised the group, saying that he did not know of any bad Klansmen and that most were successful men, but refused to join because he felt some of their ideas were misguided. In the autumn of 1923, the imperial wizard, Hiram Evans of Dallas, spoke at a Dallas rally protected by police officers wearing Klan ribbons. The rally drew an estimated 73,000 attendees, about one-third the city's population but far below the leadership's expected crowd of 250,000.[15]

The 1922 election also cemented the Klan's political power in Fort Worth, where its candidates won every race from constable to state senator. The huge victory created a political position so powerful and pervasive that Klan backing became a political essential, forcing many contractors to become Klansmen simply to help win city contracts. Membership in Klavern No. 101, the local Klan chapter, swelled to 6,500 and included notables such as Brown Harwood, who became the klazik, the Klan's second-highest national officer; Marvin Leonard, owner of Leonard's Department Store; Tarrant County Sheriff Sterling Clark; County Judge Hugh Small; Mayor E. R. Cockrell; George W. Armstrong, owner of Texas Steel on Hemphill Street; and prominent local lawyer William A. Hanger, who became the kleagle, or local chapter president. Hanger, a well-known lawyer, represented prominent people such as Governor Pat Neff and Governor Miriam "Ma" Ferguson during her impeachment (although he opposed Ferguson politically). Hanger also served as a state senator, rising to become a political power in statewide Democratic politics in which he played a key role in blocking the 1924 presidential nomination of Al Smith, Catholic governor of New York.[16] Another important Klan supporter, George W. Armstrong, arrived in Fort Worth in 1890 from Jasper County and was elected as a Fort Worth alderman the same year. A lawyer, Armstrong partnered with Hanger but left the law in 1904 after becoming the owner of Fort Worth Rolling Mill. He became one of the most vocal Klan advocates, calling the group the hope of the nation, but never joined due to a personal objection to secret societies. Armstrong was also a virulent anti-Semite who published several books exposing supposed Jewish conspiracies as well as articles in the *Dearborn Independent*, Henry Ford's newspaper, blaming most of the world's ills on International Jewry, which, he claimed, ruled most of the world. He remained an active, repressive force on many fronts, firing strikers during a 1920s strike at Texas Steel and financially supporting various right-wing causes until his death.[17]

The Klan's considerable sway affected jurisprudence and law enforcement. Joe Laverty, a local Catholic lawyer, complained that the Klan did whatever it wanted with little interference, and Ted Mack, a Jewish lawyer, gave up on local courts where Klan-dominated juries made fair trials impossible, focusing instead on appellate work. Judge Hal Lattimore became so annoyed about Klan influence perverting the legal process that he threatened prosecution for any juror who failed to disclose Klan links (those who did were removed from the jury pool). In fact, the Klan's influence was so strong in Tarrant County courts that it became a sufficient legal basis for appeals or changes of venue. In 1921, a defense attorney added that Klan membership and

Fort Worth Ku Klux Klan, Klavern No. 101, early 1920s. Courtesy Special Collections, the University of Texas at Arlington Libraries.

sympathies not only corrupted potential jurors but also extended to the district attorney's staff and the police, both with substantial staff known to be Klansmen. Many public officials disclosed their affiliations, but membership rolls remained secret, hiding the names of many members. Still, there is no doubt that many Tarrant County peace officers besides Sheriff Clark belonged to the Klan.[18]

Membership rolls may have been secret, but the Klan and its ideology were openly displayed in many forms. The *American Citizen*, a Klan newspaper published in Fort Worth, claimed a readership of twenty-five thousand, but no one had to go to newsstands to see the Klan's presence. Klansmen, as well as Klanswomen and children, appeared in uniform during selected events and occasionally marched proudly in downtown parades dressed in full robes. In January 1923, approximately nine hundred Fort Worth Klansmen departed for Waco on two special trains, one pulled by a locomotive with a twelve-foot cross tied to its smokestack. Klansmen also marched boldly in Dallas, and on February 16, 1922, some five thousand hooded members—many arriving on eighteen trains from Dallas, Waco, and beyond—gathered in Fort Worth to march down Main and Houston Streets, assisted by police who stopped traffic and turned off streetlights to highlight their burning crosses. In June 1923, Klanswomen, many carrying signs proclaiming, "We Stand for Protection of the Home," marched in a parade that stretched twenty-five blocks while an airplane towing a cross circled overhead. In 1924, Imperial Wizard Hiram Evans reviewed a large downtown parade that took fifty minutes to pass, the route beginning at Worth Field and ending at the courthouse.[19]

Klansmen tried to broaden their appeal by participating in local cultural activities and events. On February 8, 1923, the local chapter began broadcasting over WBAP Radio from 9:30 p.m. to 11:45 p.m., becoming one of the first Klan groups to adopt the new medium. A bugle call and prayer opened the show that featured music from the Klan orchestra and the Kavalier Quartet singers as well as soloists performing songs such as "Joy to the World" and "Toot, Toot, Tootsie." Listeners from as far away as Illinois and Ohio wrote commending the program. The Klan also fielded a semipro baseball team that played against teams from local businesses and organizations such as Walker Bread and the electricians union, among others. Klan players, including Fire Chief Paul Fontaine, wore white uniforms trimmed in red with "Ku Klux Klan" printed across the front. The Klan was so integrated into mainstream society that the Southwestern Exposition and Fat Stock Show designated Friday, March 12, 1924, as Klan Day, following the lead of the State Fair of Texas in Dallas, which instituted a Klan Day in 1923.[20]

Nowhere were ties clearer or more pronounced than between the Klan and local churches and pastors. Reverend J. W. Bergin of the First Methodist Church was a vocal supporter known for justifying the Klan as necessary to overcome "deplorable conditions" following the Civil War. Bergin allowed Klansmen to use the church for radio broadcasts and frequently welcomed Klan officers to speak to the congregation. One of those, Joe Campo, told parishioners that 90 percent of all ministers, including Billy Sunday (the most celebrated evangelist of the era), belonged to the Klan or were sympathizers. Campo was a stark champion for Protestantism who disdained Catholicism, which he saw as un-American, alleging that every presidential assassin had been a Catholic as proof and that a deep conspiracy between Catholics and Jews controlled 80 percent of the nation's newspapers. Many Baptist ministers also lent support, including J. Frank Norris, who offered the First Baptist Church's auditorium for Klan use. Some Fort Worth clergy went beyond mere support to become Klan officers. L. P. Bloodworth, a Methodist minister and confidant of Norris, served as grand dragon of the Texas Klan, and Reverend C. A. Ridley, a Baptist minister, was a national Klan officer. In August 1924, at the Chamber of Commerce Auditorium (the local Klan chapter received its mail at the chamber), Ridley, surrounded by sixty-five robed Klansmen, told the crowd that the Klan had been a good friend of African Americans. In the audience sat Reverend Lee Heaton, an open Klansman and rector of Saint Andrews Episcopal Church. Cross allegiances between churchmen and Klansmen were also common in most other southern cities, including Dallas, where many pastors openly supported the organization and one, Alex C.

Parker of Rosemont Christian Church, served as the Dallas cyclops, or local head.[21]

Fort Worth's chapter grew large enough to build a grand Klan hall. At the beginning of the 1920s, Fort Worth Klansmen maintained a small office at 209½ Commerce Street but conducted large meetings, including initiation ceremonies, in large fields outside the city limits. One such event in 1922 brought a stream of six hundred cars traveling north on Main Street to a remote location where 6,000 stood by while 932 new members underwent a secret swearing-in ceremony. In 1923, the Klan owned an auditorium on twenty-eight acres in the Tyler Lake area, named for developer James L. Tyler, that was located off Evans and East Terrell Avenues, just south of the terminus of the streetcar line (in Glenwood Park, near what is today Riverside Drive, south of Vickery Boulevard). Imperial Wizard Hiram Evans spoke at the hall that June, and in October, the chapter held its first public initiation ceremony in which 720 inductees took the Klan oath while thousands of members and nonmembers watched and police officers stood as security. At the time of the initiation, the Klan had sold the property to the city of Fort Worth for $20,000, using the money toward the construction of a new three-story hall at 1006 North Main Street. The grand edifice, costing $100,000 and seating 4,000, opened in March 1924 during a combined dedication and initiation ceremony for 600 new members, all highlighted with speeches from W. A. Hanger, a noted pro-Klan lawyer, and Reverend J. W. Underwood. The hall was also let for shows, such as Harry Houdini, who appeared on October 18, 1924, but a minstrel show scheduled for November 6, 1924, had to be moved to the First Baptist Church after a suspicious fire on November 5 did $45,000 in damages—almost half the property's total value. The cyclops (local Klan leader), Julian Hyer, and many members, suspecting arson, offered a $500 reward for information. Their suspicions seemed confirmed by an anonymous note that threatened more violence, although closer examinations raised suspicions that the missive was a crude ploy to blame African Americans. Doubters pointed to the note's signature, "the blacks," an awkward but perhaps revealing use of the third person.[22]

Klansmen were most widely known for aggressive repression of nonwhites, Jews, and Catholics, but they also occasionally dealt harshly with Protestant whites. In 1921, robed men whipped two white men known to beat their wives, pummeled an unidentified man accused of abusing his children, and severely beat W. T. Ralls, who they took from his rooming house on Taylor Street. In another case, Benny Pinto, described as an Anglo gambler known to have "immoral relations with women," was tarred and feathered. The Klan warned Pinto to leave the county, and when he failed to comply, they administered sixty lashes with a whip. Reprisals against white women were rare but did occur. Mrs. I. C. Tatum reported that several Klanswomen took her from her home to a remote location where they beat her, accusing her of teaching her daughter "immorality." The Klan developed a harsh reputation from such tactics that had somewhat of a deterrent effect. Two men charged with robbery told police that they would leave Fort Worth rather than face the Klan's wrath, indicating a preference for Denver, Colorado, where they said many of their colleagues had relocated to escape similar fates.[23]

For all its spread and power, the Klan did face some organized opposition. In June 1921, some 1,500 persons gathered at Marine Park forged a loose coalition dedicated to counteracting Klan violence and influence. One of the main groups to emerge from the meeting, the Citizens' Liberty League, was a progressive group (Fire Chief W. E. Bideker was a member) that advocated nonviolence, but others, like the Anti-Klan, were more confrontational, promising retaliation in kind if the Klan followed through on a flyer sent to hotel bellhops in August threatening to beat any who provided prostitutes for guests. In 1922, twelve businessmen met at the Westbrook Hotel to unite Klan opposition into a single organization with clear leadership. They adopted the Anti-Klan name and made J. W. Estes, a member of both groups, the chair. Their charter defined the Klan as an unlawful assembly acting in contravention of society and its laws, and they worked to counter the Klan on a broad front, including the political—at one point, demanding and receiving equal time to respond to a speech at the chamber of commerce by a high-ranking Klan official from Atlanta,

Georgia. During the rebuttal, W. W. Witcher warned of a reign of terror if the Klan were not checked and demanded that all political candidates confirm or deny Klan membership. Dallas developed a similar opposition group that same year that struggled to blunt the Klan's power, a tough job anywhere in the South in the 1920s.[24]

Even as the Klan's power peaked, signs appeared suggesting future problems. The big political victory of the 1922 general election was tempered by the realization that it came from a paltry turnout in which only 50 percent of eligible Democrats voted, a poor participation rate that many saw as a reflection of diminished enthusiasm for the largely pro-Klan slate. In addition, the Klan candidate for senator, Mayfield, ran poorly, winning the nomination while receiving one hundred thousand fewer votes than the rest of the Democratic ticket despite running unopposed. Texas' Klan leadership hoped to reassert itself in the 1924 election by nominating either William Gibbs McAdoo or W. A. Hangar of Fort Worth for governor but instead backed Judge Felix Robertson, a Klansman with less popular appeal. As the Democratic primary neared, the Klan so feared defeat that it scrambled to find votes among nontraditional sources, even to the point of asking candidates to tone down anti-Jewish and anti-Catholic rhetoric and campaigning for Jewish votes at a Fort Worth rally. Those fears proved well justified as Klan candidates lost every statewide primary race, including governor, won by Miriam "Ma" Ferguson (her campaign manager was Homer T. Brannon of Fort Worth), spoiling a planned Robertson victory celebration in Dallas with a float parade. The loss had results, as Governor Ferguson, the first woman to serve as Texas governor, signed an Anti-Klan bill prohibiting secret organizations from wearing hoods, masks, or other costumes. "Ma" was far from a progressive, campaigning for reelection in 1926 on the boast that she kept evolution out of textbooks. Still, by 1926, the tide had turned so much to the antis that Governor Ferguson lost the Democratic nomination not to a Klan-backed candidate but to Dan Moody, a district attorney known for prosecuting Klansmen. The 1926 election, just four years after the remarkable success in 1922, represented a profound, statewide fall from grace that was so substantial, the *New*

York Times reported that the Klan was dead in Texas. That may have represented an overstatement, but the group's influence had clearly waned, its membership declining from a peak of 97,000 statewide to just 18,000 in 1926, while the Dallas chapter fell to only 1,200 members from a high of 13,000.[25]

The Klan's political sway in Fort Worth also began to crack in the 1924 election, the first under the city manager scheme of government. Klansmen lost control of the new city council, a costly defeat that left them unable to control the appointment of the new city manager, a failure that carried significant costs. O. R. Carr of Iowa, Fort Worth's first city manager, drew bitter Klan opposition, including a recall election, after he fired many Klansmen hired during earlier, Klan-friendly administrations. Carr's anti-Klan actions stemmed not so much from doctrinal differences—he openly sympathized with many Klan ideas—but from his determination to end Klan influence on municipal affairs, vowing that he would not allow any outside organization to run the city.[26]

The Klan hoped to rebound using a multifaceted approach to spin a positive public image as a defender of traditional values. They began as early as 1922 with a $700 donation to the Welfare Association and a gift of $50 each to three destitute persons—one a young, unwed mother in a local sanitarium. In 1924, the local chapter, using the Chamber of Commerce Auditorium, presented two performances of *The Flaming Cross*, a drama based on the Klan's postwar rise that ended with a dramatic scene as Klan riders raced to the rescue just as a group of African Americans and "low whites" rushed against a white man defending Klan virtues and southern womanhood. A reviewer called the message blatant, stating in ironic language that the drama tended to "call a spade a spade." In 1924, the Klan bought Ruth Lubin Camp on Lake Worth, turning a section into the Ku Klux Klan Kiddies Kamp, providing a summer camp for hundreds of poor children. They also hosted lake barbecues that drew thousands from all over the state. The softer, gentler image did not mean they abandoned force. In 1926, witnesses reported seeing six men in white robes with red crosses abduct a man off a Fort Worth street.[27]

Although the Klan declined after 1924, it and other institutions remained so formidable that few hardy souls dared to challenge racial standards. One of the few exceptions involved a black man arrested in November 1921 for refusing to sit in the "negro [*sic*] section" of a streetcar. In the face of overwhelming force and severe consequences, most African Americans adapted to survive and, at times, prosper in the existing highly stratified system. Remarkable though they were, few of their personal struggles earned public notice in the existing media or chronicles. One exception, Mose Ruffin, was lauded in 1928 for thirty-seven years of service to the Fort Worth Gas Company. Ruffin, beginning as a lowly mule driver, rose to become the main operator of the company's largest truck and oversaw the laying of more than three hundred miles of pipe, enough to stretch to the Gulf of Mexico. Another successful African American, William M. McDonald, the son of a slave who became one of the most successful black businessmen in Texas, may have been the wealthiest black in the Southwest. Known as "Gooseneck Bill," McDonald built the Fraternal Bank and Trust at Ninth and Jones Streets, a landmark institution that became a catalyst for a vibrant black business district and a home to black fraternal organizations.[28]

Most African Americans did not do so well and, cut completely out of white society, concentrated on developing a separate cultural infrastructure. Local churches became one of the most important forces sustaining and advancing African American culture. The oldest organized black congregation in Fort Worth, Mount Gilead Baptist Church, was established in 1875 in the southeast quadrant at Crump and Fifteenth Streets but relocated by 1912 to 600 Grove Street, a magnificent neoclassical red brick building featuring a front portico with six columns facing east that still dominates the eastern approach to downtown. In addition, the Holiness Church of God Church scored a major advance with the first broadcast of an African American church service on January 1, 1925. The service, aired over WBAP Radio, drew listeners from as far away as Michigan and Utah who sent congratulatory telegrams. Many secular organizations also supported the community. The Negro Welfare Committee opened the Home for Negro

Girls on West Peter Smith Street to teach young ladies domestic science and vocations, and the Colored YMCA at 912 Jones Street, headed by S. H. Fowler, provided important employment services such as job placement assistance, guidance in filing out business forms, and training for careers in automobile mechanics and other trades as well as providing access to necessities such as restrooms and food service at its cafeteria, accommodations not readily available for blacks in the segregated South. Fort Worth's Colored YMCA organized in 1903 but lapsed for several years before reforming in 1915. After 1915, the YMCA occupied several sites, including Sixth and Grove Streets; the Knights of Pythias building on Second Street, purchased for $200 in 1924; to Fifth and Jones Streets in 1929; then Crump Street in 1934; before finally achieving a degree of geographic stability in 1939 at 1600 Jones Street at a building owned by William McDonald. Other black fraternal organizations developed local chapters, including the First District Woodmen of the World, whose members paraded eight hundred strong through downtown Fort Worth in 1928.[29]

Blacks also built separate entertainment outlets—a necessity, since segregation shut them out of most facilities. In 1923, a black man, identified as both Tedd Johnson and Jess Johnson, filed for a permit to build a "negro swimming pool" in the Lakeview Addition, part of the city's Seventh Ward, and the project was surprisingly approved in a plebiscite, 170 for to 124 against. Segregation ruled city parks, but the park board set aside a few parks or sections of parks despite facing serious opposition. In 1925, the board applied for $2,000 from the Harmon Foundation of New York for a black park, promising the city would also contribute $1,000 and appropriate $200 for annual maintenance for four years.[30] Indoor entertainment centered on the Jim Hotel at 413 East Fourth Street, opened by McDonald in the late 1920s, which provided accommodations and dining for black guests and achieved lasting fame for the fabulous lineup of musicians and entertainers appearing on its stage, a list that included the biggest names in show business.[31]

Health care for African Americans made some important advances in the decade but still suffered from segregation. In 1925, the city council hired an architect to design an addition to the City-County Hospital for "negro charity patients," stipulating that until its completion, black indigent care would continue at the Negro Baptist Hospital. In 1928, the Negro Community Hospital, the first facility providing accredited care for blacks, opened at 509 Grove Street thanks to the efforts of Dr. George Munchus and Dr. R. A. Ransom. Despite that expansion, blacks continued to suffer higher mortality rates. In 1928, Fort Worth, rated the healthiest city in Texas and fourth nationally thanks to a low overall mortality rate of 10.7 per 1,000, had a much higher death rate for blacks, a whopping 18.1 per 1,000, almost twice as high as whites (9.7 per 1,000). In an effort to correct some of the environmental factors responsible for the disparity, the local African American community formed a committee, chaired by Dr. Jerome S. Harris, a dentist, to encourage general neighborhood cleanups, and the city established "Negro Health Week" in April 1928, during which students at Fort Worth's ten "colored schools" could receive free health examinations at several clinics established by the Negro Parent Teacher Association, including the Negro Community Hospital on Grove Street.[32] African Americans in Fort Worth and the nation struggled to survive and make incremental progress. Those who prospered were the rare exceptions. For most, the strength and nature of racism prevented any reasonable expectation of meaningful change or advancement. In the 1920s, that was still years away.

Race relations made few advancements in the 1920s. Nonwhites had never enjoyed more than limited, bare access to Fort Worth's white-dominated society that prized their labor but little else. Conditions did not improve in the 1920s as African Americans faced institutionalized segregation in every sector, displayed publicly in housing conflicts, where whites resisted even minor incursions into their separate neighborhoods, and in politics, where the Ku Klux Klan controlled state and local government for much of the decade. The Klan's virtual total control of political power waned after 1924, but its ideas continued unabated. In response, black communities developed their own infrastructure, creating an impressive separate culture.

CHAPTER FOUR

A Struggling Economy

The Fort Worth economy that had done very well during World War I struggled during the 1920s. In 1919, Tarrant County's $155,299,159 in industrial production ranked first among Texas counties and was larger than the combined totals of Dallas County ($116,160,150) and Bexar County ($37,045,244). The Fort Worth area reached such lofty heights through remarkable business growth that began soon after war broke out in Europe in 1914 and continued unchecked until 1925, producing an incredible 906 percent increase in manufacturing output between 1911 and 1925, almost quadruple the rate of increase experienced by Dallas. That growth turned Fort Worth from an industrial infant into Texas' second-largest industrial center, accounting for 8 percent of the state's total output. Industrial growth created a general economic upswing that almost doubled Fort Worth's property valuations from $68,104,154 in 1917 to $128,203,419 in 1920, a remarkable surge in just three years. Property valuation growth slowed the next five years to a still respectable average increase of 4 percent per annum, rising to $153,588,962 in 1925. Bank clearings, which had risen 30 percent in 1919 over 1918, grew at a marginally faster rate of 33.9 percent in the first five months of 1920, an increase made even more remarkable in comparison to Dallas, where clearings rose but 2.4 percent. In the same period, Fort Worth was one of only two cities in the Eleventh Federal Reserve District to increase in bank deposits, and its growth rate of 17.1 percent was far greater than that of second-place Tucson, Arizona.[1]

Fort Worth's remarkable economic growth in the 1910s owed a lot to the economic impact of World War I. The war's stimulating effect was national, but it played an especially significant role in jump-starting industry in the mostly agrarian Texas. The US Census of 1920 credited Texas' large increases in wages and value of production between 1914 and 1919 to changes brought on by the war.[2] (See table 4.1.)

Fort Worth benefited from the war's stimulus more than any other Texas city, becoming the state leader in industrial production, but the Treaty of Versailles in November 1918 brought not only peace but the unraveling of that stimulus. The undoing of the war economy was displayed most blatantly in the closure of Fort Worth's military bases. By 1921, only remnants remained of Camp Bowie, the vast military complex where one hundred thousand soldiers trained, while the three airfields where thousands of army pilots learned to fly were either shuttered, being sold, or bare skeletons of their former selves: Carruthers Field at Benbrook lay leveled; Barron Field, near Everman, was scheduled for auction; and Taliaferro Airfield to the north, the largest of three, had only four officers and 4 airplanes, a shadow of its grand past when two thousand officers and six hundred enlisted men flew and cared for 332 airplanes.[3]

Table 4.1. Percentage increases in Texas industrial production between 1914 and 1919

	1919 statistics	Percentage increase over 1914
Establishments	5,724	12.6
Persons employed	130,911	43.7
Salaries and wages	$147,907,778	149.9
Value of production	$999,995,796	176.8
Value added	$298,824,898	176.3

Source: *Fourteenth Census of the United States* (Washington, DC: Government Printing Office, 1922), p. 9:1448.

The three airfields may have become mere shells, but their legacy eased Fort Worth's entry into commercial aviation. Military aviation landed again in November 1923, when the Army Air Service began regularly scheduled flights of mail and military passengers into Barron Field, the flights arriving from San Antonio and departing for St. Louis, Missouri. In early 1925, the army ended its lease at Barron, shifting flights to Aviation Garden near Lake Worth until a fire destroyed the field's hangar and storage buildings, leaving Fort Worth without a suitable airport. In May 1925, the Fort Worth Flying Club, made up of former army pilots, proposed a new airfield on one hundred acres situated between Fortieth Street and Decatur Road, a half-mile west of the US Helium Plant and four and one-half miles north of the courthouse. The plan drew enthusiastic support from Amon Carter and Mayor Henry Meacham, the latter investing $1,200 of his own money to defray initial costs, a bequest that allowed the city council to fast-track a five-year lease with the landowner, T. B. White of Keller, for a $750 annual fee, recouping that outlay by granting Trans-Air Company, owned by Leslie Dief and J. R. Meeker, operational concessions for the same $750. Trans-Air, in turn, planned to profit by charging commercial planes a landing fee, excepting those of the army. Work began immediately on the field, personnel quarters, and equipment storage facilities, as well as hangars for fifteen commercial airplanes already contracted. After only a month, Army Major H. C. Burwell approved the field for use, but the official opening was delayed until July 3, 1925.[4]

The airport grew rapidly, spurred by civilian companies that took over airmail service, then expanded into passenger service. National Air Transport (NAT) began handling airmail service to Chicago on May 12, 1926, following a ceremony that drew ten thousand celebrants who watched the company christen one of its planes as "Miss Fort Worth." NAT established six regular routes with connections to most major cities, making Fort Worth Field the nation's third-largest airmail center, behind Chicago and New York, providing rapid transit that could take packages from Fort Worth to New York City in just one day. Many credited the early successes to Mayor Meacham and

A. P. Barrett, the founder of American Airways, the two men cited for having done the most to advance aviation in Fort Worth. On July 16–17, 1927, Fort Worth Field was renamed in honor of the mayor, becoming Meacham Field during a grand celebration that drew fifteen thousand spectators and more than sixty planes, including forty military aircraft.[5]

Passenger service grew as the field developed, hastening and expanding infrastructure improvements. In November 1926, NAT began carrying passengers to and from Chicago in $40,000 Ford Tri motors capable of carrying eight persons and two pilots. The company boasted that for $90, anyone could leave Fort Worth in the morning and be in Chicago that evening. Passenger service increased the need for more planes, driving facility expansion that in 1927 brought a $30,000 hangar housing thirty planes as well as office space and sleeping quarters for pilots. In 1927, the city council offered Meacham's facilities to the Department of Commerce as a regional aviation center, a major step in the development of passenger service. Texas Air, a forerunner of American Airlines, was an early leader in air passenger service, carrying 5,446 passengers out of Meacham in 1929. Their success drew the attention of Dallas leaders who attempted to lure the company, but timely intervention by Fort Worth backers convinced Texas Air to not only remain but add hangars, offices, and an aviation school three hundred yards east of Meacham on 100 acres where the helium plant had stood. Texas Air also planned a downtown aviation building, but Southern Air, another predecessor of American Airlines, stole the initiative, building at Seventh and Main Streets where the Byers Building had stood. Southern also paid W. A. McLean $93,000 for 380 acres two miles north of Meacham for an operations center.[6]

The rise of aviation complemented Fort Worth's position as the transportation hub of the Southwest. By 1929, Meacham had regularly scheduled passenger service with National Air Transit, Texas Air Transit (serving larger Texas cities), Cromwell Airlines, Bowen Airlines, Delta Airlines, Pickwick Airlines (travel to Los Angeles), Braniff Airlines, and Southwest Fast Air Express, which bragged that its expanded Ford Tri motors could take fourteen passengers to St. Louis in only eight hours. Air transit developed rapidly, but its economic

Interurban Trolley at Main and Lancaster, 1920s. Courtesy Special Collections, the University of Texas at Arlington Libraries.

impact remained minuscule in comparison to Fort Worth's rail facilities, the largest in the Southwest, carrying passengers over twelve trunk lines radiating in all directions. Those services were the clear bedrock of an impressive external transportation system that included two interurban lines and intercity bus services. The only transportation mode unexploited, large-scale water navigation, had been and would continue to be advocated, but the realities, especially the cost, of digging a canal to the Gulf of Mexico via the Trinity River proved insurmountable.[7]

Aviation would become a major economic force for Fort Worth, but in the interwar period, the economy depended on its traditional commercial mainstays. In 1920, some five hundred factories employed 10,694 industrial workers, paying them an average monthly wage of $122. Approximately seventy-five of those five hundred businesses were in Industrial City, a commercial area north of downtown across the Trinity River that stretched to Panther Park and the Beltline

Railway serving the packinghouses (then outside Fort Worth). The concentration of a large industrial area adjacent to the packinghouses reflected a high degree of commercial focus to the north, but the near west side, also outside the city limits, drew increasing commercial attention after the Chevrolet plant, shuttered in November 1920, reopened on March 1, 1921. In truth, few, if any, neighborhoods escaped commercialization thanks to nine railroads with local offices and shops spread citywide. Railways were major employers of 5,047 people, almost half of all industrial workers. Texas and Pacific Railway, with 1,700 staff, the city's largest employer, paid relatively high wages averaging $126 monthly. Railroad employees, especially the lower paid, tended to settle near their workplaces, creating industrial neighborhoods that grew and spread. That industrially defined pattern began to slowly change in the twentieth century, when Fort Worth's impressive interurban system offered quick access around town, to the suburbs, and even to surrounding cities, a development that allowed workers to commute from residential neighborhoods free of industrial ill effects. The interurban transit system was truly remarkable. The Dallas Interurban Line, opened in 1902, operated from 6:00 a.m. to 8:30 p.m., serving forty-nine stations, while the Cleburne line, opened in 1912, served twenty-seven. Combined, the two lines provided transit to and from seventy-five surrounding communities, moving not only people but goods at affordable rates. That service complemented the external rail service, helping make Fort Worth, miles removed from large grain production, the largest grain market in the South. In the 1920s, local grain capacity expanded significantly with the construction of Kimball Milling's 500,000-bushel elevator and Jule G. Smith Milling Company's addition of 1,500,000 bushels to its storage, raising overall grain volume to nine million bushels.[8]

Commodity transportation also benefited retail trade, contributing significantly in the 1920s to remarkable growth in the grocery trade and nascent automotive shops. More than half of 442 new businesses that opened between 1918 and 1921 dealt in either groceries (147 new shops) or the automobile market (104 new shops). The new grocery market openings included Piggly Wiggly, the nation's first grocery chain, which by 1924 boasted of thirteen general groceries and one butcher shop in Fort Worth. The surge in automotive-related businesses was fueled mostly by rapid expansion in gasoline fueling stations. At its peak, Fort Worth city hall averaged four permit applications for new gasoline stations daily—apparently needed to handle the 18,498 cars registered in Fort Worth in 1920, the fourth-highest total in Texas, although well behind number one Dallas's 26,090. Many Fort Worthians thought the rankings would change, noting that Tarrant County recorded Texas' largest car sales in 1920. That proved overly optimistic and more an aberration fueled by West Texas buyers flush with oil money.[9]

Construction, released from wartime restrictions, boomed so much in the early 1920s that nail shortages were reported. Annual building permits, which had dropped to $1,790,612 in 1917, when the war limited nondefense construction, surged to $19,053,157 in 1919, the largest total of any Texas city and more than $4 million over second-place Dallas. Building continued to grow in 1920, when Fort Worth issued $22,500,000 in permits, the largest in the South and $5 million more than any city south of St. Louis, but that figure fell dramatically in 1921 to $4,604,377 before leveling thereafter to the $8 million to $11 million range. All the building created some notable structures: a new home for the *Star Telegram* at Seventh and Taylor Streets, dubbed the finest in the Southwest; the Farmers and Merchants Bank building of twenty-eight stories, one of the tallest in the Southwest; and the Texas Hotel, costing $4 million, which opened formally on September 30, 1921, to throngs in the streets and a few lucky celebrants in the hotel's clubs who danced past 2:00 a.m. Other important but less lofty projects included a new union depot on the Texas and Pacific reservation as well as a $300,000 addition to the Chevrolet plant and $600,000 in work at Swift's Packinghouse, the latter two outside Fort Worth limits and not covered by city permit totals. The new depot forced the Texas and Pacific to move some of its yards to leased lands west of downtown, creating the El TP neighborhood.[10]

In 1924 and 1925, construction took off again with several major projects announced or begun. The impressive list for 1924 included

Monnig's Department Store at Fifth and Throckmorton Streets, valued at $300,000; a $750,000 administration building for the Southwestern Theological Seminary at Fifth and Lamar Streets, built on land donated by Mrs. Winfield Scott; the Fort Worth Club's twelve-story headquarters at Sixth and Throckmorton Streets; and the Worth Mills's plant, employing five hundred on Old Cleburne Road just south of the Belt Line Railway. One major concern, the Chevrolet plant, closed again but was bought by Montgomery Ward for its mail-order operations. The next year proved even more impressive, with construction permits reaching $15 million thanks in large part to an eight-story Montgomery Ward's retail store being built on fifteen acres across Seventh Street from their mail-order house. The new facility would boost Ward's local employment to two thousand, making the operation one of the area's largest employers.[11] In addition, work began on the eighteen-story Medical Arts Building on Tenth Street, with almost half of its planned 250 offices leased by the grand opening on May 1, 1927.[12]

Packinghouses continued to be the largest industry in both in the Fort Worth area and in Texas. Some five thousand workers toiled at Armour and Swift and a few smaller packers, and many others worked at supporting businesses such as the stockyards and the stockyards rail service, all supported by sizable profits produced by the slaughterhouses during the war and afterward. In the nine-year period from the start of the European War in 1914 to 1923, Swift reported an average net profit of $1.07 per head of cattle after all costs were paid. In 1924, the company's return improved slightly to $1.10 per cow based on an average income of $80.52 per animal (receiving $68.35 for the beef and $12.17 for byproducts) versus costs averaging $79.42 ($66.97 for the animal and $12.45 for processing). That profit margin, only 1.4 percent, created substantial profits thanks to the large numbers involved. In 1925, Armour and Swift bought 480,000 cattle and 485,000 calves (smaller concerns bought another 18,000 and 25,000, respectively) in addition to 315,000 hogs and 320,000 sheep.[13]

Many thought the future for Fort Worth, Texas, and the nation lay in oil, seeing petroleum as the next great economic force. The oil industry, like the rest of the economy, went through a period of depressed prices postwar that saw oil drop to $1 a barrel, but by 1922, prices had rebounded to $2.25, high enough to stimulate explorations. On June 28, 1925, a special fourteen-page section of the *Star Telegram*, "Twenty Years of Progress," that highlighted Fort Worth's growth credited oil as the most important factor separating Fort Worth, the "town" of 1905, from the twice-as-large "city" of 1925. The question of transformative primacy among railroads, meatpacking, and oil is debatable, but no one seriously questioned oil's role in Fort Worth's transition to a major city.[14]

The irony is that Fort Worth became a major oil center despite being located in Tarrant County, one of only twenty Texas counties (including Dallas County) producing neither oil nor gas (until recently). Fortunately, oil gushed from several nearby fields. The first significant oil production in the extended Fort Worth area came in 1906, when five existing wells around Corsicana, eighty miles southeast of Fort Worth, increased their output by a factor of 30 to 1,450 barrels daily. The Corsicana fields were followed in 1916 by Breckinridge (100 miles west of Fort Worth), in 1917 by Ranger (90 miles west), in 1918 by Burkburnett (135 miles northwest) and Desdemona (90 miles southwest), and in 1926 by Mitchell County (225 miles west). All were important, but none had such a transformative effect as Fort Worth–based Texas and Pacific Coal and Oil Company's McClesky No. 1 Oil Well strike at Ranger on October 17, 1917, which produced 1,700 barrels daily. Oil production at Ranger came along at a critical point, alleviating looming shortages during World War I and making Fort Worth into an oil town. In 1918, after only one year of operation, Ranger's output ranked seventh nationally, making it a major player in West Texas' daily production of 248,625 barrels (worth $2.50 each) from 2,542 wells, a figure certain to rise thanks to 1,014 operating drilling rigs. Texas oil created many of Fort Worth's most important businessmen, such as Sid Richardson (patriarch of the Bass family), W. T. Waggoner, and William "Tex" Moncrief.[15]

Oil became another economic force cementing historical economic ties between Fort Worth and West Texas, a huge trade area larger than Pennsylvania, New York, and Indiana combined that produced $225 million in oil and natural gas in addition to $350 million in agricultural commodities and $175 million in livestock. For many years, Fort Worth had benefited from close economic connections as the nearest large city (before the rise of Midland and Odessa)—all made possible, in large part, by Fort Worth's vast railways providing the cheap transit important to commodity producers. Oil augmented those West Texas connections thanks to thirteen oil and four natural gas pipelines converging in Fort Worth, the most of any point in the world. Many of those conduits carried West Texas petroleum to Fort Worth's nascent refining infrastructure, which got an early start thanks to the proximity of oil fields, especially Ranger, which in 1919 pumped 54,320,844 barrels.[16] By 1924, Fort Worth had 9 refineries; by 1929, it boasted of 22, making it the nation's largest petroleum refining center, drawing local offices for all the major oil companies as well as many local companies of varying capital. The Fort Worth experience was part of a statewide development that by 1929 had built 390 refineries and employed 94,405 workers, the most of any state.[17]

The center of the oil universe was found in the lobby of the Westbrook Hotel at Main and Fourth Streets, a seven-story building with 247 rooms. The site had been developed in 1877 as the El Paso Hotel before becoming the Pickwick Hotel, then the Delaware Hotel, and then the Westbrook (the area now forms part of the Sundance Square fountains). The concentration of so much oil activity, much of it involving wild speculation, made the Westbrook the "oil lease center of the world," filled with legitimate businessmen making huge deals as well as shady operators dealing in unfulfilled promises and fraudulent stock certificates. Between 1918 and 1923, Texas oil swindlers bilked five hundred thousand investors out of more than $100 million, often by selling stock in oil exploration companies that suggested, if not promised, huge returns when the companies existed largely on paper with little or no capital or intent to drill. Occasionally, an unscrupulous operator would go through the motions, drilling a shallow hole to give the pretense of effort at the least cost, but more often, scam artists just pocketed the money and delivered empty promises. By 1921, authorities were busy prosecuting fraudulent operations, although it was a constant struggle to stay ahead of scammers. One of the cases filed in 1921 involved ten men indicted for a Ponzi scheme in which they sold $750,000 in shares of the Penn Burkburnett Oil Company, an imaginary company whose name was chosen to resemble the Burkburnett Oil Company, a legitimate operation. Swindlers used common tactics, suggesting annual returns of 24 percent but paying out 2 percent monthly dividends to a few early investors, all drawn from later investment capital. The number of filed cases expanded so dramatically that in January 1922, Fort Worth courts held 129 pending fraud cases at the same time that a federal grand jury investigation sought indictments against 13 additional persons. In 1923, federal investigators in Fort Worth reported more than 200 cases against oil swindlers, many discovered during 400 mail fraud investigations into worthless oil stocks sent through the post. Prosecutions became so aggressive that some accused resorted to desperate measures, including a robbery at the Fort Worth office of the US district attorney in which the robbers asked not for money but for papers pertaining to federal oil fraud investigations. Prosecutions eventually took a toll, the effect evidenced by a sharp fall in local postal receipts brought about by a drop in brochures mailed to potential investors, or suckers.[18]

Convictions were wide-ranging in geographic scope and in personalities. One notable prosecution involved Dr. Frederick A. Cook, an Arctic explorer from Wyoming who came to Fort Worth in 1919 and began speculating in oil leases and stocks as sole trustee of Petroleum Producers Associates. Dr. Cook made the local news on February 1, 1923, when his estranged wife, Marie Cook, who had filed for divorce a few days earlier, summoned Fort Worth police to Dr. Cook's hotel room, where officers found him with a young woman and a quantity of liquor (during Prohibition). Cook sued the *Fort Worth Press* for $1 million over their reporting of the matter, but that summer, he faced more serious charges after being indicted by federal courts in Cleveland, Ohio, for mail fraud involving fraudulent stocks sent through the post. Cook, tried and convicted in Fort Worth, received a fourteen-year sentence and a $12,500 fine.[19]

Many factors indicated a thriving 1920s economy, but some coexisting markers suggested that all was not so wonderful, especially for the middle and lower classes. At the start of the decade, Fort Worth's automobile manufacturing, already reeling from the closures of the Ford plant at First and Commerce Streets during World War I and the Chevrolet plant on West Seventh Street in 1920 (which would reopen and then close again), suffered another blow in 1921, when the Texan Automobile Plant at 3600 McCart Avenue shuttered, aggravating a postwar unemployment problem that abated but persisted through the 1920s. In January 1920, the US Department of Labor rated labor demand in Fort Worth practically nonexistent, and in 1922, Fort Worth reported the highest unemployment rate of Texas' seven largest cities. The effects of the depressed labor market could be seen in homeownership rates and home valuations that stagnated at relatively low levels or decreased. In 1921, almost half, 43.7 percent, of Fort Worth's 28,042 homes carried a mortgage and only 35.8 percent were owner-occupied, while more than half, 58.1 percent, were renter-occupied (we assume the other 6 percent were unoccupied). Perhaps more troubling, Fort Worth's average home value, $4,125, was substantially lower than Dallas's $5,553 or Houston's $5,173 and declined further in 1922, dropping to only $2,902.[20]

Unemployment became such a critical issue that the city of Fort Worth took aggressive steps during the winter of 1921–22, including the adoption of some innovative proposals that were remarkable given the dearth of direct government relief available. The most noticeable, and perhaps only, program for adults was the Poor Farm on Kimbo Road that in 1921 stood packed with eighty-seven men and thirteen women (the home later became a home for the aged before closing in 1965). More effort went into business stimulation, including the city council's joint agreement with property owners along the east valley of the Trinity River to convert an adjacent dump into an industrial area, contingent on the Texas and Pacific running a rail line to East First Street—an early cooperative effort among the city, private business, and a neighborhood. The council also took some initial exploratory steps toward providing job security for city employees with discussions on extending civil service protection, then covering only firefighters, to all city employees. Both plans were well-intentioned but designed more for long-range results than to provide the quick relief needed by destitute families facing long winter months. In a laudable effort to ease deprivations, the city of Fort Worth accelerated the issuance of $150,000 in work contracts to extend sewer mains across the Trinity River and build Forest Park Pool. Unfortunately, in 1923, city finances were already strained to the breaking point, and the added outgo created monetary shortfalls that sent overdrafts soaring to $900,000. Being overdrawn was nothing new for Fort Worth; local banks had covered temporary overdrafts for years, but now they balked, warning that the numbers had gotten so large that they would refuse future drafts. Facing bankruptcy, Mayor Cockrell instituted a multifaceted program, raising taxes while also cutting the city workforce, including a reduction in police ranks from 185 to 165, and at the same time scheduling a plebiscite for a $1,250,000 bond package. Still, the cash flow deteriorated, forcing administrators to end free garbage collection and eliminate 120 more staff, including 30 more from the police, reducing officer strength to 135 for a city of more than one hundred thousand. Even with austerity, Fort Worth failed to meet its first payroll in 1924 and could not issue the second and third paychecks until February 23, and the fourth payday, due February 20, did not appear until the end of March. The financial crunch eased that summer, allowing the police in June to announce thirty-six openings. The problems were, in part, a reflection of a generally weak economy transitioning from war to peacetime while also confronting developing technologies that replaced some jobs and changed others. In 1926, Southwestern Bell Telephone began converting its operator-assisted system with dial phones that routed calls automatically, thereby reducing the need for operators. The company announced the change in newspaper advertisements along with operating instructions, and businesses rushed to publish their new direct numbers. The changeover took several years; some five years later, in February 1931, Bell announced that 22,820 phones lines had been changed over but 15,611 still required operator assistance, a pace of nine hundred conversions a month that suggested another eighteen months would be needed to complete the transition.[21]

Unemployment brought dire poverty and hardships that challenged private relief organizations such as the Union Gospel Mission (UGM). Religious salvation was the mission's primary focus; it estimated having made twenty-five thousand conversions since its founding in 1889, but poor relief became an important part of its services, taking up a large part of the two main buildings on lower Main Street. The mission building at Main and Fourteenth Streets housed a ground-floor meeting hall with dormitories on the second and third floors, while Fifteenth and Main Streets offered indigent services such as a cafeteria, barbershop, reading room, and employment office as well as a dormitory reserved for railroad men who paid $0.50 a night. Finding jobs proved difficult, but the UGM did what it could, in one instance finding work for 17 of 135 men arrested for vagrancy during a 1922 police roundup. The mission also provided large holiday dinners for the destitute. In 1921, banquet organizers appealed for donations of calves, chickens, hogs, opossums, and rabbits for one thousand Christmas Eve meals. They also reached beyond unemployed adults to help reconnect runaway or displaced youths, often paying for telegraphs or, in some cases, providing train tickets home. In too many cases, all family connections had been lost. In 1922, UGM took in an abandoned twelve-year-old boy clothed only in rags they found on the streets, scraping out a bare existence selling newspapers.[22]

Economic troubles struck first and most severely at those at the economic bottom, a group that included a disproportionate percentage of nonwhites. Little information documents the hardships faced by African Americans, but the evidence concerning Mexicans and Mexican Americans is somewhat better. In April 1921, the Welfare Association reported feeding two hundred "Mexicans" daily at its north-side office adjacent to the Wesley House, plus another fifty around Dallas Alley and Pacific Street. The men, including many recently laid-off packinghouse workers, received sandwiches as well as sacks of potatoes, rice, beans, and onions to take home to their families. Much of the food was donated by private citizens, people such as

Sam Joseph, owner of Joseph's Café, who provided five hundred loaves of bread weekly. Despite the community's efforts, demand outpaced supply, leaving hundreds unfed while coffers at the Welfare Association and the Red Cross sat empty. Fort Worth city officials stepped in, filling some of the gap, but they required that the men work cleaning Edwards Park or on a road to connect Trinity Park to Stove Foundry Road. Those work crews, which on some days counted as many as six hundred men, included many Mexican immigrants or Americans classed as such due to ethnicity. The Mexican government contributed generously to support the program, reimbursing the city $5,000 in June 1921 for relief provided to Mexican labor as well as spending $1,200 on train tickets for returning nationals. Thanks to that assistance, 250 Mexicans left for Laredo, Texas, on May 10, 1921, the first leg of their repatriation, with more scheduled to leave the next day.[23]

Unemployment put additional stresses on labor relations. Fort Worth had a significant history of labor unrest in the nineteenth century, especially during the Great Southwestern Railroad Strike of 1886, but except for a 1903 strike, labor and management had remained relatively strife-free in the twentieth century, especially after 1917, when war needs subsumed labor disputes. The chamber of commerce attributed calm labor-management relations to race and culture, crediting a labor force that was 80 percent native-born whites who were disinclined to tolerate agitators, a view that meshed with an antiunionism linked to nativism that identified union organizers as outside, often foreign, agitators opposed to true Americanism. The *Star Telegram* seconded the argument, writing that Fort Worth had "no Bolsheviks and less trouble with labor than any other Texas city," a remarkable claim for the largest railroad center of the Southwest with a rich history of labor upheaval. Part of the explanation lay in local union men who adopted conservative approaches, championing accommodation over conflict. In 1921, C. W. Woodman, head of the Trades Assembly and editor of the *Union Banner*, tied Fort Worth's calm labor relations after 1903 to its unemployment rate, which was one-tenth that of Dallas. Woodman admitted that unemployment had recently become a problem, but he argued it was temporary, brought on by two thousand recent layoffs by railroads and packinghouses. He added that the problem appeared worse due to idle "Mexicans" and transient oil field workers clogging the streets. Whatever had been the case, the end of the war in 1918 and a resulting decline in labor demand brought an end to Fort Worth's extended period of labor tranquility.[24]

It did not take long for labor unrest to become evident. In April 1920, a walkout by 650 switchmen idled local rail traffic, paralyzing freight trains across much of the Fort Worth region and leaving railcars laden with rotting perishables sitting on suburban sidetracks. The rail stoppage was isolated, short-lived, and quickly overshadowed by a walkout pursuant to wage cuts by the big four national meatpackers, Swift's, Armour, Cudahy, and Wilson (the fifth, Morris Brothers, was believed ready to follow). The cuts were particularly insidious because they fell hardest on unskilled workers, almost 40 percent of the workforce at Swift and Armour, whose hourly pay dropped $0.07,

Labor Leader C. W. Woodman, 1946 (George Farmer, C. W. Woodman, and Marvin Rall). Courtesy Special Collections, the University of Texas at Arlington Libraries.

from $0.42½ to $0.35, while skilled laborers, who earned much more, lost only $0.03 to $0.05. Despite the severity, Swift and Armour management deemed resistance unlikely, given that unskilled laborers were unorganized. They discovered they had miscalculated labor solidarity. Led by the Butcher Workmen's Union, local skilled workers struck, joining fellow unions in Omaha, Nebraska; East St. Louis, Illinois; and Milwaukee, Wisconsin. The strike garnered widespread support, including Niles City Mayor W. H. Brown, who stated that all the city council stood 100 percent prolabor. At the end of the first day, the two sides presented vastly different evaluations of its effectiveness—union representatives claiming 90 percent of the workforce refused to cross the picket line, while Armour management reported more than one thousand at work, only two hundred less than a normal shift. In addition, the company noted that 130 applicants waited for jobs at the company gate, although they did admit skilled workers were in short supply. As the strike wore on, the steady supply of substitutes willing to cross picket lines grew, becoming a serious threat to the union cause and leading to violent clashes between strikers and applicants. Armour used that violence in obtaining a district court injunction that enjoined interference with or threatening workers. The ready availability of workers willing to cross picket lines and no effective means to interfere doomed the strike, leaving the union little choice but to surrender to company demands.[25]

The local labor movement survived and flirted with radicalization. In 1922, a walkout temporarily shut down the Majestic Theater, but a strike at Miller Manufacturing, a garment manufacturer employing mostly women, endured, becoming confrontational as clashes once again broke out between pickets and nonunion workers. This time women union supporters were the aggressors, taking a woman known to cross their picket lines, Hollie Hinkle of 1041 East Allen Avenue, from her home to an unknown location and flogging her. Incidents away from the strike ground presented challenges for the company, making it harder to tie labor directly to violence, but that changed to the company's advantage when an organizer from the Industrial Workers of the World (IWW), a union noted for aggressive tactics including violence, arrived. Charles Smith (also known as Callo Costeello), who emigrated from Sweden in 1900, became so involved in and well known for aggressive union activities that he had been run out of Arkansas and scheduled for deportation. Miller used Smith's presence as proof of insidious outside influences to pressure the city to intervene, threatening they would relocate the plant if it was not made safe. Miller's economic blackmail brought not only increased Fort Worth police patrols but also the Texas Rangers. The presence of the IWW was significant in turning opinion from the union to the company. Many local police officers held decided prounion sympathies, some even voicing their distaste at protecting picket-line crossers, but they harbored no such qualms about the IWW, who they regarded as radical agitators. During the 1920 railroad strike, Fort Worth police arrested several IWW representatives, and in 1923, they arrested two IWW organizers for vagrancy the moment they stepped off an incoming freight train. After Smith was arrested, the union, facing the loss of most outside support, ended the walkout on company terms.[26]

Strikes and their associated violence may well have contributed to a general waning of philanthropic spirit that grew as burgeoning relief payouts drained financial resources. An early sign of donation fatigue appeared in 1923, when, for the first time in its history, the *Star Telegram's* Goodfellow Fund, a Christmas fund for needy families, failed to meet expenses, raising only $6,339—approximately $2,000 less than it spent. Hardening attitudes found an easy target in Hispanics, who were seen as outsiders and therefore as financial burdens dumped on the mainstream community. Police Chief Henry Lee asked US District Attorney Henry Zweifel to investigate reports of paid agents bringing hundreds of "peons" to Fort Worth, an allegation that Immigration Inspector Guy Smith rejected as patently false, noting that the local Hispanic population had fallen from fifteen thousand in 1921 to only five thousand in 1923, most leaving voluntarily, including some four thousand repatriated by the Mexican government. Mexican nationals may have left voluntarily but not without persuasion. Unemployed persons of all types, but especially nonwhites, faced prosecution under vagrancy statutes that carried sentences of forced labor. The

Mexican consul at San Antonio complained that one hundred Mexicans arrested in Fort Worth were not vagrants but simply victims of the "acute economic situation" beyond their control. Poor whites were also singled out at depots where police officers routinely scrutinized arriving passengers, letting the prosperous pass but interrogating the poorly dressed about their employment status, warning those without jobs to continue traveling or face arrest as vagrants. A group sensitive to human rights issues reported that most men on county convict road crews were guilty only of being unemployed and poor.[27]

Vagrancy laws were widely used because they offered multiple advantages in dealing with the disadvantaged. They were local charges, keeping jurisdiction, and fines, with city and county courts; they granted broad powers to arrest anyone who could not prove a means of support; and they largely affected only those at the bottom of the economic ladder without encumbering the rest of society. They also provided a source of virtually free labor. Convictions brought fines that most convicts, by definition, could not pay, forcing a choice between lengthy jail time and "volunteering" for work gangs constituting little more than forced labor. The racial dimension of vagrancy codes was clear, as in 1923, when Police Commissioner Alderman ordered the arrest of all unemployed black men. The order filled the city jail with the sons and grandsons of slaves who were given the choice of serving lengthy sentences or working West Texas farms in dire need of 4,500 cotton pickers. An arrest was so certain that C. W. Woodman of the Labor Bureau suggested that African American men avoid the process (but not the consequences) by reporting to the Colored YMCA for transport to the fields, adding inducement by assuring that the "volunteers" could take their families, provided they all worked. Cotton picking as a jail option was normally reserved only for African Americans. During the great picker scarcity of 1923, Woodman reported only one order for Mexicans and stated he would accept whites reluctantly, noting that they would require arrangements for separate transportation and housing. Fort Worth was not unique in its use of the legal system to provide forced labor. A special train transporting blacks, required by segregation laws, was delayed getting to Fort Worth after it stopped in Waco to pick up one hundred workers committed by their courts.[28]

Economic struggles subsided somewhat in the second half of the 1920s as the economy stabilized. Retail trade grew significantly, sparked in part by the arrival of national chains such as the Piggly Wiggly groceries that stressed self-service and lower prices, although they also made life more difficult for locally owned shops offering amenities like full service and credit but higher prices. One local shop not only survived but became Fort Worth's largest retailer. On April 25, 1918, brothers Marvin and O. P. Leonard opened Leonard Brother's Department Store in a twenty-five-by-sixty-foot-space at 111 Houston Street. That first day they rang up a respectable $195.26 and grew from there, expanding to cover two blocks and reaching $1 million in sales by 1926. In 1929 they covered four blocks (twice the size of a Walmart) and racked up $2.5 million in sales, becoming the Southwest's largest

Leonard Brothers Dry Goods, Houston and Weatherford Streets, early 1930s. Courtesy Special Collections, the University of Texas at Arlington Libraries.

grocery and Texas' largest purveyor of meat, groceries, baked goods, and produce. Leonard's rise was exceptional, but many other retailers also did well, thanks to healthy growth in the livestock market, oil trade, and milling, all bolstered by the release of pent-up construction demand following the end of World War I.[29]

Retail success trickled down to other businesses, such as wholesalers and commodity producers, and to Fort Worth's railways, which transported much of the trade. A significant portion of Fort Worth's retail sales came from $6,040,782 in agricultural goods produced in 1929 by 3,553 Tarrant County farms, a symbiotic relationship enriching local farmers and ranchers who then spent a large part of those earnings in local shops. However, Fort Worth's trade area extended well beyond Tarrant County, going out along well-developed wholesale trade routes that stretched into West Texas and beyond to Arizona as well as Oklahoma. That trade was also bilateral in that wholesalers not only sold but also bought goods in their service area, especially in West Texas, a bountiful region producing $175 million in cotton, $125 million in livestock, $100 million in grain, and by 1929, $265 million in oil. Moving those goods put great demands on rail service, driving an expansion that in 1928 and 1929 consumed more than one-third of all the railroad construction in the United States. Much of that traffic ran to Fort Worth, the nearest large city, establishing and cementing interregional links of enormous economic importance.[30]

Fort Worth maintained its position as the state leader in much of the agricultural market despite a mid-decade drought that wreaked havoc on farmers and ranchers. Arid conditions killed pasture grass, forcing ranchers to sell off large herds that cost too much to feed. Local banker R. E. Harding cited the drought for Fort Worth packinghouses experiencing their biggest year ever in 1925, the surge driven by ranchers selling stock they could not afford to feed. Harding also predicted that the drought's effect would reduce crop yields for agricultural commodities such as cotton and feed grains, sending prices soaring. Grain production did suffer, reducing the volume of trade at Fort Worth's Grain and Cotton Exchange by 20 percent in 1926 compared to 1925, although the exchange still handled $45 million (wheat being the most common grain), and production recovered quickly as the drought waned. Conditions improved so rapidly that Kimbell Milling Company began construction in 1930 of a one-million-bushel elevator that doubled its storage capacity, helping make Fort Worth the largest grain center in Texas (accounting for half of Texas' total) and the nation's third-largest (behind Chicago, Illinois, and Kansas City, Missouri).[31]

The most obvious sign of economic development was seen in construction, which took off in 1927 with a record $17,111,430 in building permits, the seventh-largest total in the nation. A big part of that increase came from the construction of Lancaster Yards, a massive $5 million Texas and Pacific project that included a new downtown terminal that forced the relocation of repair shops two miles west to a large site parallel to Brooklyn Heights and Factory Place Additions. The new facilities in the west, which eventually employed 2,000, opened on June 12, 1928, to a crowd of 5,000. In addition, on September 27, 1927, the Worth Hotel moved from Main Street to West Seventh and Taylor Streets to a new eighteen-story, $2.5 million building with modern conveniences such as private baths and circulating ice water. Two months later, on November 26, 1927, the Worth Theater opened on the hotel's ground floor, presenting movies and live performances in its Egyptian-motif auditorium seating 2,800 (the author worked as a teenage usher at the Worth in the 1960s; the theater closed in 1971).[32] In 1928, construction slumped slightly with 3,337 building permits worth $11,324,845, a figure that still represented $50.83 per capita (based on a population of 227,800, which was exaggerated), the eighth highest nationally and far eclipsing Dallas's $14.81 and San Antonio's $18.59. Much of Fort Worth's work came from five hundred new businesses, including ninety oil-related concerns, further evidence of the importance of petroleum to the overall economy. Continued growth seemed so assured that the local association of commerce predicted that new commercial expansion would drive construction to $26,320,000 in 1929, a huge figure. The year did get off to a good start, thanks to Texas and Pacific Railway's construction of a thirteen-story passenger terminal and two freight terminals costing $8 million, almost as much as all construction in 1928. The railroad conditioned its building plans on Fort Worth voters passing a $2 million bond package for grading improvements. Fortunately, the bond referendum passed easily.[33]

Many large projects begun earlier were finished in the last half of the 1920s. The massive Montgomery Ward's Department Store, announced in 1924, opened on September 29, 1928, to a grand celebration with twenty-five thousand balloons festooning the building and a fifteen-piece orchestra entertaining fifty thousand in attendance and others listening via a live remote broadcast by local radio station WBAP, all celebrated by a sixteen-page commemorative section in the *Star Telegram.* The eighteen-story Electric Building opened early in 1929 at Seventh and Lamar Streets (the first floor had space reserved for a theater), and the Blackstone Hotel followed on October 10, 1929, at Fifth and Main Streets, replacing the Rialto Theater. The Blackstone boasted three hundred rooms with ceiling fans, radios, and circulating

Worth Theater Marquee, 1928. Courtesy of the Genealogy, History and Archives Unit, Fort Worth Library (Historic Photograph Collection, box B, folder B0015).

ice water, all available at daily rates that began at $2.50. The hotel's top floor housed WBAP Radio.[34]

By 1929, the value of all postwar construction reached $127,424,698, an amazing total celebrated in a special newspaper section on July 27, 1929. The public effect was visible for all to see thanks to thirteen buildings of eight stories or more built downtown and a fourteenth, the Forest Park Apartments, on the near south side. The new skyscrapers and year they opened were as follows (number of stories for each in parentheses):

1919	Texas Hotel (14)
	Fort Worth National Bank (24)
	W. T. Waggoner (20)
1920	Neal P. Anderson (10)
1924	Fort Worth Club (12)
1926	Medical Arts (18)
	Worth Hotel and Theater (18)
	Petroleum (14)
1927	Electric (18)
	Blackstone (23)
	Forest Park Apartments (12)
1929	The Fair Department Store (18)
	Office Building (formerly the Van Zandt) (14)
	Texas and Pacific Passenger Station and Offices (13)
	Texas and Pacific Terminal (8)[35]

While downtown skyscrapers extended Fort Worth vertically, suburban residential development stretched the population horizontally to reach largely middle- and upper-class housing. In 1924, W. F. White, owner of White Lake Farm, east of downtown, announced the Scenery Hill development with relaxed restrictions on lot sizes to ensure greater livability. Two years later, on August 8, 1926, a syndicate led by William Bryce opened Park Hill Addition on land investors had bought as open prairie in 1910 and held in anticipation of future growth. While they waited, they enhanced their investment by selling land for what would become Forest Park as well as donating land and money to lure Texas Christian University (TCU) from Waco. TCU had a major indirect impact, especially on residential housing, stimulating the southwest movement of Fort Worth's population, and a direct effect through its own construction, including plans in 1929 for a new stadium, largely funded by the Burnet estate, to be built on 68 acres west of the campus and north of the municipal golf course. In 1928, W. C. Guthrie opened Monticello as a restricted subdivision of 125 acres west of downtown with 406 homes. Guthrie had been responsible for or contributed to the development of much of Fort Worth's nicer neighborhoods, including Park Hill, Kensington, Forest Highlands, Country Club Heights, University Place, and River Crest. All were nice neighborhoods, but the most economically exclusive was Westover Hills, advertised as a "distinctive home district" in the style of Houston's River Oaks and Dallas's Highland Park. Westover Hill added many glamorous homes, including the W. A. Moncrief estate.[36]

As the 1920s neared their end, Fort Worthians had good reasons to expect a continuation of general economic health. New construction projects seemed to be opening almost daily, including a $250,000 public market on Henderson Street slated for May 15, 1930, and several major projects stood well along in development. In December 1929, the Tarrant County Water Control District announced it had acquired all the necessary land and was prepared to begin work on dams to create Lake Bridgeport and Eagle Mountain Lake, and TCU trustees approved plans for the new football stadium. TCU's decision to a build new stadium came after an unbeaten Frog team played rival Southern Methodist University (located in Dallas) for the conference championship before a standing-room-only crowd on November 30, 1929.[37] Several signs posited that the economy was holding its own, with at least a portion of that wealth trickling down. In 1928, Tarrant County registered 54,738 motor vehicles, more than one for every four persons, suggesting that most families could afford personal transportation. A large majority, 85.6 percent in 1928, could also afford to live in single-family residences, indicating the availability of affordable housing. Of the remainder, 4.3 percent lived in rooming houses, 3.9 percent in apartments, 2.9 percent in duplexes, 2.6 percent in servant housing, and 0.6 percent in hotels. City finances, which had struggled in the middle years, revived thanks to a rise in assessed valuations to $180,384,107 in 1928 that, coupled with an estimated annual tax rate of 4.39 percent (county, city, school, and associated taxes), produced sufficient revenue that the 1927 city council proposed a raise for common laborers, most of whom received wages only and no benefits. In 1930, Fort Worth boasted of 256 police officers and 215 firefighters, a major increase from a few years before, when staffing had been radically cut. Many people felt that Fort Worth was on the move, some claiming net immigration of five thousand monthly, an unrealistic number, although the population did increase more than 53 percent in the 1920s to reach 163,447 in 1930, a significantly higher percentage increase than the 45 percent in the 1910s.[38]

After doing so well in the 1910s, the Fort Worth economy struggled throughout the 1920s. The decade began with a significant downturn as the economy transitioned from its war footing, a major event with multiple effects, including creating unemployment concerns after years of labor scarcity, a condition that put greater demands on relief rolls, leading to intensified hostility shown to outsiders, including Americans of Mexican descent. By the middle years, Fort Worth's economic pillars—railroads, packinghouses, and to a degree, oil—had weathered the worst and stabilized, bringing a steady if not vibrant economy in which the middle and upper classes prospered while the working class struggled. Associated unemployment effects could be seen in Fort Worth's housing market issues, with its low percentage of homeownership and falling home values, the latter having a crippling impact on the municipal budget. Those economic fault lines remained largely obscured thanks to the aggressive construction program that added fourteen skyscrapers, making it seem that Fort Worth still had an expanding economy that was competitive with Texas' other large cities. The next decade would remove that illusion.

CHAPTER FIVE

The 1920s Come to an End

The 1920s were eventful for Fort Worth. Several of the most important civic leaders died, most notably B. B. Paddock, but new boosters emerged. City government occasioned major changes, switching from the commission form to the city manager system that is still in place today (and still with eight council seats plus a mayor), undertaking an aggressive annexation program that doubled the geographic size and added fifty thousand to the population, and making important advances in professionalizing the fire and police departments. In addition, Fort Worth added significantly to its outdoor entertainment venues through expansion and improvements to the municipal park system and private development of Casino Beach, all while dealing with the transition from a war to peace economy, the rise of Ku Klux Klan as a major political force, motor vehicle traffic problems, and Prohibition, the latter two presenting especially significant challenges for the police.

Raw statistics indicate that Fort Worth's population grew significantly, but closer analysis suggests that the actual increase was small and that growth was stagnant. In 1930, the Census counted a population of 163,447, an addition of almost 57,000, or more than 53 percent since 1920, a seemingly significant increase but one that was almost totally due to annexations bringing 50,000 into the city limits. Likewise, the raw data on Fort Worth manufacturing suggest the city experienced tremendous growth in the 1920s, recording double-digit increases in the number of workers and wages and triple-digit increases in the value of production and the value added by manufacturing, all accomplished while the number of establishments declined. In addition, in 1930, Fort Worth manufacturing represented a much larger percentage of Tarrant County production than in 1920. For example, in 1920, Fort Worth accounted for 25 percent of Tarrant County's value of production, but in 1930 that share had grown to 87 percent. (See table 5.1.)

The problem with the numbers is that they compare two different cities, the Fort Worth of the 1920s and that of the 1930s, which covered twice the geographic area. Fort Worth's huge annexations in the 1920s added the Swift and Armour packinghouses as well as supporting concerns in Niles City, large factories that greatly enhanced production statistics at the same time that the number of businesses actually decreased. Far from growing, the evidence suggests that Fort Worth's commercial development actually regressed. Tarrant County industrial data provide a broader picture, taking in Fort Worth and all the annexed sections in both 1920 and 1930. Those statistics show declines in every category, most dramatically an almost 16 percent drop in the value of production, indicating that Fort Worth–area manufacturing suffered a significant fall in the 1920s. (See table 5.2.)

A similar conclusion can be seen by comparing Fort Worth and Tarrant County statistics to the city and county of Dallas, both of

Table 5.1. Fort Worth manufacturing statistics

	1920	1930	Percentage change
Establishments	229	228	–.4
Workers	4,452	6461	+45.1
Wages	$5,082,000	$8,273,505	+62.8
Value of production	$38,160,092	$113,614,152	+197.7
Value added	$12,502,858	$27,693,891	+121.5

Source: *Fourteenth Census of the United States* (Washington, DC: Government Printing Office, 1922), pp. 9:1449, 1461, 1470; *Fifteenth Census of the United States* (Washington, DC: Government Printing Office, 1930), p. 8:507.

Table 5.2. Tarrant County manufacturing statistics

	1920	1930	Percentage change
Establishments	257	246	–4.2
Workers	9,196	8,600	–6.5
Wages	$10,563,246	$10,607,560	–.4
Value of production	$155,299,159	$131,336,433	–15.4
Value added	$33,706,354	$33,181,026	–1.6

Source: *Fourteenth Census of the United States* (Washington, DC: Government Printing Office, 1922), pp. 8:271–73; *Fifteenth Census of the United States* (Washington, DC: Government Printing Office, 1930), pp. 3:508–9.

which recorded double-digit increases in establishments, workers, wages, and value of production and triple-digit increases in the value added. That manufacturing in both Dallas city and county increased almost identically indicates that the effect did not come from an extraneous force such as annexation but represented real growth. Clearly, Dallas manufacturing did very well in the 1920s and Fort Worth did not, widening the gap between the two, which had narrowed in the 1910s. (See table 5.3.)

Table 5.3. Percentage changes in Dallas city and county manufacturing statistics between 1920 and 1930

	Dallas City	Dallas County
Establishments	+17.1	+16.3
Workers	+52.3	+59
Wages	+71.2	+77.3
Value of production	+52.4	+44.8
Value added	+109.1	+100

Source: *Fourteenth Census of the United States* (Washington, DC, Government Printing Office, 1922), pp. 8:271–73, 9:1449, 1461, 1470; *Fifteenth Census of the United States* (Washington, DC: Government Printing Office, 1930), pp. 3:508–9.

Dallas's economic success was consistent with stateside statistics showing that between 1920 and 1930, Texas manufacturing experienced double-digit increases in workers, wages, the value added, and the value of production but declined 9.2 percent in the number of establishments. The across-the-board fall in establishments may have been an effect of the loss of war funding, forcing the closure of many smaller concerns while larger, more established businesses were able to adapt and survive. (See table 5.4.)

The concurrent increase in manufacturing recorded in Dallas and stateside suggests that Fort Worth's economy stagnated in the 1920s, while Dallas and most of Texas experienced double-digit growth. That disparity meant that Fort Worth, which had outperformed every major Texas city in the 1910s, fell behind in the 1920s. Something was clearly wrong, and the timing could not have been worse.

Table 5.4. Percentage changes in Texas manufacturing between 1920 and 1930

	1920	1930	Percentage change
Establishments	5,724	5,198	–9.2
Workers	107,522	134,498	+25.1
Wages	$116,403,800	$151,827,257	+30.4
Value of production	$999,995,796	$1,450,246,431	+45
Value added	$298,824,898	$460,306,803	+54

Source: *Fourteenth Census of the United States* (Washington, DC: Government Printing Office, 1922), pp. 3:271, 9:1448; *Fifteenth Census of the United States* (Washington, DC: Government Printing Office, 1930), p. 3:507.

PART TWO

To Pearl Harbor

CHAPTER SIX

The Economy Stalls

Economic troubles plaguing the 1920s foreshadowed the Great Depression, the defining issue of the 1930s that dominated the age to a degree that few events have. Other issues both old and new arose, but none matched the impact poverty had on average Americans who struggled to survive. The economy had dipped prior to the stock market crash, but after 1929, the downturn deepened, reaching a nadir in the winter of 1932–33 that persisted throughout the decade and into the 1940s. The effects were ubiquitous, clear for all to see in the gaunt faces of the unemployed, the ill-housed, and the ill-fed who loitered in the streets and waited in long lines at soup kitchens. A fortunate few avoided harsh personal realities, but they could not escape seeing the Depression's public scars.

By 1930, Fort Worth's growth and development had clearly begun to wane. The Census reported a population of 163,447, a 53.5 percent increase since 1920, which, while significant, was well below Houston's 110 percent rise to 292,352 or Dallas's 69.5 percent growth to 269,475 but better than third-place San Antonio, which added just 43.5 percent to reach 231,542. Despite relatively healthy increases in the 1920s, Texas cities still ranked comparatively low compared to other American cities. The largest, Houston, came in at only the twenty-eighth largest, Dallas was thirty-third, and Fort Worth lingered at forty-ninth. In addition, Texas' overall population increased much slower than its four urban centers, growing just 24.6 percent, indicating that smaller cities and rural populations either stagnated or increased at much slower rates. Fort Worth's percentage increase in the 1920s was slightly better than the 45.2 percent in the 1910s but far below the 175 percent rate in the 1900s. Of course, percentages can be misleading. Fort Worth added more people in the 1920s—almost 57,000—than in any previous decade, but its larger population base reduced its percentage rate.[1]

Municipal population growth engendered suburbanization as the sheer mass of numbers pushed people outside the inner city, a transition made possible by the development of a mass transit system (streetcars) that was complemented and then replaced by automobiles. The population shift so changed the face of Fort Worth so that in 1930, downtown was no longer the most populous sector, having surrendered that distinction to the south side, as it was known, which now held 26 percent of Fort Worth's total, or 42,224, in a large expanse that stretched from the Texas and Pacific tracks in the north to the city limits in the south and from the Katy tracks in the east all the way west to the Frisco tracks. Growth and changing boundaries would eventually expand the eastern limits to the International and Great Northern tracks and the western limits to the Clear Fork of the Trinity River, and its percentage of the total grew to 36.8 percent. The common use of rail tracks as neighborhood boundaries reflected the degree to which railroads dominated Fort Worth's landscape. A 1931 study praised Fort Worth for its clean geographic divisions, noting that they had not developed from planning but were imposed naturally by the Trinity River and the twelve railroad lines radiating in all directions. The population shift southward was just one facet of a general trend away from the business district to suburbs such as Arlington Heights, Riverside, Polytechnic, Meadowbrook, and Texas Christian University (TCU). With suburbanization and automobiles came traffic congestion. A 1930 survey of twelve main Fort Worth arteries between 6:00 a.m. and 12:00 p.m. on weekdays counted 142,000 vehicles—up from 102,000 in 1926, an almost 40 percent increase. The rise in automobile use coincided with a corresponding decline in streetcar traffic, leading to the eventual dismantling of Fort Worth's interurban system. In August 1941, Tarrant County accepted a $5,097 bid for removal of the last of its interurban rails, some 354 tons going to salvage.[2]

By the 1930 Census, the Depression was well under way, but its effects were delayed in Fort Worth, thanks largely to several commercial construction programs begun at the end of the 1920s. In February 1930, the chamber of commerce credited lingering 1920s construction projects for Fort Worth's low unemployment rate of only 2.3 percent. Building permits reached $17 million in 1927, Fort Worth's highest total to that point, but declined to just more than $10 million in 1930, a still respectable figure. In fact, Fort Worth led Texas in new construction in both 1929 and 1930, thanks to projects such as a $700,000 Bell Telephone building; the $800,000 Texas and Pacific Union Passenger Station, serving many railways; and TCU's football stadium. TCU began preparing for a new stadium at the end of the 1920s, buying land west of the campus and starting a $400,000 fund drive. A building committee compared stadia at several colleges—including Ohio State, Michigan, Illinois, Northwestern, and Chicago—before selecting the University of Nebraska as the model for its twenty-thousand-seat football stadium. Actual work began in March 1930 and finished just eight months later, on October 11, 1930, with a formal dedication held just before a Horned Frogs victory over the Arkansas Razorbacks. In 1930, work was completed on the $1 million, sixteen-story Sinclair Building at Fifth and Main Streets, with modern amenities like automatic elevators and air cooling for the basement and first two floors. The eighteen-story Fair Building at Seventh and Throckmorton Streets opened in 1931, housing the Fair Department Store in the first six floors, while the Fort Worth Grain and Cotton Exchange occupied the top two.[3]

A few more existing projects finished in the early 1930s, but new construction, which had kept the local economy going, dropped precipitously before virtually ending in 1932. The completion of a few existing buildings masked how dire the construction situation had become. A cornerstone was laid in 1931 for a new $1 million Masonic temple just west of downtown (opened in 1932), and R. E. Cox's Department Store at Fifth, Main, and Houston Streets opened in 1933. Cox's began in 1915 in Stephenville, Texas, about seventy miles southwest, and spread to the nearby cities of Waco and Marlin before making the jump to Fort Worth. In 1934, Burrus Mills, located at Jennings and Lancaster Avenues, announced a $500,000 grain elevator on eighty acres adjacent to the Santa Fe tracks in Saginaw, Texas, just north of Fort Worth. Civic leaders boasted of the new openings, but nothing could hide the coming construction stall as building permits nosedived from $10,121,774 in 1930 to $1,430,000 in 1932, a drop of 86 percent. The slowdown affected home construction dramatically, as Fort Worth issued only 110 residential building permits in 1932, a steep cut from 1,998 in 1928. With construction at a standstill and no jobs forthcoming, local building trades unions lowered daily wages 30 percent but got little response. Other economic indicators performed similarly. Bank clearings, a good reflection of commercial activity, sagged from $744,519,000 in 1929 to $520,254,095 in 1930 before crashing to $242,650,000 in 1932—a decline of two-thirds from 1928—and remained stunted through 1935. Postal receipts suffered less severely but still declined from $1,908,221 in 1927 to $1,324,517 in 1933, a drop of more than 30 percent. Somehow, Fort Worth still reported an addition of 158 businesses in 1932 over 1931, a remarkable achievement given the high mortality rate for businesses between 1930 and 1932.[4]

Government construction took up some of the decline from the commercial slump. The city of Fort Worth had signed off in 1928 on a five-year program from the chamber of commerce containing several major objectives designed to spur industrial development, including additions to the county road system and a new union depot. The city fathers backed that commitment with a $100 million bond package in 1931 that, among other items, funded paving forty-seven miles of streets. In addition, the state of Texas chipped in, budgeting $50 million for regional projects. Much of the state money, along with federal dollars, funded the $5.6 million needed for Possum Kingdom Lake and Lake Bridgeport, important additions to Fort Worth's water supply. Lake Bridgeport was completed on December 15, 1931, and Eagle Mountain Lake on October 24, 1932. Federal appropriations spent on the two lakes represented only a portion of substantial local expenditures made by the US government. In 1930, the US Postal Service paid $200,000 for a site at Jennings and Front (Lancaster) Streets

by the First State Bank of Polytechnic, the two failures creating a mild panic that sent crowds to both, although bank officials assured depositors they would receive their full holdings. The unease ticked upward when Louis W. Ward, an assistant teller at Texas National, walked into the police garage and shot himself in the head, leaving a note blaming the loss of his job, along with other problems. First State of Polytechnic was saved by larger depositors with more than $200 on the books who agreed to contribute 25 percent to a $75,000 trust fund covering the bank's red ink, a timely intervention that forestalled inquiries into whispered allegations. The situation at Texas National was messier, especially after Turner Locke, the bank's bookkeeper, admitted keeping a dummy ledger and hiding shortages from examiners. Those revelations and subsequent investigations led to criminal charges against B. B. Samuels and A. L. "Lon" Baker, bank president and vice-president, respectively, for misapplication of $1,297,363 in bank funds. Vice-President Baker received a ten-year sentence, and bank officials W. C. Smallwood and Claude C. Johnson received three years each, all at Leavenworth Penitentiary (Baker was scheduled for parole in 1935 after serving four years). Later, employees at Stockyards National Bank and Continental National were also charged for various forms of malfeasance, although the banks were not threatened.[9]

In the early 1930s, banking problems, regardless of the causes, became rampant, spreading uncertainty among nervous accountholders whose deposits sat unprotected. In that precarious environment, the merest rumors would send nervous clients rushing to withdraw money from solid institutions. Such was the case on February 18, 1930, when one thousand anxious depositors gathered at First National Bank, Fort Worth's second-largest bank and one of three—along with Fort Worth National, the largest, and Continental National—that dominated Fort Worth banking. As closing time neared, a large crowd still spilled out the front doors and into the street, all waiting to withdraw their deposits in cash. Bank officers kept the bank open past closing time and brought in an orchestra to play, all designed to reassure and calm. They were joined by Fort Worth's leading citizens, men such as W. T. Waggoner and Amon Carter, who circled the crowd with assurances that all was fine, Carter providing cheese sandwiches and donuts. Every withdrawal was honored, although it took until 11:00 p.m. and $6.5 million expressed over from the Federal Reserve in Dallas. The next day, the Fort Worth Clearinghouse Association ran a full-page ad promising that every Fort Worth bank was solid and that fundamentals had never been sounder, the latter an overly rosy assessment. Bank closures became so commonplace that a three-week period in 1932 without one failure in Texas sparked hopes that the worst was over and that conditions had turned for the better. The threat to common depositors eased somewhat after 1933, when the Federal Deposit Insurance Corporation began insuring deposits up to $2,500, an important advance that saved George V. Schmidt, a successful Fort Worth businessman, half of his $5,000 savings in a failed bank.[10]

The oil industry, a major economic force for Fort Worth, also declined dramatically as demand and prices plummeted below profitability. Oil producers meeting in Fort Worth in 1930 sought to shore up prices by calling for a cut of 126,000 barrels from the average daily production of 863,450, creating a 50,000 shortfall that would stabilize prices. State governments also intervened. Texas Governor Ross Sterling, Oklahoma Governor William H. Murray, and representatives from Kansas proposed barring foreign oil importation. Still, prices continued their descent, hitting just $0.61 a barrel in 1932 despite appeals from Fort Worth's Charles Roeser, vice-president of the American Petroleum Institute, that oil companies refuse to sell for less than $1.00. Hard times in the oil industry had wide-ranging national effects that fell disproportionately hard on Texas, responsible for 40 percent of the nation's output, and the Fort Worth trade area, home to two-thirds of the state's oil production. At the time, Texas oil production was divided into four regions: Fort Worth, Dallas, Houston, and San Antonio. The Fort Worth region, stretching west to El Paso and north though the Panhandle, had more operating drilling rigs than the other three combined and produced the most oil, accounting for 25 percent of the nation's total production compared to 16 percent for the Dallas region, 7 percent for Houston, and 9 percent for San Antonio. Fort

Worth had so much oil commerce that it laid claim to being one of the world's four most important oil centers—a bit of a stretch given that most of the production occurred three hundred miles west in the Midland-Odessa Permian basin. The geographic dissonance between Fort Worth and oil production centers would occasion a shift in commercial focus that was already well under way in the early 1930s, a transition that would cost Fort Worth dearly.[11]

Declines in commercial construction and the oil trade finally brought the Depression to Fort Worth's doorstep in the winter of 1932–33. The only business of size to close initially, Henderson Grain Company, was declared insolvent and removed from the Chicago Board of Trade, but many others cut hours and personnel as their revenue dropped. The chamber of commerce tried to maintain an optimistic outlook, boasting of 327 factories paying $22 million in wages, especially noting the stockyards, the South's largest livestock market, and the two big packinghouses. In fact, the livestock trade soldiered on during the Depression despite many difficulties, including a drought that left so many cattle without water or feed that sixty-one thousand were destroyed in the field and thousands more were forced into slaughterhouses, depressing prices so much that ranchers struggled to survive. Fort Worth could do little about the oil trade or the drought but tried to stimulate construction through the Emergency Employment Committee, chaired by Walter B. Scott and staffed by volunteers who maintained a workers' registry and encouraged businesses and individuals to build. The program experienced less than a stirring success, receiving commitments for only $110,000 in new work, including $20,000 from W. T. Waggoner.[12]

The Depression drove Harris Hospital, a private institution affiliated with the Methodist Church, to a serious cash flow crisis that threatened bankruptcy and auctioning on the courthouse steps. Facing an existential crisis, the hospital's founder, Dr. Charles H. Harris, scrambled to find investors who would guarantee loans, at the same time trying to cut costs by merging the hospital with his sanitarium. Dr. C. O. Terrell, Harris Hospital's medical director and administrator since 1932, used the circumstances to suggest eliminating church ties

Swift's Cattle and Sheep Killing Department, 1934. Courtesy Special Collections, the University of Texas at Arlington Libraries.

but relented when Methodist Bishop Hiram Abiff Boaz threatened divine retribution, warning Terrell that "the curse of God would rest upon him," saving Harris as a Methodist institution.[13]

Franklin Roosevelt's New Deal programs were more successful at having significant impacts on the local economy, but even they only ameliorated and did not end the Depression. The combined efforts of the Public Works Administration (PWA), the Works Progress Administration (WPA), the Civilian Conservation Corps (CCC), and the National Recovery Administration (NRA) created more than two thousand local jobs, although many were only temporary, and the effect was never as successful as supporters claimed. General Hugh Johnson, the head of the NRA, told a 1933 Fort Worth crowd of seven thousand that the agency had alleviated 25 percent of the Depression, a clear overstatement. Still, some positive signs began to appear, including $2,822,405 in building permits issued during the first ten months of 1935, a 274 percent increase over the same period in 1934 and more than Dallas registered.[14] The CCC, one of the more popular New Deal programs, established an early presence with Sunset Camp, which opened on May 1, 1934, on the north shore of Lake Worth. Sunset Camp housed two hundred men and boys clearing underbrush and doing general work around the underdeveloped area north of Nine Mile Bridge. In 1936, the CCC built a regional office, adding one hundred semipermanent jobs. The PWA had a tremendous impact on construction through its funding of projects such as Arlington Heights High School and an orphans' home as well as contributing $500,000 for the construction of a new city hall, $400,000 for a library, and $687,000 for Fort Worth's Texas Centennial Celebration in 1936. In 1935, the WPA picked up where the PWA left off in creating construction jobs. Karl Wallace, WPA district director, announced in 1939 that since its inception in 1935, the agency had spent $7,851,501 in the Fort Worth area with only $944,046 going for materials and $5,907,738 for wages, a figure he claimed was sufficient to support 4,500 families (twenty thousand people) for four years—a bit of stretch, since that only amounted to $436 per year per family, but it was still a sizable boost to the local economy. The WPA funded many endeavors, including the arts. In 1939, Will Rogers Coliseum hosted a WPA exhibition, "American Hands in Action," highlighting the agency's nonconstruction projects employing artists, writers, musicians, folk artists, and others. Over the course of three weeks, 26,349 persons toured displays of canning, sewing, historic records, music, and other arts.[15]

The Depression even drove Fort Worth to the brink of cooperation with Dallas. In 1933, mayors William Bryce of Fort Worth and Charles E. Turner of Dallas attended the Third Annual Banquet of the Trinity River Canal Association, a group promoting dredging the Trinity River to create a commercial waterway to the Gulf of Mexico. The two mayors agreed on the benefits of mutual cooperation in industrial development—a propitious decision, since their two cities were (and are) inexorably linked. A 1941 state survey found that the Dallas–Fort Worth Pike, the main intercity link, carried 11,350 vehicles daily, second in Texas only to Houston's Highway 59 with 13,920 daily users. (In 2013, an average of 66,000 vehicles traveled daily on I-20, one of three major linking arteries.) Bryce and Turner also acknowledged the historic competition shared by both cities, suggesting it had made each better. That competitiveness was on display in 1938, when Dallas and Fort Worth both sought a regional veterans' hospital of 250 beds and costing $1.2 million. Dallas won, a decision the *Dallas Times Herald* applauded as overdue, complaining that Fort Worth had taken

New City Hall, financed by PWA, 1938. Courtesy Special Collections, the University of Texas at Arlington Libraries.

the "lion's share" of federal contracts. The *Star Telegram* agreed but argued Fort Worth had won its share because of its careful planning and intelligent sponsorships.[16]

The most poignant effect of the Depression lay in its devastating impact on people. Unemployment began to creep upward very early, even as the overall economy, buoyed in the early 1930s by construction, struggled to hold its own. Before 1932, the Fort Worth area experienced some down cycles, including in 1927, when C. W. Woodman, assistant director of the US Employment Service, reported a large surplus of labor created by overbuilding and low cotton prices, but those were temporary problems that passed quickly. After 1931, unemployment accelerated rapidly, affecting large segments of the economy, and remained a problem throughout the decade. Economic stagnation left able-bodied people with no job and no hope of a job, forcing so many into relief that resources were soon overwhelmed. In

1931, the city of Fort Worth tried to offer basic assistance in providing food and rent assistance to women and children as well as limited numbers of unemployed men who were required to work—usually cleaning alleys, parks, or vacant lots. Unfortunately, demand quickly overwhelmed the city welfare department funding. In 1931, Fort Worth budgeted just $50,000 for welfare relief, a ridiculously paltry figure considering $15,003 was spent in February alone, with $12,823 just for food to feed an estimated 6,100 needy families. The funding versus expenditures ratio did not improve in 1932, when the budget rose to only $60,000 and expenditures reached $11,700 in February, leaving the funding depleted by April 15, six months before the next budget in October. February, the coldest month, traditionally experienced the highest demand on assistance as the poor faced both hunger and extreme cold, twin conditions that aggravated serious infectious diseases such as pneumonia, which in 1937 ranked second only to heart disease as the leading cause of natural death in Fort Worth. With no public funding and no hope of any additional money, relief workers could do little more than pray for spring to come early. In the winter of 1932–33, the poor bore the brunt of the Depression's worst effects while facing dire conditions as the weather turned bitterly cold. At the peak, 8,500 families and 14,000 vagrant men swelled relief rolls; the enormity of demand was so great that local relief expenditures, both private and public, soared from $195,254 in 1932 to $664,978 in 1933. Things did not ease in 1934 as an estimated 14,000 families received an astounding $240,000 in monthly relief, providing each an average of only $17 for food and rent. In 1934, Tarrant County was rated as the poorest urban county in Texas, having 25 percent of its families on relief compared to 22 percent in Bexar County, 19 percent in Dallas County, and 17 percent in Harris County. The demand became overwhelming. In December 1933, work relief counted 7,237 men on its rolls, an unsustainable figure given the available funding, necessitating cutbacks as the only option. That meant limiting the number on work relief. For example, one day, 927 men sought work to earn merely a $2 food order when funding existed to provide for only 145 vouchers.[17] Even in the face of obvious deprivation, some continued to believe that welfare rolls were full of lazy people who chose to live off the state rather than work. In 1935, Floyd Helm, district relief administrator for a five-county region of North Texas, ordered employable persons off relief, stating he had been told that local poultry plants had five hundred open jobs plucking turkeys at $0.05 per fowl.[18]

Faced with staggering demands, relief organizations, private and public, local and national, struggled to keep up with the demand for food and services. Tarrant County offered a home for paupers (near the current location of the Juvenile Detention Center on Kimbo Road) with housing, separated by gender, for 150, a mere fraction of demand, and the county relief program suffered from dire underfunding. Federal assistance through the Reconstruction Finance Corporation budgeted $340,000 for local relief for the fiscal year beginning October 1, 1932, contingent on state participation. That proved difficult, as Texas experienced problems in selling $2,750,000 in supporting bonds, part of a $20 million state package covering several programs. Tarrant County Relief Administrator A. H. Flickwir, MD, expressed confidence that the setback was only temporary and that money would soon be flowing to the four thousand families on county rolls. When the funding finally arrived, the resulting rush overwhelmed the downtown relief office, forcing the opening of substations in closed police stations on the north side and on Missouri Avenue on the south and quickly emptying coffers. Private organizations such as the Union Gospel Mission, American Legion, Salvation Army, Community Chest (which donated $12,000), and St. Joseph Hospital tried to keep the relief offices open, but they faced the same insurmountable problems. Many businesses also made large cash contributions, especially the Missouri Pacific Railroad, which donated $25,000 one month and $50,000 the next. Some donations were earmarked, such as $200 raised by the Knights of Columbus for the relief of Mexican families. The efforts helped, but the demand was simply too great, leaving many hungry, including schoolchildren, who were often sent to school without breakfast or lunch, which led to students collapsing from hunger. In response, the school district began funding free lunches for the indigent, paying

$0.10 for each meal. Ellis Boyd, president of the Fort Worth Board of Education, reported the district provided 534 free lunches, the maximum the budget could support, while teachers and parents contributed to feeding another 236, but that still left 348 hungry. Fortunately, Leonard's Department Store, the Community Chest, the Kiwanis, the Lion's Club, and several churches joined forces to buy 500 lunches, all supplemented by milk donated by local dairies. The Depression brought desperate suffering as well as remarkable human decency.[19]

Private citizens donated food and money to feed the destitute who gathered in parks and other open areas. At first, a few individuals began offering various forms of sustenance, such as an anonymous woman who in 1932 donated one hundred bread loaves and one hundred quarts of milk to feed unemployed men who regularly congregated at Burnet Park. Those individual, uncoordinated efforts were supplemented in 1932 with a soup kitchen organized by Alice Leavy of the American Legion's War Nurses Auxiliary, who launched the initiative with $10 donated by a lawyer during a luncheon. Leavy spread her appeal, receiving numerous small cash gifts as well as donated food: chicken wings, necks, and backs from J. W. Nichols Poultry; canned goods from Waples Platter; and bread from Mrs. Baird's Bakery (Baird's required the slices be taken out of the original packaging and put in paper bags to prevent reselling). Other items came from various sources, including two copper vats used to cook soup that had been seized from bootleggers. On October 8, 1932, Fort Worth's soup kitchen opened at 111 South Florence Street, providing a pint of soup and bread that cost less than one cent to produce to more than three hundred waiting men, women, and children. That first day, the cauldrons emptied before all were fed, but those left waiting were given meat bones and vegetables to make their own soup. The kitchen fed an average of between four hundred and five hundred between 11:30 a.m. and 2:00 p.m. each day. In December 1932, the city of Fort Worth began contributing $100 to $150 each month to cover utilities and other expenses.[20]

Charities concentrated much of their efforts on children's assistance. The Goodfellow Fund, a *Star Telegram* Christmas charity, faced mounting demand in 1932 as the list of needy families climbed to 2,300—so overwhelming was the demand that the fund ran a $1,500 deficit, its first since its start in 1911. The next year, 1933, contributions sank to their lowest level in years, limiting distributions to only $8,422, almost all going to food, with only $225 spent on candy and nothing spent on toys. The newspaper also started the Free Milk and Ice Fund (before refrigerators were common, ice was needed to preserve food). Several other organizations worked to improve the welfare of poor children. The Panther Boys Club (PBC), organized in 1926 at 111½ East Third Street, originally focused on newsboys and other indigent downtown youth but expanded its reach to cover impoverished youth anywhere in the city. Their associates often dealt with abject circumstances at the most intimate level. A worker delivering clothing to 410 Northwest Twenty-First Street found four young boys locked out of their home by their mother, who worked at a packinghouse and feared the boys would start a fire. Latchkey children were a major factor leading Hazel Vaughn Leigh, along with support from the Kiwanis Club of North Fort Worth, to establish the Fort Worth Boys Club (FWBC). The FWBC opened on February 1, 1935, at Boulevard Methodist Church, providing after-school care and classes for boys between six and fourteen. Their after-school programs were so successful that they were credited for a 75 percent reduction in north side juvenile delinquency. In September 1937, the club moved to 100 NW 20th Street to a building with a gym, library, game room, showers, and kitchen. While the FWBC concentrated on young boys, Edna Gladney cared for unmarried mothers, many of whom were young girls, providing medical care and assistance in adoptions for three thousand babies. Ms. Gladney also worked at the state legislative level to remove the stigma of illegitimacy from birth certificates. Hollywood immortalized Ms. Gladney in a 1941 movie, *Blossoms in the Dust*, starring Greer Garson. Everything helped, but nothing erased all the pain associated with poverty. All the efforts helped but could not cure all ills. In 1937, the Fort Worth Health Department reported 163 infant deaths, almost one every other day.[21]

Mary Rossman of Fort Worth Welfare looks through Goodfellow Letters, 1937. Courtesy Special Collections, the University of Texas at Arlington Libraries.

Some of the most serious cases involved homeless children, many abandoned by parents unable to feed them. In 1930, the city of Fort Worth established Ruth Lubin Camp at Lake Worth to provide shelter for 400 destitute children. Private entities like the Riverside Civic League, Veterans League, Community Chest, and Leonard Brothers pitched in, donating food and money to the camp, but the most enduring contribution may have come from Lena Pope, who, along with her Sunday school class at Broadway Baptist Church, opened a children's home at 1215 Washington Avenue. On opening day, January 1, 1930, the home took in 25 children, four times the 6 expected, and the number continued to grow, reaching 100 within a year. The growth forced four relocations before Pope and her staff settled into the W. T. Waggoner home at the corner of El Paso and Summit Avenues.[22] Significant financial support came from individuals such as C. A. Lupton, who funded the home's food budget for an entire year, as well as Tarrant County and Fort Worth, which contributed a fixed monthly payment in compensation for Pope's care of destitute children. In 1939, a women's group led by Mrs. James Cook argued that county funds would be better spent improving the county's home, but County Judge Miller disagreed, noting that expanding the home, then at the maximum capacity of 65 children, would be costlier than the flat $200 monthly stipend that Lena Pope received for keeping some 75 wards of the county. Mrs. Pope charged that the complaint represented a crass effort to grab county funding by a rival organization, the All Church Home, which charged $0.50 per child per day, a rate that would have amounted to $1,125 a month for the 75 children Lena Pope kept for only $200. Fort Worth also contributed $400 monthly, but the controversy surrounding the All Church Home matter sparked a reconsideration that ended the flat stipend effective November 1939, replacing it with a per diem of $0.50 per child for the 4 children then housed pursuant to a municipal court commitment, the city arguing that the other 113 children were the county's responsibility. Fort Worth may have had a valid legal argument, but that did little to help Mrs. Pope feed the children.[23]

Homelessness affected children, adults, and complete families. Fort Worth, as a rail center, had always had more than its share of traveling unemployed, or hoboes. On an average day, some 150 men populated the rail yards and various camps, especially a large area south of Lancaster Avenue and east of Hemphill Street (near what would later be the site of Frank Kent Cadillac). Many were attracted to the camps for the freer lifestyle they offered, especially more seasoned travelers who harbored little hope of finding jobs, but younger men still hoping for work tended to seek out one of many local shelters. The Salvation Army, with one thousand beds, was the largest provider, but smaller facilities such as the Wesley Community House at 2131 North Commerce Street, the San Jose Mexican Center at Fourteenth and Calhoun Streets, the YMCA, and the Panther Boys Club also furnished overnight accommodations. Women and girls found rooms, or at least beds, at the Girls Service League, Young Women's Christian Association, Lassiter Lodge at 1008 Penn Street, and Worth Cottage at

917 North Henderson Street. They were the lucky ones; others, such as Ann Williams, were left outside. Ms. Williams, just twenty-two when she came to Fort Worth in 1936 looking for work, found only an offer to be a "hostess" at a taxi dance club, dives where men paid a dime to dance with girls who earned only tips, gifts that often came with strings attached. The first night she danced until 3:00 a.m. but made no money, leaving her broke, homeless, and with no recourse but to sleep in Burnet Park, where the police found her.[24] Housing became an especially critical issue in winter. February 1933 was a bitterly cold month, with temperatures hovering near zero, creating such dangerous conditions that the city turned an old fire station at Throckmorton and Monroe Streets into a dormitory housing 130 men, all of whom were required to bathe before getting into the bedding. Winter was hard, but even in summer, people searched for indoor access at night to avoid the elements. In June 1932, for the first time ever, Fort Worth began locking city hall doors nightly after the police found more than one hundred sleeping in empty offices.[25]

The lack of sufficient long-term accommodations forced some families to camp, many doing so around the Trinity River bottom and its bridges. In November 1934, two families consisting of eleven members were discovered under the Henderson Street Bridge, where they had lived for weeks, getting by on $7 in groceries received from the Transient Bureau, a one-time grant to out-of-towners meant to last three days, and from occasional work plucking turkeys at $0.04 per bird. The adults and children shared just four pairs of shoes among them. The next month, a reporter found a half dozen people under the Belknap Street overpass, occupying shacks made of cardboard, tin, and scrap lumber. In 1935, police picked up Billie Bob Story, eight years old, begging door-to-door late at night. Young Billie led the officers to his parents and three siblings camped on the Trinity River bottoms, where they had been for the past month after arriving from Lawton, Oklahoma. The family scratched out a bare existence selling junk picked out of garbage, but even that had dried up, leaving them without food all day. The officers fed Billie Bob and arranged for relief intervention. Dire conditions brought dire consequences—in

September 1936, the four-year-old son of G. E. Harper drowned in the Trinity River while under the care of his ten-year-old sister, the two left while both parents worked. The couple and their five children had sheltered in a shack on a concrete ledge under the Paddock Viaduct since the previous year, living in a hovel furnished with crude furniture fashioned from packing boxes and discarded lumber and bathing in the river. The family had maintained a bare existence from sporadic work and food begged from restaurants as well as from a few chickens and calves penned between the river and levee.[26]

Sometimes people were pushed to desperate measures. Officers S. P. Jones and D. G. Hodge followed two men they saw stealing four bread loaves to a dilapidated rooming house shared with two women and a child. The adults told a common story about leaving home in Haskell, Texas, to seek work but finding nothing and ending up broke, hungry, and desperate. The officers bought food for the families. E. J. Durham, thirty-seven years old, who lived in rooms at 211½ West Weatherford Street, was jailed after assaulting a woman caseworker who refused food vouchers until she had inspected their home the next day despite Mr. Durham's statement that he, his wife, and their three children had not eaten that day and were facing eviction the next day. Mrs. Durham affirmed the dire account, adding that E. J. often walked the streets because he could not bear to hear the children crying from hunger. Good Samaritans supplied milk and bread. In the face of so much poverty and so little hope, it was not surprising that some resorted to the ultimate step, although the suicide rate was not excessively high; only twenty-eight were recorded in 1931 and twenty-five in 1935. Still, a few gave up and took not only their own lives but those of family members. In November 1938, Oliver Harper, owner of Harper's Bakery, closed the windows tightly before turning on the gas, killing himself, his wife, and their three children while they slept. Mr. Harper left a note warning of the gas and asking that relatives be notified.[27]

Some of the unemployed joined protests, and others took more aggressive action. In 1932, F. R. Compton and T. W. Conner organized one hundred local World War I veterans to participate in the Bonus

Army March in Washington, DC, an effort to pressure Congress into the immediate payment of bonuses scheduled to be paid World War I veterans in 1943. When the railroads refused to grant passes, many of the group simply hopped boxcars. While those left Fort Worth to protest in Washington, DC, others came to the city to do the same. On June 20, 1933, Thomas Earl Barlow led a large group opposing the eviction of Jack Daniel, an unemployed refinery worker, from his home at 1204 Lagonda Avenue. Barlow and twenty-four other men and four women were arrested for unlawful assembly. Being arrested was not an uncommon experience for Barlow, originally from Kentucky, who joined the National Unemployed Council in Houston, an organization of the American Communist Party. The council sent him to Fort Worth to organize the six thousand unemployed workers reported to be without hope of jobs, and he had considerable success, enrolling eight hundred members. Barlow persisted, continuing the fight even after being arrested on Lagonda, organizing a rally on August 31, 1933, to protest the suspension of relief funds that drew one thousand people to Bluff Park. Barlow told the crowd that letting people go hungry would bring consequences—a threat he, along with two supporters, telegraphed to Governor Miriam Ferguson. As they left the Western Union office, they were arrested by A. C. Howerton, a city detective assigned to investigate communist activities. Two days later, on September 2, 1939, jailers found Barlow unconscious in a Tarrant County jail cell, and he died shortly thereafter from a fractured skull. The injury occurred, according to jail officials, the day before at the city jail during a fight with Charley Morgan, also an inmate and an amateur boxer. Witnesses, including E. E. Hardy and H. N. Macomb (arrested with Barlow), supported the account, stating that Morgan and Barlow fought after the labor leader tried to reclaim a quarter he had chipped into a fund for snacks and cigarettes. A grand jury investigation found no basis for claims that Barlow had been tortured or shot in the head, finding that he most likely died from injuries received striking a cell bar as he fell. Reverend J. Frank Norris conducted Barlow's funeral at the First Baptist Church, and Hy Gordon, Texas chairman of the Communist Party, eulogized him before burial in Mount Olivet Cemetery in a coffin bearing a red flag with a hammer and sickle.[28]

For a brief, intense period, Fort Worth reeled from aggressive labor action. In 1937, strikers seized the Monroe Street offices and South Main Street shops of Lone Star Gas, holding the facilities from May 27 to June 12 before the city manager and police chief negotiated their withdrawals, although the strike continued with sporadic violence breaking out as strikers battled nonunion workers crossing picket lines, including one incident in which three strikers assaulted one worker. As violence continued, authorities increased the police presence and called in the Texas Rangers. During the next week, officers arrested ten strikers and one employee during several confrontations, but the violence eventually subsided. The next year, a minor, nonviolent flap developed when twenty members of Painters Local 318 walked off the job and picketed the Blackstone Hotel over allegations that the hotel used nonunion workers.[29]

Management, as well as workers, also found nontraditional responses to counter low commodity prices. In March 1940, Johnson County (Tarrant County's southern neighbor) dairymen cut prices below market value, a move that threatened Tarrant County farmers, many of whom remembered the 1933 milk war, which drove the cost of a quart of milk to drop to $0.03, below the cost of production. A few men confronted the cut-rate operators, leading to a fistfight and the arrest of several Tarrant County men by Johnson County authorities. On March 20, Fort Worth milkmen changed tactics, using five cars to block Highway 81 two miles south of Fort Worth (Highway 81 was the main traffic route between Johnson and Tarrant Counties). The blockade stopped a dairy truck belonging to Sixty Oaks Farm, located near Burleson, and participants dumped its milk. The next day, carloads of armed men escorted the Sixty Oaks truck unhindered. With violence threatening, the Tarrant County district attorney negotiated a settlement between W. J. Wilkes, the owner of Sixty Oaks, and representatives from the Producer-Distributor Dairymen of Tarrant County, led by W. J. Horner.[30]

The battle over milk prices reflected the lingering effects of the Depression that persisted through the 1930s and even into the 1940s. Although the number of idle people declined from the worst years, the 1940 Census still showed 5,110,270 Americans unemployed in March 1940. Fort Worth still had its share of the jobless well into 1940. In the winter of 1938–39, the Texas Relief Fund announced it would pass out coats to WPA workers, bringing 150 men who waited all night to discover only sixty coats available, resulting in squabbles and fistfights over places in the queue. To forestall a recurrence, the 300 men who showed up at the next free coat event were given numbered cards indicating their order. In January 1940, 30 who had been out of work for months appeared before the Tarrant County Commissioners Court seeking relief. Their spokesman, Raymond Bland of 201½ East First Street, claimed that hundreds faced eviction and hunger without hope of work of any kind.[31] In 1940, homeless people still lived in makeshift shelters under bridges. In January 1940, a dozen families under the Belknap Street bridge survived thanks to donated firewood needed to heat their dwellings and to fuel an open fire for men building rustic tables they hoped to sell. Several other families were found living in trailers and shacks adjacent to the Trinity River, north of downtown off White Settlement Road, including an elderly couple without food or much clothing living in a cardboard-and-wood shack. As late as November 1940, civic leaders touring the Trinity River bottoms reported people in the same living squalid conditions as those from earlier reports: children without shoes despite the cold, an eleven-year-old child caring for four younger siblings while their parents worked, and a jobless father and mother of seven living on what two older sons earned selling newspapers.[32]

Fort Worth's Great Depression experience was similar to that of most of the nation. The worst effects were delayed a few years thanks to a healthy construction economy, but they then struck with great force, crippling the main economic mainstays of meatpacking, oil, and banking. The need overwhelmed charitable efforts by governments (local, state, and national), businesses, and citizens, leaving many people destitute of the basic necessities of food, clothing, and shelter. Circumstances created horrible conditions in which grown men, women, and children were left hungry and homeless, many condemned to a bare existence in camps along the Trinity River. A few people reacted violently, but such incidents remained relatively rare.

CHAPTER SEVEN

Politics and Other Entertainment

1930s Edition

Fort Worth entered the 1930s with a remarkably stable political environment but encountered considerable upheaval after 1936. Stability flowed from a single power source, the Good Government League (GGL), whose candidates dominated elected offices. The GGL's base of supporters included many city employees who owed their jobs to the group and who, in turn, contributed lavishly to candidates, creating a self-perpetuating political climate inclined to reelect incumbents such as Mayor William Bryce, who served six years, or Van Zandt Jarvis, who served four years. The cozy arrangement was broken in 1936 by a challenge from the People's Progressive League (PPL), a group of residents convinced that the GGL was a pawn of powerful utilities that controlled city government and the local press. PPL supporters charged that the utilities lawyer, W. A. Hanger, authored many editorials in both the *Fort Worth Press* and *Fort Worth Star Telegram*. The 1936 election split along clear class lines, with the GGL running strongest in upscale sections such as Texas Christian University (TCU), Mistletoe Heights, Forest Park, and Arlington Heights, while the PPL gathered enough votes in the north side and other working-class neighborhoods to win a majority of city council seats and name one of their own, W. J. Hammond, as mayor (at the time, the council selected the mayor). Hammond rose from a poor background in Ellis County to earn an AB and an MA from TCU and a PhD from the University of California before returning to his alma mater as a history professor and becoming an active progressive. He was known for harshly criticizing the police over the 1933 arrest and in-custody death of a labor leader (Barlow), causing Police Chief Henry B. Lewis to label him a communist and call for his removal from the TCU faculty.[1]

Internal strife proved more threatening than external criticism as Hammond's progressivism proved too advanced for the rest of the council. Rancor developed after Hammond balked at doling out city jobs to PPL supporters, especially over his rejection of S. Barney Edwards as city manager in favor of L. W. Hoelscher. PPL's insistence on sharing in municipal spoils resulted in council bickering so intense that Hoelscher demanded a vote of confidence, a move that backfired when the aldermen demoted him and made Edwards city manager. Hoelscher refused the demotion and resigned, but the breach between mayor and council persisted despite pleas for harmony from the General Ministerial Alliance. In July 1937, three councilmen initiated a recall petition for Hammond and one of his chief supporters, a councilman identified only as Hull. In the recall vote on December 3, 1937, Hammond defeated Dr. Clary Johnson, and Hull won over H. C. McCart, a lawyer and former city attorney. Just five months later, on May 11, 1938, Hammond resigned, complaining the mayor's job limited his ability to promote a progressive agenda (he retained his council seat). Dr. R. H. W. Dreschsel replaced Hammond as mayor, but the rift continued with a second recall petition in June 1938 that targeted Hammond as well as five other councilmen, all PPL men. The petition garnered sufficient signatures and withstood a legal challenge in the Texas Supreme Court, but by now, Hammond had had enough and resigned, citing tremendous pressure and persecution. The recall election on July 23 brought six new councilmen, five who defeated the five named incumbents and one who ran unopposed for Hammond's vacant seat. Ousted councilman George Seaman and a councilman named Martin, contending the vote was illegal, vowed not to surrender their seats, but the other three—Hull, (unknown) Oglesby, and (unknown) Hooper—were uncertain about their futures.[2] The loss doomed the PPL but also ended council divisions and returned stability to city politics. In February 1940, Thomas Jefferson Harrell, originally from Grandview, Texas (thirty miles south), and a graduate of Baylor University before becoming president of Traders Oil Company, was named mayor but served only seventeen months before being replaced in July 1941 by I. N. McCrary, noted for his rotundity.[3]

The city manager's position also experienced flux, with personnel passing through like a revolving door. Six men served as manager from 1925 and 1939, an average tenure of just more than two years. The sixth to go, Dudley L. Lewis, a twenty-seven-year city employee, was fired in 1939 after proposing a draconian budget that eliminated fifty-eight positions and closed three fire stations. Sam H. Bothwell Lewis, city manager in Sweetwater, Texas, replaced Lewis, receiving a salary of $10,000. Fort Worth had gone outside the ranks before, luring George Fairtrace away from Wichita Falls in 1931 for $12,000 a year.[4]

In 1937, political uproar spread to the suburbs when Fort Worth tried but failed to annex Westover Hills. The process began when Westover Hills, population 212, scheduled a plebiscite on incorporation as a municipality—a move Fort Worth Mayor Hammond described as a crass move to avoid Fort Worth taxes while still reaping the benefits of city services available from a larger city. Fort Worth was familiar with the tactic; years before, Niles City, home to the packinghouses, had incorporated for the same reasons. Hammond suggested that Fort Worth annex its smaller neighbor before it could act, noting that two of Westover Hills's seventy-two homes already lay within Fort Worth city limits. He also applied pressure, threatening to cut off Westover Hills's water supply, furnished by Fort Worth, and to deny rights-of-way for other utilities. At the same time, Fort Worth tried, but failed, to push legislation through the state legislature authorizing annexation without consent of towns with fewer than seven thousand residents, a tactic it had used years earlier with Niles City. Westover Hills remained steadfast, voting thirty-five to zero in May to support incorporation and naming John Farrell as mayor. Fort Worth responded by cutting the water supply, although they resumed service after only one day, all the while warning that the service was subject to permanent revocation. The matter seemed sure to end up in litigation as Westover Hills prepared to seek an injunction based on the threat to public welfare posed by water service interruption. Fortunately, cooler heads prevailed, permitting an agreement in which Westover Hills remained separate and intact but agreed to pay doubled water rates, the same rate charged other outside users. The settlement displeased many Fort Worthians bent on expansion through annexation.[5]

Two other suburban communities bickered over which was the real White Settlement, an antebellum community approximately ten miles west of Fort Worth. A popular legend claimed the community's name distinguished it from a nearby community of freed slaves and/or an American Indian camp near the current stockyards, but Mrs. C. K. Normand, a longtime resident, reported that the name White Settlement, already in use when her grandfather arrived in 1851, referred to three families named White who settled the area. The dispute over naming rights developed in 1941, when a two-mile area near Lake Worth incorporated as White Settlement Village, angering neighbors to the west who argued that they were White Settlement and that the incorporated area was actually Tartar Hill. The newly incorporated mayor disagreed, countering that the western area was Sunset Gardens and that the true White Settlement stretched from Raymond Buck's place to just west of Powder Hill, some distance east. The western group, refusing to concede, scheduled a vote on May 24 to incorporate as White Settlement Community.[6]

The biggest issue confronting city politics concerned not boundaries or annexation but the Depression. The financial crunch on municipal government became evident as early as 1930, when Fort Worth reduced the workweek for laborers from six to five days while holding their wages static at $0.40 an hour, a net one-sixth reduction in weekly pay for each worker. Things did not improve in 1931. That year, Fort Worth's government faced a $500,000 drop in revenue, beginning a downward trend that continued until 1935, when municipal tax revenue garnered only $1,908,087, which was $284,679, or 13 percent, less than in 1927 (eight years earlier), when receipts reached $2,291,087. The 1931 budget forced the council to reduce wages by 10 percent and dismiss seventy-five staff, including twenty firefighters and thirty police officers, effective October 1, 1931. Several factors contributed to the decline, but delinquent taxes were a major component as the accumulated unpaid taxes increased from $1,602,630 in 1926 to $3,962,155 in 1935, a figure larger than annual expenditures.[7]

In 1932, things only got worse. In April, city accounts were overdrawn $937,522—an amount so high that banks refused more advances or loan relief, especially with $100,000 in municipal bonds languishing unsold. Part of the bond difficulty stemmed from Fort Worth's bond rating falling to "Baa," or "highly speculative," denoting that its financial stability might be satisfactory but not noteworthy. That meant that Fort Worth was in worse financial straits than Dallas, Houston, and Waco, all of which retained "a" bond ratings. The lack of options for increasing revenue brought more cuts, which meant further reductions in salaries. On June 1, the Parks Department cut wages from 5 to 15 percent, and wages for general city laborers fell from $84.82 to $75.00 monthly, an 11 percent drop, with another round of cuts looming for the new fiscal year beginning October 1, 1932. As cash flow slowed to a stop, Fort Worth began issuing warrants, or scrips, in lieu of cash wages, a practice it had used thirty years earlier during the lingering effects of the Panic of 1893. At first, banks honored scrips at face value, but that ended on October 13, 1932, when the city stopped paying 6 percent interest for the delayed redemption period, notifying employees they had to deal with their bank on terms of discount. That meant that banks immediately discounted city scrips, usually 10 to 15 percent, a move that saved the city money but at workers' expense. In addition, another eighty workers were laid off and then recalled after a public outcry, although their wages were cut 21 percent (the author's own grandfather was one of the furloughed staff).[8]

Throughout the rest of the decade, city employees faced more deprivations. In 1934, the council eliminated paid vacations but required employees to take two weeks unpaid annual leave, saving $39,000, although they later amended the order to grant pay for one of the two weeks. They also eliminated blanket pension coverage for non–civil service employees, although continuing to grant exceptions on a case-by-case basis until June 1, 1935, when that option ended, as did civil service pensions for firefighters and police. Thereafter, pensions were restricted to workers rendered unable to work due to on-the-job injuries and to dependents of employees killed on duty. The council and city manager rejected some cost-cutting proposals, including a gender-based initiative to end employment of married women and terminate all married women with a working husband. The proposal had a laudable motive, to spread jobs by eliminating two-income families, but was poorly conceptualized and unworkable, even in the 1930s.[9]

The economic crunch touched every part of government, including education. Public school enrollment slumped, declining from 30,723 in the 1929–30 school year to 28,827 (25,731 whites and 3,096 blacks) in September 1939, a loss of 1,896 students, while the population increased more than 8 percent. School attendance was also poor, averaging only 24,326 daily, or 79.2 percent in 1929–30. No strict causation ties an incongruent decline in the student body and low attendance to the Depression, but it seems very likely. In contrast, the Depression's impact on faculty salaries was as clear as figures on a pay stub. In 1932, the average annual wage for white Fort Worth elementary teachers, $1,639, was less but comparable to Dallas and Houston at $1,746 and $1,743, respectively, but Fort Worth salaries declined significantly thereafter to 40 percent below the 1932 level by 1939. In that year, the school district tried to correct some of the loss by granting 900 of its 952 teachers a lump-sum payment equal to 40 percent of the decrease sustained since 1932. The 52 excluded employees included 20 blacks whose salaries were already below the state minimum of $1,020 in 1932 and therefore not reduced. The payment and other advances brought teachers' salaries within 2.5 percent of what they had earned in 1932–33, seven years prior. In contrast, per-student expenditures remained rather constant, amounting to $81.20 in 1937, a respectable rate that ranked forty-fourth nationally, ahead of Dallas ($71.73), Houston ($70.36), and San Antonio ($75.35). In the larger context of Tarrant County, schools experienced large disparities in per-student spending, ranging from $8.49 to $109.42, and in the school year, which varied from 125 to 184 days. Fort Worth's school tax rate of $1.17 per $100 valuation placed it midway between $0.89 in Dallas and $1.42 in San Antonio.[10]

Budget constraints aggravated overcrowding issues at the City-County Hospital at the same time that indigent care demand soared. Charity cases increased fivefold in just one year, from 7,510 in 1930 to 36,433 in 1931, overwhelming hospital staff and facilities. In 1932, the hospital treated 42,980 and admitted 8,675 patients to its 134 beds, which were so tightly packed together that nurses had difficulty passing between them. To free bed space for the most serious cases, new mothers were dismissed only four hours after delivery, and patients with chronic but incurable conditions were turned away. Those efforts helped but did not stem the flow as almost 50,000 sought treatment in 1935, one-fourth of Tarrant County's population (197,553 in the 1930 Census). Much of the hospital's resources treated infectious diseases that are now largely eliminated, including pneumonia, the second leading cause of death (heart disease was the first), afflictions that hit the old and young especially hard. Many of the 163 infant mortalities in 1937 were due to infections.[11]

Overcrowding intensified existing plans to relocate City-County Hospital medical services from downtown to South Main Street, where sixty years earlier John Peter Smith had donated 4.15 acres specifically for a hospital. Many in the medical community preferred that location when the hospital was first built, but the downtown space prevailed because it benefited a nearby medical school at Fourth and Jones Streets. By the 1930s, the school was gone, and most doctors supported relocating to a larger, more modern facility wherever it could be built, although a few thought that South Main Street was too remote. A majority of Fort Worth councilmen and Tarrant County commissioners supported relocation, although they preferred more acreage to accommodate future growth. Construction finally became possible in 1937, when the Public Works Administration (PWA) included partial funding in a large block of PWA appropriations that included a new city hall and library. Work began soon after, allowing John Peter Smith Hospital to open in July 1939 to 55 patients moved from downtown. Just a few months later, in November 1939, the patient load reached 153, all cared for by a staff of two hundred plus forty-one student nurses funded by the

National Youth Administration, who earned only $35 monthly plus room and board.[12]

John Peter Smith Hospital was just one part of a large body of federally funded construction projects during the 1930s that reduced unemployment while also significantly improving Fort Worth's municipal infrastructure. The remarkable success Fort Worth experienced receiving federal largesse was no accident but rather the product of initiatives that began even before FDR and the New Deal. In 1931, Will Rogers wrote in his syndicated column that, although times were bad in Washington, DC, Amon Carter and "his gang" were hard at work seeking federal plunder, noting that Fort Worth was the only American town that still had lobbyists. Lobbying did not slow after Roosevelt took office in March 1933 but accelerated to secure a $519,000 PWA package in 1934 that included $279,000 to expand Rosedale Street into an artery, giving Poly (an eastside neighborhood) access to downtown via South Main Street as well as a much-needed renovation of the eastside sewage treatment plant needed to eliminate odors. Nearby residents, who had complained about malodorous fumes since the plant's opening in 1924, were fed up to the point that some threatened to withhold tax payments. Others took a lighthearted approach, claiming that if the German army had used the gas in World War I, it could have pushed the French into the sea or that a cow jumped to its death from a cliff while trying to escape.[13] Sensing a problem in the air, the council formed a committee that applied for and won the federal funding. One of the sewage contracts, awarded in December 1935 to McKenzie Construction of San Antonio, totaled $147,470, 30 percent of which (up to $45,200) was supplied by the PWA. The contract stipulated minimum hourly wages ranging from $0.30 for messengers, $0.40 for common laborers, to a high of $1.38 for foremen.[14] Federal funds built or contributed to the building of many other sites, including several facilities for Fort Worth schools. For example, in 1934, school construction received $4,167,000 of $5,379,000 federal dollars allocated locally. The PWA also funded at least part of Arlington Heights High School in 1936 and paid $160,000 toward the $244,000 cost of Farrington Field (named for Athletic Director K. S. Farrington), an athletic stadium seating twenty thousand on thirty-six acres south of Lancaster Avenue and across from Casa Mañana.[15]

The boast that Fort Worth received more than its share of federal largesse carried a lot of weight. The 1936 PWA grant behind Arlington Heights School also included $225,000 toward a new city hall costing $500,000 ($275,000 added from the city) and $180,000 for a new library costing $400,000 ($220,000 from city), all city contributions derived from a large 1935 bond proposal that included $127,500 for the City-County Hospital, $91,000 for the sewage plant, and $275,000 for a tuberculosis sanitarium. The new four-story city hall, built using the same Texas limestone used in the Lancaster Post Office that opened in 1933, became operational on January 2, 1939, but was not formally dedicated until March 25. The new library ran into considerable controversy in site selection. The original prospectus called for moving a few blocks west from the existing Carnegie Building site near city hall to Burnet Park, but donors associated with both sites raised objections. The existing library had been built in 1901 on land donated in 1892 by Mrs. Sarah Stripling with the stipulation that it be used only for a library, with discretions allowed at the donor's pleasure, an allowance her heirs were not disposed to grant. Their reluctance was understandable, given that the land reverted to them if the library left. The proposed location in Burnet Park also ran into problems, since Captain Samuel B. Burnet donated the land for use as a park to memorialize his two deceased children. Burnet's heirs, objecting to the library as contrary to those intentions, obtained an injunction from the Ninety-Sixth District Court enjoining construction, a move the city appealed to the Texas Supreme Court but lost. With Burnet Park no longer feasible, the plan moved to demolishing the Carnegie Building and building in its place, drawing complaints from preservationists who opposed razing the thirty-six-year-old structure. One of the dissenters, F. W. Rosson of 1723 Gould Avenue, filed an unsuccessful last-minute court challenge. The new library in the old spot was dedicated on June 16, 1939.[16]

The list of federally funded projects went beyond the traditional to include Fort Worth's 1936 Centennial Celebration celebrating Texas' independence from Mexico. In 1936, the PWA approved $687,000 for Fort Worth's Centennial Celebration, a multiweek event that was the entertainment event of the decade and beyond, eclipsing every spectacular event before, including the Spring Palace Exhibitions of 1889 and 1890. Ironically, the idea for the show sprang from defeat after Fort Worth lost its bid to host the official state festival to Dallas. Losing to Dallas infuriated Amon Carter, a fierce Fort Worth booster and publisher of the *Star Telegram* who was known to love a big party almost as much as he hated Dallas. Carter's socializing earned national notice from Will Rogers, who wrote that Carter and his "gang" were the life of the party at the 1932 Democratic National Convention in Chicago. Carter's other legendary characteristic, an intense distaste for Dallas, was an outgrowth of a historical competition between the two cities that the *New York Times* compared to the relationship between the Montagues and Capulets (warring families in Shakespeare's *Romeo and Juliet*). Carter was so incensed over the snub that he proposed a separate Fort Worth centennial event that, he somewhat disingenuously claimed, would complement rather than compete with what happened in Dallas. The Fort Worth Centennial Board of Control, a group of local businessmen who took their cue from Carter, at first linked the celebration to the fortieth anniversary of the Fort Worth Southwestern Exposition and Fat Stock Show (Stock Show) also occurring in 1936, dubbing it the Centennial Livestock Exposition, later opting for the Frontier Centennial Celebration. The committee considered nine locations but focused on the stockyards where the Stock Show was held. An ambitious proposal developed to enlarge Cowtown Coliseum and add exhibit halls and thirty-two acres to the grounds, but the plan became untenable when the Fort Worth Stockyards Company, producer of the Stock Show, withdrew its support over terms of the land purchase. Six other sites were eliminated for one reason or another, leaving only an area north of White Settlement Road and the eventual choice, some 138 acres along University Drive in the Van Zandt property, bought for $150,000 in a contract that carried deed restrictions forbidding its resale to "negroes."[17]

Funding was an early priority, especially given the scope of a project originally estimated to cost $1,612,000—approximately the same as Fort Worth's annual city budget. Carter and William Jarvis petitioned the state for $300,000 and received a commitment for $250,000, contingent on Fort Worth securing at least $1,200,000 from other sources. On September 3, 1935, voters approved a $687,500 dedicated bond package despite strong opposition, especially from north-side interests who won a temporary injunction barring the use of bond funds for land or buildings pending adjudication. Fortunately, the courts moved quickly, removing the injunction in December, thereby clearing the way for construction to begin. The already ambitious proposal included construction of a new home for the Stock Show, Will Rogers Memorial Center, designed by Herman Koeppe and local architect Wyatt C. Hedrick, the latter responsible for Amon Carter Stadium and the main post office and who would later design the Texas and Pacific Railroad Passenger Terminal. Will Rogers Coliseum's dedication on March 7, 1937, featured eighteen circus acts, a concert by the Fort Worth Symphony Orchestra, and a speech by Amon Carter.[18] Carter was chiefly responsible for obtaining federal funds for the showcase, personally writing Harold Ickes, secretary of the interior and head of the PWA, seeking $700,000 to be combined with $250,000 from the state. After the PWA approved funding, Jesse H. Jones, head of the Reconstruction Finance Corporation, cabled Carter that "your cowshed has been approved." Carter also helped raise investor financing through the sale of private bonds totaling almost $1 million. The Fort Worth National Bank was the largest single investor, buying $70,123 worth, followed by the *Star Telegram* with $58,450. So much money came in from so many sources that determining the show's actual cost became difficult, although it seems certain that the final bill was considerably more than the original $1.6 million. Estimates of city funding varied from $887,000 to $1,188,000; the PWA contributed $725,727, the Texas Centennial Commission $250,000, and private funding perhaps another $1 million, a total of $2,862,727, but the actual figure may have been more. The *New York Times* estimated the combined cost for both Dallas and Fort Worth celebrations at $20 million.[19]

With sufficient funding assured, the actual work of building and producing began in earnest to meet a July 1 scheduled opening. In March 1936, contracts totaling $1,051,589 were let for the construction of the coliseum, auditorium, memorial tower, exhibit hall, and animal sheds that would become Will Rogers Memorial Center (all dedicated on January 10, 1937), which became Fort Worth's first large public performance center. There was much to do besides putting up brick and mortar to prepare the show. Billy Rose, known as the successor to entertainment entrepreneurs Florenz Ziegfield and P. T. Barnum, was hired at $1,000 a day for one hundred days to create, design, develop, and direct the Frontier Centennial. Rose began work on March 10 in the Sinclair Building, announcing that beautiful "girls" should apply, in bathing suits, between 5:00 p.m. and 6:00 p.m. He dismissed one aspiring dancer from Weatherford, Texas, telling Mary Martin she wasn't good enough for a feature spot but too good for the chorus. Carter launched a grand publicity campaign that stressed Fort Worth's advantages over Dallas show, all despite his earlier assurance that his production would complement, not compete. The competitive intent was clearly displayed in highway billboards proclaiming, "Dallas for Education, Fort Worth for Entertainment," and most blatantly, in the world's second-largest neon sign, 130 feet by 60 feet, stating, "Wild and Whoopee, 45 minutes West. Fort Worth Frontier," which Carter placed just outside the entrance to the Dallas fair. Subtler promotions also went out, including more than two million folders sent to railroads to be distributed nationally as an inducement to travel to Fort Worth. All the hustle and bustle proved too much to accomplish so quickly, delaying the opening until July 18, a move that cost the appearance of Shirley Temple, booked to appear July 1 through July 9. Even with the extra days, the police still had to rush to get thirty new police officers on the job, the men starting July 13, just five days before opening and working with a senior officer only a few days before being released. On July 18, President Franklin D. Roosevelt, on board the presidential yacht, opened the celebration by pressing a button that snipped a lariat stretched across the main gate.[20]

View of Frontier Centennial from Jumbo Circus Building looking east to Pioneer Palace and Casa Mañana arches, 1936. Courtesy Special Collections, the University of Texas at Arlington Libraries.

Visitors, including several honored guests arriving via stagecoach, entered a remarkable entertainment extravaganza. The entrance, adorned with signs touting "Where the West Begins," featured gateposts that looked like fort blockhouses that opened to the primary showcase, Casa Mañana, a café theater with a 50-foot bar, and a dining area seating four thousand, all attended by a staff of three hundred, all overseen by the managing director of Dallas's Adolphus Hotel. Casa Mañana's centerpiece was its 130-foot revolving stage, the largest in the world and three times the size of New York City's Radio City Music Hall. Between shows, the stage receded, revealing golden gondolas floating in a 40-foot lagoon. Rose at first planned to have the theater revolve around a stationary stage but reversed the plan. The premiere show at 8:00 p.m. that evening began

Casa Mañana and Pioneer Palace Showgirls, 1936 (Jerry Richards, Jean Stuart, and Gipsy Sheppard). Courtesy Special Collections, the University of Texas at Arlington Libraries.

as the stage turned to reveal two hundred showgirls portraying scenes from the St. Louis Fair of 1904, the Paris Exposition of 1925, Chicago's Century of Progress Exhibition, and the Frontier Centennial while the Casa Mañana Revue singers featuring Everett Marshall sang "The Night Is Young and You're So Beautiful," the show's theme song that had been hastily composed in the Worth Hotel by Miss Dana Seusse. The Paul Whiteman Orchestra, a nationally known dance band, played nightly, except for Sundays, when they broadcast nationally from the Ringside Club until November 3, when Ed Venuti and the Ed Lally–Ben Young Orchestra replaced them. Following the opening, two grand shows were presented nightly, at 6:30 p.m. and 10:00 p.m., running for two hours, charging $1.00 for adults or $0.50 for children for a seat under an open sky, a blessing when temperatures hit 112 degrees that summer. On especially hot nights, Rose would abbreviate some acts to protect performers.[21]

As magnificent as Casa Mañana was, there was much more to see, including lots of flesh. Carter and his pals presented a stark contrast to Dallas's emphasis on education and advancement with their brawling, noisy jamboree offering sides of debauchery served with risqué sauce. Prurient suggestions began at the entrance, where women ticket takers appeared behind a facade resembling a barrel that covered their midsections, exposing only their heads and bare shoulders and bare legs, making it appear that they were nude. The shows, and the sex appeal, came thanks to hundreds of dancers, many earning just $30 weekly, although their base pay was eventually raised to $36. While Casa tended to showcase legitimate theater, it did present Sally Rand performing her famous fan dance, albeit a less revealing version achieved by strategically placed balloons. When Rand's run ended, she was replaced by Ann Pennington, a Ziegfeld girl who performed a "Little Egypt" belly dance made famous at the 1893 Columbian Exposition in Chicago, an act that was also performed by Mary Lou Bentley, a local girl from nearby Weatherford, Texas, who took over after Pennington left. Raucous themes suggested at Casa Mañana were shouted at the Pioneer Palace of Pleasure, a western-themed saloon with dining, a large dance floor, slot machines, and a forty-foot mirrored bar. The Palace presented the "Honky Tonk Parade," a revue with a torch singer, a comedian, spoon musicians, and the "Six Tiny Rosebuds," a popular dance troupe whose members ranged from 215 to 340 pounds. In addition, the venue offered legitimate musical theater: "The Last Frontier," a rowdy show with singers, dramatic actors, two hundred square dancing couples, and rodeo sports portraying the settling of Texas and the Southwest, all narrated by Irving O'Hay, a soldier of fortune of many conflicts, including the Spanish American War and the Boer War. Interestingly, the only Fort Worth woman in the original Pioneer Palace Revue was Jeanette Bacon of 2626 Travis Avenue. Several dignitaries and celebrities attended "The Last Frontier," including Vice-President John Nance Gardner (on August 6, 1936), Ernest Hemingway, Jimmy Doolittle, and J. Edgar Hoover. In addition, small sideshows offered considerable variety, from family entertainment at the Jumbo Circus to the salacious with bare-chested women dancing in a cage with lions or taking milk baths, but the most notorious and most popular of all was Sally Rand's Nude Ranch with a marquee that originally read "Dude Ranch" with an *N* written over the *D*. Sally did not perform at the ranch but often greeted customers, who paid $0.50 to witness fifteen young women perform several athletic exercises while topless, save for bandanas prone to slippage.[22]

The Centennial had a clear economic impact, but its profitability for investors was questionable. The show closed on November 14 after a run of 120 days, during which it drew 986,128 visitors, an average daily attendance of more than 8,200—a grand crowd that provided several hundred local jobs, temporary though they were, and boosted business for local grocers and other suppliers who reported a 20 percent trade increase during the four-month run, the best sales

Six Tiny Rosebuds of Pioneer Palace, 1936. Courtesy Special Collections, the University of Texas at Arlington Libraries.

Jeanette Bacon, only Fort Worth woman in Pioneer Palace Revue, 1936. Courtesy Special Collections, the University of Texas at Arlington Libraries.

performance since 1930. At the close of the first week, the official books showed a $26,000 profit, but as weeks wore on and the opening hoopla withered, profits tended to disappear, as costs, which were substantial, outstripped income. Monetary concerns were significant enough to produce unintended consequences, such as the admission of African Americans, originally barred from the grounds except for some 250 employed as waiters and other helpers. The change was

Barkers outside Sally Rand's Nude Ranch, 1936. Courtesy of the Genealogy, History and Archives Unit, Fort Worth Library (Fox Photograph Collection, binder 1, plate 65, photo 3).

limited, offering only segregated seating for Jumbo and "The Last Frontier," while Casa Mañana remained whites only. Balancing the budget still proved difficult. The final accounting listed an operating profit of $289,000, but late costs wiped out the surplus and more, leaving a $100,000 shortfall.[23]

After 1936, the celebration revived annually for three years before closing permanently. The 1937 event, called the Frontier Fiesta, closely mirrored the original, with Billy Rose and the Paul Whiteman Orchestra returning to Casa Mañana, which was expanded to seat six thousand guests before a million-pound moveable stage, the world's largest dining-dancing facility. Rose, given a $10,000 weekly budget, produced five shows, previewed for 2,500 press and radio journalists during a thirteen-hour marathon on June 26, 1937, a week before opening. The rush to production so occupied Rose that he was unable to greet his wife, Fanny Brice, arriving by train, although he found time in his schedule to judge sixty-five young women at Hotel Texas, selecting Grey Downs of Temple, Texas, as the new Texas Sweetheart No. 1. Ms. Downs received a featured role in one of the five shows. President Roosevelt again opened the run by activating a device that cut a lariat strung across the entrance. The second year featured more local musical talent, including Fort Worth's own Euday Bowman and his Twelfth Street Rag Band plus seven other local bands or musicians, and the midway added a popular attraction, the Ride of Flaming Death. The sophomore run closed early, after only ninety-three days, on Sunday, September 26, 1937, after lawsuits sent Rose packing. The legal troubles involved a suit by Margaret Mitchell, author of *Gone with the Wind*, filed in Fort Worth's federal court charging Rose, the Frontier Fiesta Association, and Territorial Production Corporation of Fort Worth with copyright infringement of her novel. Rose denied the allegation, saying that the only commonalties were a southern plantation and a house fire, neither part of Mitchell's copyright. Despite not doing as well as the inaugural season, the second year was considered enough of a success to justify a toned-down third season of just two weeks with the Wayne King Orchestra, Irish tenor Morton Downey, and dancer Edna Sedgewith along with forty dancers and twelve showgirls appearing in four productions. Despite being downsized, the 1938 show retained some of the glamour, especially when the stage revolved into view each night to the orchestra playing "The Night Is Young and You're So Beautiful." In 1939, the celebration stumbled on with a thirty-day run featuring Ray Bolger performing as both an emcee and a dancer in a minstrel show supported by the Wayne King Orchestra, but the biggest stars, Edgar Bergen with his puppet Charlie McCarthy and singer Eddie Cantor, appeared for only one week beginning August 25, 1939. Like the earlier versions, the Casa Mañana production was considered rather tame, and most found the real action at the Pioneer Palace, where 280-pound Johnnie Perkins emceed stripteases, and Belva White sang lusty melodies at the piano.[24]

The Frontier Celebration and Casa Mañana were the biggest entertainment news of the decade, but Fort Worthians found many outlets for their entertainment dollar. In 1938, a Dallas newspaper called Fort Worth the amusement center of Texas, but local boosters thought they were too modest and that Fort Worth's supremacy extended over the entire Southwest. One of the main attractions, Casino Park's pavilion and boardwalk, had been destroyed by fire in the spring of 1929 but was rebuilt at a cost of $250,000. It reopened on May 7, 1930, the same day that workers completed an expansion of the Lake Worth Bridge, the main route from Fort Worth. In 1934, the chamber of commerce boasted that Casino's large dance pavilion and scores of carnival attractions were among the largest and finest in the United States. The same article also touted top-notch dance clubs such as the Showboat and the Den as well as the Ringside and Blackstone Hotel's Venetian Room, both closed but scheduled to reopen in the autumn of 1934. The Show Boat, the newest and grandest dance club offering dining and dancing to the wee hours, resembled a ship but sat on a hill overlooking Lake Worth. Fort Worth was a center for western swing music thanks to Bob Wills and Milton Brown, who played together locally in the Aladdin Laddies Band and the Lightcrust Doughboys before becoming famous bandleaders for the Texas Playboys and Musical Brownies, respectively. The local golf game got a huge boost on January 29, 1936, when Marvin Leonard, of Leonard's Department Store, opened Colonial Country Club. Colonial began with just one hundred members but included a grand golf course that would host the US Open in 1941 and continues to host an annual Professional Golfers Association tournament.[25]

Other forms of entertainment flourished. Several movie theaters opened in the 1930s, including the Hollywood Theater with seating for 1,724 at 408 West Seventh Street that opened on April 17, 1930. Attendees that first night were greeted by the Texas Christian University Band before settling into their seats under five chandeliers to watch *Flight*, directed by Frank Capra. The Isis Theater on North Main Street in the stockyards originally opened in 1914 as a venue for both movies and vaudeville but burned in 1935 and was rebuilt, becoming the New

Isis. In 1940, the *Westerner* premiered simultaneously at the Worth, Hollywood, and Texas (1111 North Main Street) Theaters following parades and appearances by the movie's leading man, Gary Cooper, and other celebrities, including Samuel Goldwyn. The next day they all moved on to Dallas for a second premier. On July 18, 1941, the Bowie Boulevard Drive-In Theater, the sixth drive-in in Texas and managed by Henry Brownlee, began showing movies on six acres of land near the intersection of Granbury Road and Camp Bowie Boulevard (near the present Benbrook traffic circle). First-night customers paid $0.30 per adult, $0.10 for children for a Mickey Mouse cartoon, a newsreel, and the main feature, *A Night in the Tropics* with Abbot and Costello. Attendants washed the windshield of all 408 vehicles before guiding drivers to parking spaces.[26] Radio was in its heyday in the 1930s, and *Amos and Andy*, a comedy in which stars Charles Correll and Freeman Gosden imitated African Americans using crass stereotypes, was the most popular show on the air. In May 1934, Correll and Gosden broadcast their entire show live for four nights from the Worth Theater. On August 24, 1938, Edgar Bergen and Charlie McCarthy, ventriloquist and puppet, respectively, put on two sold-out shows at the Municipal Auditorium, drawing six thousand. In 1941, the Major Bowes Amateur Hour featured Fort Worth. The popular show presented snippets of local history about different sections of the United States sandwiched around amateur talents, with a winner selected by telephone callers. The talent winner for Fort Worth's broadcast was a violin performance by Miss Lurames Reynolds, daughter of a Southwestern Baptist Seminary professor, who won over fourteen other contestants thanks to a deluge of calls from local supporters.[27] Baseball remained big, highlighted by the New York Yankees playing a three-game series at La Grave Field in 1938. The 1930s were perhaps the greatest decade yet for TCU college football. In March 1934, Leo "Dutch" Myer, part of the TCU coaching staff for over a decade, took over as head football and basketball coach after Francis A. Schmidt left for Ohio State University, leading the team to national championships in 1935 and 1938. The Forest Park Zoo survived steep budget cuts, a remarkable achievement during the Depression. A zoo attendant, James Brown, also survived being knocked down and trampled by Sugar, a four-thousand-pound elephant, thanks to the intervention of another elephant, Queen Tut, that pushed Sugar aside until help arrived. Sugar was destroyed by rifle fire. In 1935, Kay Kimbell, owner of Kimbell Mills, paid $10,000 for *The Artist's Children* by Sir William Beechey, an early step that would lead to Fort Worth's Kimbell Museum, a world-class institution.[28]

The big issue for municipal government in the 1930s was to survive in a period of dramatically declining revenue. Fort Worth city government succeeded only by cutting staff and wages, measures that made the depression worse for many. Fort Worth blunted, at least temporarily, some of the worst effects by obtaining a disproportionately large share of federal relief funds, especially for construction projects, including the Centennial Celebration of 1936, the biggest entertainment event in city history. Through all the suffering and misery, Fort Worthians continued to pursue entertainment options.

CHAPTER EIGHT

Good Guys and Bad Guys

1930s Edition

The Depression may have been a factor leading to a surge in overall crime rates that more than doubled the number of offenses reported by Fort Worth police between 1929 and 1932, rising from 3,039 to 6,767. Statistics from the period leave much untold, but the department's annual reports suggest that property crimes and minor offenses accounted for most arrests, although definitive statements are difficult, since the most frequent charge, investigation, accounting for 9,481 arrests in 1932, could have been in relation to any offense from petty theft to murder. Despite Prohibition, drunkenness ranked as the second most frequent charge. In December 1931, almost two years before alcohol once more became legally available, Fort Worth officers made 380 arrests for drunkenness, an average of more than 12 per day. After repeal in 1933, the number of arrested drunks increased dramatically, climbing to 6,015 in 1934 and 7,364 in 1935, an average of 558 per month, or more than 18 per day. More serious crimes, such as burglaries and automobile thefts, declined dramatically after 1936 and 1935, respectively. In 1930, Fort Worth reported 1,030 burglaries; in 1931, the count climbed slightly to 1,194 but soared to 1,600 in 1936 before plummeting to 315 in 1938, a decline of 80 percent. The cause of such a precipitous drop remains a mystery, although if statistics from 1931 were consistent, it is unlikely that apprehensions played a major role; police cleared only 285 of the 1,194 burglary offenses that year. Automobile thefts followed a similar trend, with 1,576 reported in 1930, climbing to a then all-time high of 1,611 in 1932 (only 95, or 6 percent, cleared), falling to 956 in 1934 and nose-diving to 300 in

1936 and 250 in 1938. The good news is that most stolen vehicles were found. Officers recovered 811 of the 956 cars taken in 1934, including 311 that had been stripped. No conclusive evidence explains an 84 percent reduction in auto theft between 1932 and 1938, but it is possible that some new approaches contributed. In 1931, six dayshift officers selected from twenty who volunteered began working nights in two-man night scout teams, using personal cars donated by four of the six. That special squad was the first step in a general move from foot patrols to patrol cars in the 1930s (see below).[1]

Inconsistent and infrequent records make analyzing Fort Worth's homicide rate especially difficult. Some statistics covered fiscal years ending in March, while others relied on calendar years, and some reports excluded persons killed by police, a sometimes not insignificant figure, such as in 1932, when five people died by police action. The best statistics probably come from the annual chief's report—covering twelve-month periods ending in March—that in 1931 showed thirty-nine homicides, five unsolved; forty-seven in 1932, with only two not cleared; forty in 1934 with one unsolved; thirty-two (seventeen whites and fifteen blacks) in 1935; and forty in 1937, twenty-five by firearms, including twelve justified as self-defense and four shot by law enforcement (another thirty-two people committed suicide). The broadest perspective came from the chief's report of 1938, which calculated that Fort Worth averaged just under thirty-five homicides annually from 1931 to 1938.[2]

Fort Worth's homicides ranked remarkably above the national average but were comparable with other Texas cities and lower than many other southern cities. The 47 murders in 1932 represented a homicide rate of 26.7 per 100,000, which was comparable to 29.7 for Dallas (with 81 murders) but was substantially above the national rate of 10.5 (4,533 total). In the first quarter of 1934, Fort Worth's homicide rate, 5.5 per 100,000 (which would, if continued, have produced an annual rate of 22 per 100,000), was higher than that of New York City but comparable to Dallas, which led large Texas cities with 7.7 (30.8 annually), and El Paso, second with 5.9 (23.6 annually), but greater than San Antonio, 5.2 (20.8 annually), and Houston, 4.4 (17.4 annually).

Many southern cities outside Texas experienced higher rates, some much higher. Nashville, Tennessee, with 5.8 (23.2 annually) was similar, but Memphis, Tennessee, with 9.1 (36.4 annually) and Birmingham, Alabama, with 11.2 (44.8 annually) far exceeded rates for Fort Worth and Texas. Chief Henry Lewis argued that the South's higher rates were due to the "heavy proportion of negro [*sic*] population in southern cities."[3]

Murders ran the gamut from gangland murders to crimes of passion. In 1930, Homer Rodgers was found near the Glen Garden Country Club alive but mortally wounded in what police described as a gangland slaying. Rodgers remained conscious for some time before succumbing but refused to name his assailants. Earl Penix, an ex–Fort Worth police officer who owned the State, Texas, and Capitol Theaters, shot and killed Ted Adams after Penix spotted him in a car with Penix's wife, who had recently filed for divorce. Adams was a known radio crooner who had gotten his start after being discovered in a Memphis jail. At the time of the shooting, he lived with his pregnant wife at 2317 Ellis Avenue. Mrs. Adams refused to blame Mrs. Penix, saying she did not know Ted was married. Penix was no-billed by the grand jury, probably an example of the unwritten law excusing the killing of a wife's lover.[4]

Other violent crimes remained relatively uncommon. Only five rapes were reported in all of 1932, an unreasonably small figure that could not have been accurate, being more a reflection of social mores that stigmatized sexual assaults than the actual number of incidents. Robberies were reported in greater numbers than sexual assaults and were seemingly difficult to investigate; only 59 of 189 robberies were solved in 1931, a closure rate of 31 percent. Like burglaries and automobile thefts, robberies declined in the second half of the decade; only 60 were reported in all of 1938, although temporary spikes occurred. Many robberies involved rather small amounts. In January 1930, a total of 28 reported incidents netted a total of just $461.44, an average haul of under $17.00. The low monetary return rate was likely a consequence of the Depression and the involvement of a large proportion of juvenile or young offenders. The most common ages of arrested robbers ranged from twenty to twenty-four, but many were even younger. In November and December 1934, Theodore Eggleston, Grady Lee Huffman, and an unidentified third accomplice, all seventeen, committed a series of robberies and a kidnapping that became known as the "kindergarten robberies" because of their youth. In one incident, on November 21, 1934, Eggleston and several others forced cabman W. H. Gentry to drive them to Higgs Novel Nook on White Settlement Road, telling him to wait or face reprisals while they robbed the business. The plan went awry when Gentry escaped by running away on foot. The courts dealt harshly with young offenders, sentencing Eggleston to fifteen years and Huffman to twenty years. In 1940, several robberies earned Robert Myers, age eighteen, and Glenn Harris Wooten, seventeen, several five-year sentences and their three juvenile accomplices a trip to Gatesville Reformatory for Boys.[5]

Not all robberies were small affairs. Bank robbery became such a problem that in 1928, the Texas State Bank Association (TSBA) offered a $5,000 reward to anyone killing a bank robber in the act, advertising the program as "$5,000 for Dead Bank Robbers—Not One Cent for Live Ones." Between 1928 and 1934, the association paid out $35,000, suggesting seven robbers were killed; however, some of the incidents were found to have been the product of schemers with lots of initiative but few scruples. Famed Texas Ranger Frank Hamer, not known for softness, predicted at the inception that the program would spawn frame-ups. Two robbers killed in Rankin, Texas, were believed to have been set up by such opportunists, as were two African American men who were killed while robbing the Polytechnic Bank of Fort Worth on April 10, 1930, in which they wounded a teller, J. M. Fry, before being shot to death. Police arrested two white men, A. P. Boyt and John Alsup, a former Fort Worth police officer, a few days later, charging them with setting up the dead men in order to collect the standing reward. Investigators alleged that Boyt and Alsup convinced Isaac (also known as Will) Tate and George Terrell of 1300 East Third Street to rob the bank, telling them it was an easy target, but once the arrangements were made, Alsup tipped off the police, who stationed him as a special officer across the street from the bank and put

Detective H. E. Weatherford inside with the tellers. Alsup and Weatherford began shooting as the robbers entered, continuing to fire as they ran away, but Alsup left the bank, pursuing Tate to 3015 Avenue E, where he shot him several times despite Tate's putting his hands up to surrender. The former officer then flagged down a passing car, riding on the running boards to catch and kill Terrell at the Polytechnic Methodist Church. Corroborating witnesses, William Trower of 900 East Fourth Street and Joe Harper of East Second Street, stated that Boyt and Alsup also approached them about doing the robbery, but they refused. Alsup went through several trials in Fort Worth, Dallas, and Wichita Falls, but in every trial, either the jury deadlocked or the conviction was overturned on appeal.[6] Frustrated, Tarrant County district attorney Will Parker dismissed charges in January 1935, arguing that further prosecutions would violate the double jeopardy clause of the Constitution. Ironically, the TSBA refused to pay the reward; Polytechnic Bank had not contributed to the fund.[7]

Another sensational robbery occurred at the Stockyards Bank on Exchange Avenue. On August 8, 1930, Nathan Martin of 4301 Avenue M, armed with a vial containing nitroglycerine, demanded $10,000 from Bank President W. L. Pier, who agreed to gather the money but managed to covertly contact police while collecting cash. When officers arrived, Martin either hurled or dropped the explosive, killing himself and Fred Pelton, a bank vice-president, and injuring a cashier, an eight-year-old boy, and a police officer. Police later exploded more than sixteen pounds of dynamite found in the dead man's garage.[8] The incident may have spawned a copycat who committed several robberies using a small bottle purported to hold nitroglycerin. On March 8, 1937, a white male twenty-five to thirty years old took $350 from the Texas Electric Service Company in Fort Worth. The same MO was employed during a robbery at the Union Bank and Trust Company on December 2, 1937; the Morris Plan Bank on January 21, 1943; the Continental Bank on June 22, 1944; and the Dallas Morris Plan Bank on August 6, 1943. In each case, the actor's description remained similar, except for progressively aging, but the actor or actors were never caught.[9]

A sensational robbery led to several murders involving some of the most infamous of Fort Worth's underworld figures. The story broke when J. R. Rutherford of Eula, Texas; his brother, Harry; and Jack Sturdivant of Abilene, Texas—all ex-cons and known police characters—went missing in July 1933 shortly after they were seen talking to several men, including W. D. May (reputed to be the biggest dope dealer in Texas) at May's home near Handley, Texas, just east of Fort Worth. A few days later, their bloody clothing along with wallets containing money and other valuables were found in the Trinity River, raising concerns for their welfare. A subsequent search of May's home uncovered $500,000 in narcotics but no evidence related to the disappearance. Shortly thereafter, all three bodies were recovered from the Trinity, and authorities charged May, O. D. Stevens, M. T. Howard, and M. D. "Blackie" Howard, all known hoodlums, with their murders. May was widely known as the muscle behind O. D. Stevens, a gangster who lived in east Fort Worth at 1408 Morrison Drive, a home described as a fortress with a hidden room used for stashing loot or Stevens himself. Detectives learned the three dead men and the suspects had all been involved in the February 1933 robbery of a mail truck at Fort Worth's Texas and Pacific Terminal, which netted $72,000. The heist required a bit of derring-do, requiring that the robbers jump from a billboard above the Main Street overpass and then overpower a guard and another employee before taking mail pouches arriving from the Dallas Federal Reserve Bank. It was timely, coming just one week before the new post office opened, an important point because the new facility eliminated the manual carting of cash pouches several blocks to the old post office. The job had been scheduled on two earlier dates that were scrubbed, once because their car stalled and again because the men got too drunk. The case may well have remained unsolved had Stevens not proved reluctant to split the money, a sore issue that bought Harry Rutherford and Jack Sturdivant to a Handley drug store, purchased by Stevens with some of the stolen loot. The two, along with Harry's brother, J. R., were last seen alive at the drug store before driving away with Stevens and were killed soon thereafter at W. D. May's nearby home. Neighbors reported hearing gunshots about 10:00 p.m. that evening. The grand jury no-billed Blackie Howard but indicted Stevens, May, and M. T. Howard for the murders and the robbery as well as J. R. and Harry Rutherford and Jack Sturdivant for the robbery, despite their deceased status, along with several lesser gang members. Little doubt existed about the robbery—even J. R. Rutherford's wife publicly stated that her husband, his brother, Sturdivant, and May had stolen the money—but the lack of eyewitnesses, alive or unindicted, of the murders made prosecutions difficult. Prosecutors had to rely on circumstantial evidence to prove that the three had been killed at the May farm on July 8, 1933, during a quarrel over shares and that their bodies were dumped into the Trinity River near the First Street Bridge. Despite all the problems, May and O. D. Stevens were convicted and given death for the murders and, along with M. T. Pettijohn, alias M. T. Howard, convicted for the mail robbery, each receiving twenty-five years for that offense. May was executed at Huntsville on September 6, 1935, but Stevens's murder conviction was overturned on a legal issue, leading to an acquittal on retrial, but he still served sixteen years of a thirty-five-year sentence for the robbery. Paroled from Alcatraz in 1950, Stevens moved to Hot Springs, Arkansas, where he died in 1972. Most of the money was never recovered and probably spent before the murders.[10]

The 1930s were infamous for notorious bank robbers, and none was better known than Bonnie Parker and Clyde Barrow. From 1932 until their deaths in 1934, the couple roamed across Texas and the Midwest, robbing and killing several people, including peace officers. Clyde was arrested in Fort Worth on February 22, 1928, for "investigation-general principles," but no hard evidence ties him or Bonnie to robberies in Fort Worth (the arrest sheet lists Clyde's middle name as "Champion," not "Chestnut"), although a rash of sightings came in 1933 during the height of the couple's fame. Three witnesses identified Clyde Barrow from a photograph as the man who robbed a Piggly Wiggly grocery at 4085 Lancaster Avenue; Fort Worth police detained three women and three men in one vehicle after Arlington police broadcast that Bonnie Parker was in a car headed west; a special officer reported stopping Bonnie Parker on Morningside Drive,

Narcotics seized at O. D. Stevens's home during the murder investigation, 1933 (Federal Narcotic Officer Buck Nance, US Commissioner Louis Newman, and Federal District Attorney Clyde Eastus). Courtesy Special Collections, the University of Texas at Arlington Libraries.

but she escaped after pushing him; and an anonymous telephone tip reported Clyde living on West Weatherford Street. It is likely that the reports were products of public hysteria fanned by the couple's notoriety, their tendency to travel over great distances, and their propensity for violence. They were active in the Fort Worth area, being directly tied to the deaths of at least three area peace officers. On January 6, 1933, Clyde killed Tarrant County Deputy Sheriff Malcolm Davis at the Dallas home of Lillie McBride, and on April 1, 1934, he and Bonnie, along with Henry Methvin, killed two Texas highway motorcycle patrolmen four miles west of Grapevine, Texas (forty miles northwest of Fort Worth). Clyde and Bonnie were stopped on Roanoke-Dove Road, three hundred feet north of Highway 114, waiting on a confederate arranging a meeting with Bonnie's mother, the two having robbed a gasoline station near Brownwood, Texas

(150 miles southwest of Fort Worth), the day before. As they loitered in and around their car, three Texas highway motorcycle patrolmen drove by—Officers H. D. Murphy, on his first day of motorcycle patrol, accompanied senior officers E. B. Wheeler of 1101 Fairmont Street and Polk Ivy of 1220 West Bewick Street. The three had just left Highway 114, where they got in some target practice shooting at cans thrown in the air, Murphy hitting three of four and Wheeler two of three; Ivy declined to participate, saying they were too good for him. As they left, Officer Ivy, in the lead, spotted two people beside a stopped car on the side road but, thinking it was just a couple "petting," rode on. He turned around a half-mile down the road after noticing that Wheeler and Murphy were no longer following. Ivy found the men lying in the road near where he had seen the car, both grievously wounded. Wheeler was already dead, but Murphy was still breathing, although he died before arriving at a doctor's office where he had been taken by a citizen who happened by. Ivy rode off in search of the suspects, although delayed by getting aid for Murphy and by problems starting one of the injured officer's motorcycles, opting to take it instead of his own, which had a sidecar, making it slower.[11]

William Schieffer, a local farmer who witnessed the shooting from a nearby field, reported that Murphy was shot while still mounted on his motorcycle and that Wheeler was hit while loading a shotgun (he carried the weapon unloaded for fear bumps would cause a discharge). Schieffer initially identified Bonnie Parker as having shot Murphy as he lay on the ground, saying she turned the prone officer on his back before delivering a point-blank round to his torso (Murphy was found with wounds to his back and chest). However, a month later, in May 1934, Schieffer identified the killers as Bonnie's sister, Billie Mace, also known as Billie White, and Floyd Hamilton, brother of Raymond Hamilton, both known associates of the Barrow Gang. Mace and Hamilton were arrested in Gladewater, Texas, and charged with the Grapevine murders a few days before Bonnie and Clyde were killed near Acadia, Louisiana, on May 23, 1934. Barney Finn, the Fort Worth police identification expert, and two Fort Worth police detectives traveled to Louisiana to compare fingerprints from a whiskey bottle found at Grapevine and to have a New Orleans ballistics expert compare spent shells from Grapevine to weapons found in Bonnie and Clyde's car when they were killed. The examinations found that the bottle's fingerprints belonged to Clyde and Henry Methvin, a known Barrow Gang member, and that the spent rounds came from a sixteen-gauge shotgun found in the death car. Faced with compelling exculpatory evidence, authorities dropped the charges against Billie Mace and Floyd Hamilton.[12]

Two other infamous outlaws had direct ties to Fort Worth. Tarrant County Sheriff Smoot Schmidt reported he was hot on the trail of Charles Arthur "Pretty Boy" Floyd, a notorious criminal active in the Midwest known to run with Clyde Barrow. According to Schmidt, Barrow and Floyd had spent time at a "robbers nest" on the Fort Worth–Dallas Pike, perhaps referring to the Top O' Hill Terrace Club, an infamous casino located west of Arlington in a secluded spot two hundred yards off the pike connecting Fort Worth and Dallas. Floyd, known to carry a machine gun and wear a bulletproof vest, was suspected in the killing of Tarrant County Deputy Malcolm Davis, which has since been attributed to Clyde Barrow. The other gangster, George Francis Barnes Jr., better known as Machinegun Kelly, was a nationally known criminal who lived with his wife at 857 East Mulkey Street. Kelly drove a fast sixteen-cylinder automobile on graveled New York Avenue to avoid paved Evans Avenue, which was more heavily patrolled by police motorcycles. In 1933, Kelly fled Fort Worth following the arrests of several associates, including Mrs. Ora Shannon, his mother-in-law, for the abduction of Oklahoma oilman Charles Urschel. Urschel had been held at the Shannon farm near Paradise, Texas, until the family paid a $200,000 ransom.[13]

Police in the 1930s had their hands full dealing with gangsters and bootleggers, but they, like the police today, also spent a lot of their shift on mundane matters involving traffic infractions and drunkenness. Traffic control and enforcement became increasingly major police issues as the number of automobiles grew. Vehicle registrations in Tarrant County, which had fallen from 54,738 in 1929 to 47,950 in 1933, rebounded to 69,000 in 1938. The increased police attention can be seen in increasingly higher numbers of traffic citations used to control hazardous practices such as speeding. In the 1930s, traffic violations were counted as arrests, swelling the 1934 arrest total reported by Fort Worth police to 20,247 and becoming even more inflated in 1936, when parking citations were added to the total, driving reported arrests to 27,239—the majority, 15,198, from traffic-related citations. Another bump came in 1937, when Fort Worth installed 618 parking meters, making it one of only eleven cities to have the latest in parking technology (along with Dallas, which had 1,500 meters). Parking meters helped push total citations issued in 1938 to 23,401, approximately one for every seven residents. Arrests for drunkenness also rose, climbing from only 1,420 in 1924 during Prohibition to 6,015 in 1934 and 8,430 in 1936. In 1936, traffic citations and drunkenness accounted for 86 percent of the department's 27,239 total arrests. After 1936, overall arrests and arrests for drunkenness began slow declines, mirroring decreases in burglaries and automobile thefts. In 1937, intoxication arrests fell to 7,364, and total arrests fell to 21,360 and to 19,338 in 1938, mostly due to large reductions in drunkenness and vagrancy arrests.[14] Not all intoxication arrests were mundane affairs. On Sunday, January 23, 1938, the Washington Redskins played an exhibition game against the Chicago Bears in Dallas. The next morning, around 3:00 a.m., police were called to Fort Worth's Crown Bar, located at 501 Main Street, regarding a disturbance involving several Redskins players. The first two responding police officers promptly issued two calls for reinforcements, bringing in six cars and twelve officers to arrest four players. That morning, the Washington coach, Joe Flaherty, soothed feelings at police headquarters sufficiently to have the men released without charges. In appreciation, he sent the captain a box of cigars and two cartons of cigarettes.[15]

Traffic enforcement became increasingly important in the 1930s as accident fatalities surged. Vehicular deaths had been on a slow rise commensurate with increased road traffic, but in 1931, deaths spiked to forty-three before beginning a slow, gradual decline to thirty-two in 1937 and twenty-seven in 1938. The death of a police officer from traffic-related injuries may have played a role in intensifying the department's attention. In November 1935, Officer G. P. Driskill, an officer since 1918, died at home at 1613 Gould Avenue from injuries he suffered in 1931 when a car struck him as he worked downtown traffic. Driskill, maimed and able to work only sporadically afterward, was granted a $50 monthly pension on July 1, 1934, on which he survived until his death. The state also played a major role in advancing automobile safety by tightening procedures and requirements for driver's licenses. Beginning November 15, 1937, Texas driver applicants had to pass vision and hearing tests, a written exam, and a driving test conducted by a Texas Department of Public Safety officer in a vehicle furnished by the applicant. In 1939, Fort Worth Police Department (FWPD) Captain Bob Dystart announced that the Texas legislature was considering Texas' first uniform traffic code, a needed standard.[16]

For the first time, Fort Worth and Arlington developed aggressive programs to enforce laws against driving while intoxicated (DWI). In response to an uptick in traffic fatalities in 1933, Chief Henry Lee ordered a crackdown on drunk drivers, but the lack of objective, forensic evidence of intoxication made convictions difficult. At the time, prosecutors relied on a physician's testimony based solely on examinations that were often quick and inadequate and were, in the best of circumstances, subject to interpretation. The lack of clinical proof undermined the process to the extent that the Tarrant County district attorney usually reduced DWIs to lesser charges carrying only city court fines, an option popular with cities collecting the money. Steps to correct the process developed substance in 1936 after the press highlighted that six DWI cases were downgraded due to inexact and vague forensic standards, the publicity causing an uproar that led to written standards and procedures for determining intoxication, codifications that helped but did nothing about the issue of subjective interpretation.[17] Arlington took a major step forward in 1937, when its police became one of the first departments to use a device to measure alcohol in the blood—scientific and objective evidence of intoxication with a numerical scale to reflect the degree of impairment. Suspects blew up a balloon attached to a test tube with potassium permanganate, which turned yellow if the person was drunk and provided a reading of the blood alcohol content. The minimum level for drunkenness was set at .15 blood alcohol content, the equivalent of a 150-pound man having six to seven ounces of one-hundred-proof liquor (today it is .08 in Texas and most states). Arlington implemented the system on New Year's Eve 1937, using a special drunk-driving task force of four Arlington officers and four Texas highway patrolmen. In the first six months of operation, the unit charged sixty-four drivers, sixty-two of whom pled guilty. The high percentage of guilty pleas reflected the acceptance of the system's validity and reliability.[18]

In 1933, Fort Worth police went electronic, installing a central radio dispatch system with mobile receivers in automobiles. The city considered but rejected a joint system with Dallas before budgeting $3,000 for a central broadcast station, $1,500 for twenty-two car receivers, and $8,000 in annual operating expenses. Communication was one-way, allowing officers to receive but not transmit, but radios still radically changed patrol practices, accelerating a move away from foot patrols based in neighborhood substations to patrol cars dispatched from a central location. The transition proved popular with administrators because it reduced costs, allowing officers to cover more area, thereby lowering staffing demands and eliminating the need for community substations. Radio cars also had a major unintended negative consequence in isolating police officers in automobiles, insulating them from interaction with the community. Still, most welcomed the cost savings, including City Manager George Fairtrace, who trumpeted the positive economic benefits, stating that radios would bring about "virtual motorization" and eliminate foot patrols except for some members of the traffic squad, two foot-patrol officers on the north side, and a few "door shakers" on the midnight watch. Even while the broadcast equipment was being installed atop the Fort Worth National Bank building, the city rushed to reap cost reductions by closing police substations at 801 West Maddox Avenue, 1001 Missouri Avenue, and North Main and Twelfth Streets. In the first year, the six radio-equipped scout cars patrolling by day and fourteen at night traveled a combined 107,586 miles and answered 19,478 calls. The number of dispatched calls rose to 23,144 in 1936 and 23,517 in 1937, but the officers kept up with demand so well that the average response time declined from one minute and fifty-one seconds to a mere one minute and thirty-five seconds in 1939. Chief Lewis considered the operation a success, crediting patrol cars for a monetary reduction in theft losses from $77,834 in February 1933 to $9,062 in February 1934 and a decline in auto thefts from 166 cars worth $5,920 to only 66 worth $655 in the same period. The figures were impressive but may have been cooked, since the department credited 1934 stolen vehicles with an average value of $9.92 contrasted to $54.49 each in 1933.[19]

Other changes standardized patrol shifts and created specialized units within the detective bureau. In the summer of 1933, Fort Worth police announced plans to abandon quarterly rotating shifts in favor of permanent shift assignments based on seniority. Traffic, which worked 7:00 a.m. to 5:00 p.m., was the most desirable unit, followed by day watch patrol from 7:00 a.m. to 3:00 p.m. After a 1933 grand jury report criticized lax, unprofessional investigations, Chief Henry Lewis formed specialized units in the detective office, creating first a theft bureau to investigate robberies, burglaries, and thefts and, in January 1934, a two-man homicide squad assigned to murders and suspicious suicides, although the detectives took general cases when not occupied. The first homicide investigator, A. C. Howerton, who joined the force in February 1929 and made detective in October 1931, established, along with input from others, procedures requiring that field officers at homicides and suspicious deaths summon investigators as well as identification specialists who photographed crime scenes and bodies. The changes may have influenced the FBI's selection of FWPD as the nation's third-most efficient police force in 1936.[20]

The Depression hit the department hard, bringing personnel and pay cuts as Fort Worth, like many cities, slashed expenditures as revenues declined. The crunch began in 1931 with layoffs that reduced the police to only 216 officers, followed in 1932 by wage and benefit reductions. After several years operating under severe cuts, in 1937, Fort Worth officers filed a petition carrying fifteen thousand signatures seeking a referendum on returning wages to the 1931 level. Before the vote could be held, it was superseded and made superfluous by state mandates in October 1938 that set a $150 minimum monthly salary for police and firefighters, a standard that immediately increased the base monthly wage for police by $20 and $25 for firefighters. In the passage of years and inflation, $20 or $25 does not seem significant, but it meant a lot in an age when an average factory job paid $0.59 an hour, or just more than $100 monthly. In 1939, Texas expanded the mandates to higher ranks, setting a $155 minimum for sergeants and detectives, $185 for lieutenants, $210 for captains, $230 for chief of detectives, $235 for inspector, and $320 for chief. The minimums gave substantial wage increases to most officers.[21]

Several police officers faced disciplinary actions and worse. In 1931, Chief Lee fired Captain W. E. Wyatt after Mrs. Lacie Martin of 2504 Roosevelt Avenue complained Wyatt entered her home at 1:00 a.m., beating and abusing her until daylight. Wyatt admitted he went to the home but swore he was searching for liquor and remained only a few minutes. Chief Lee refused to discuss the details, saying only that Wyatt knew why he was fired. In 1932, Officer Lonnie Wilkerson, an eleven-year veteran, was charged with murder after killing Buster Grimsley, a seventeen-year-old boy, at Ridglea Golf Course. Wilkerson and his partner, dispatched on a complaint of boys stealing golf balls, saw two boys run as they approached, and Wilkerson fired several shots, one striking Grimsley in the back. Wilkerson admitted to the shooting but claimed it was an accident, stating that he fired into the ground to frighten the two and that one of the rounds must have ricocheted. Wilkerson was suspended from the police force, convicted in court, and sentenced to five years imprisonment. Wilkerson's partner on the call was also suspended at the same time for an unrelated beating of a prisoner.[22]

The Police Benevolent Association (PBA) faced difficulty involving employee theft. The PBA had existed before but lapsed before reforming in 1926 to provide life insurance for officers who paid $2 monthly dues. Problems surfaced in 1934, when an audit discovered that significant records had gone missing, but auditors were able to use bank records and insurance policies to indicate $7,187 missing. Suspicion pointed to Barney Finn, secretary of the PBA and a nationally known identification expert who organized Fort Worth's Identification Bureau in 1911 and served as director of the International Association for Identification in 1931. Finn resigned abruptly and was sued by the PBA, seeking title to a ten-acre farm and a court order to produce the missing books.[23]

In 1933, the department faced accusations of corruption linked to illegal gambling. The General Ministers Association set off the uproar during their February meeting at the First Christian Church in which they excoriated City Manager Fairtrace for overt vice operating blatantly. They complained that the police failed to see the most obvious evidence, such as a racetrack betting office on Main Street in the middle of downtown, and did not act when given solid evidence, citing the lack of response to a list of 150 bootleggers and underworld characters provided weeks earlier to vice officers. J. Frank Norris adopted his usual flamboyant style, appearing before the city council with a satchel stuffed with fifteen whiskey pints he purchased from various nearby speakeasies and bootleggers. Clay Cooke, a lawyer hired by Norris, demanded that the council investigate "graft and close allegiance" between police and criminals in which many officers received scheduled payments and gambled openly.[24] Mayor Bryce agreed to appoint an investigative committee, but before they met, Chief Henry Lee fired W. H. Hinkle, head of the vice squad, and Sergeant B. L. Seat for gambling. Seat accepted his termination, admitting that he had bet on a horse race at a bookie shop but rationalized that his action was no worse than playing the stock market and that he knew many who had done worse. Hinkle fought back, denying the charges and appealing to the civil service commission. A few days later, Hinkle confronted Lieutenant B. F. Griffith at the central police station over allegations that Griffith was responsible for the terminations. Griffith claimed that Hinkle suggested they move to the washroom for privacy, but once they entered, he pulled a pistol that discharged as the two struggled, wounding Hinkle in the hand and Griffith more seriously. Hinkle was arrested and charged with assault to murder.[25]

On March 1, 1933, the council sat as an investigating committee, armed with subpoena power and $500 in funding, most of which it spent on private detectives. City Manager Fairtrace testified first, facing a heavy grilling from Chairman Sam Galloway. Fairtrace admitted that he opposed Prohibition but that he supported gambling enforcement, specifically denying an allegation by William Monnig, a city councilman, that he had stated during a private council meeting that it was not the police's duty to enforce gambling laws. Fairtrace claimed that he had only questioned the city enforcing laws tried in county court, where the city was cut out of fine revenue, suggesting instead that gamblers be treated like liquor violators charged with vagrancy in city court, where their $25 to $100 bonds were commonly forfeited directly into the city treasury. Fairtrace made several denials, including any knowledge of slot machines and gambling halls, of officers personally collecting fines from bootleggers and others in lieu of arrest, or of officers taking payoffs, except those charges involving Hinkle. To add to the list of what he did not know, Fairtrace denied being aware of an order from Chief Lee directing captains and lieutenants to instruct officers not make arrests on vice complaints but refer violations to Hinkle at vice.[26]

Captain Henry Lewis contradicted much of Fairtrace's testimony. Lewis presented records indicating that vice arrests had declined after the November 1, 1931, order from Chief Lee directing vice officers to report directly to the chief and prohibiting high-ranking officers from mingling in vice affairs. Lewis also confirmed that vice officers routinely set and collected bonds, a procedure that allowed field release of arrested persons, and that there was not a set schedule stipulating bond amounts. The council closed some sessions, including their interview with E. M. Stephens, who ran a "do-or-don't crap game" at 100 West Ninth (just two blocks from city hall and police headquarters) where players bet on whether or not the shooter wins or loses. At the end of March 1933, the committee report confirmed "considerable" but isolated graft and corruption adversely affecting the morale of uniformed officers, many of whom felt their hands were tied in enforcing vice laws. Unfortunately, the report did not name names, although they promised to turn their evidence over to the grand jury (there is no mention appeared of any additional investigations or disclosures). A private report by the Ministerial Association asked that Fairtrace resign, that the vice squad be abolished, that the police force be reduced 25 percent, and that detectives be placed under the city manager rather than the chief, none of which happened.[27]

Hinkle's trial two months later made public some embarrassing allegations concerning police payoffs. Hinkle testified that he had been drinking beer at the Waco Hotel when Griffith telephoned, asking that he come to the station so they could talk, but as they entered the washroom, Griffith, not he, went for a gun that discharged, wounding both men. Griffith spent most of his time on the stand denying a list of allegations about accepting "gifts" from anyone in the "rackets," specifically denying that he had been given a suit by Fred Fuhlendorf or a pistol by the operator of Sans Souci Inn, a local nightclub known for gambling. Griffith did admit that someone left a gun for him at the captain's desk on Christmas night and that he had received a pistol from a Jess Petty but testified that it was not the Jess Petty who ran slots in Fort Worth but the major league pitcher with the Cleveland Browns and other teams who was then playing for a Minneapolis minor league club. He also denied defense claims that Officer John Woodruff was the "pay dirt," or the officer known for strictly enforcing Prohibition laws, who would be assigned to deal with any bootlegger who refused or delayed payoffs or that Griffin and "his crowd" had arranged for vice officers Walter Dews and Joe Johnston to be on vacation during the hearings so they would be unavailable to testify.[28]

The hearings admitted some improprieties and hinted at others without bringing direct charges, although the report still had repercussions. Chief Lee avoided testifying by taking a leave of absence, citing poor health, leading the council to appoint Henry Lewis temporary chief, a post that became permanent just two weeks later after Lee wrote from El Paso that he was unable to return for six months. Henry Lewis had been a competitive bicycle and motorcycle rider before joining FWPD, where he became the department's first motorcycle officer. He made some immediate changes, including moving detectives Joe

Johnston and Walter Dews, both implicated in the corruption charges, from vice to the north-side station, although he claimed that the transfer was only a periodic reassignment. Lewis also demoted north-side Lieutenant Ed K. Lee, the son of ousted Chief Lee, giving no reason for the action. The rest of the 1930s proved turbulent for police administration. In 1937, Lewis was demoted back to captain and replaced by A. E. Dowell, who served for less than a year before being demoted to chief of detectives and replaced by Captain Karl Howard.[29]

The chaos and related instability obscured the rest of the story—that most public servants served honorably and that six, one police officer and five firefighters, were killed in the performance of their duties. Police Officer Joe Graham, who lived at 2403 Market Street, died May 10, 1935, from injuries sustained while arresting a drunk driver. Graham, forty years old and on the force since 1926, was off duty and in his own car on March 27 when he was struck by Dee Miller at Northwest Twenty-Fifth and Market Streets. Graham arrested Miller for DWI, but Miller resisted, biting Graham so severely on the finger that he missed work for three days and only lasted three more days when he returned. On April 11, two weeks after the injury, surgeons at St. Joseph's Hospital amputated the finger but were too late to stop the infection's spread. Graham's death was broadcast over the recently installed police radio, station W5XB.[30] Firefighter H. L. Payne of 2732 St. Louis Avenue died in 1932 when a hook and ladder truck slammed into a telephone pole while responding to a vehicle fire at 2330 Medford Court East, the home of Kay Kimbell, a local miller whose estate would endow the Kimbell Museum. Only weeks later, Firefighters J. F. Powell and G. E. Wilson were killed and six others injured in a collision between two pumper trucks racing to an alarm; both were killed when the force of the crash swept them off their truck's rear step. On September 1, 1938, Captain Oscar W. McCain and Firefighter J. E. Westmoreland died from injuries suffered during a fire in the 1400 block of Commerce Street.[31]

The fire department experienced some of its own noteworthy issues in the 1930s. Until 1934, the department used a separate water supply pipeline of untreated water, the nonpotable system running alongside the potable system, but that changed when the US Health Service withdrew approval of Fort Worth's drinking water after discovering cross-contamination. City Manager George Fairtrace responded aggressively, eliminating the separate, untreated system. The department fought two major incidents in 1935, a huge fire in July at Universal Mills in Riverside that destroyed 150,000 bushels of grain worth up to $300,000 and a fire at a two-story frame house in November that killed six people and injured eleven, most from jumping from the second story. The house fire had a tragic beginning, with a gas explosion set off by a woman striking a match to light a leaky gas heater as the family prepared a Thanksgiving dinner provided by friends. The Depression took its toll on the fire department, which, like other city departments, suffered budget shortfalls that brought staff reductions and restricted equipment purchases. In 1939, the Fort Worth Fire Department's twenty-five pieces of rolling stock, including a 1910 hose wagon, averaged twenty-five years of age. Two noteworthy firefighters left the department in the 1930s. In 1932, one of the last surviving original paid firefighters, Edward L. Dunwoody, died. Dunwoody began as a volunteer while employed by the water department before becoming a full-time firefighter on December 1, 1893. Another employee of long tenure, Chief Standifer Ferguson, a veteran of fifty years, was forced into retirement in 1939 after the council found he was unable to carry on the duties and replaced him with by C. C. Killian. Later, in 1941, both the fire and police faced charges that they had become a "Mexican Army," meaning that they had many ranking officers but few privates.[32]

Fort Worth police had a difficult job in the 1930s, having to deal with the lingering effects of Prohibition and a spike in crime while losing personnel to cutbacks forced by the Depression. Bank robberies were a particularly notorious issue associated with the decade, some involving well-known gangsters and large sums. The police made some major advances, professionalizing investigation and adopting cars with radio dispatch, but they also dealt with significant corruption issues that downgraded police morale, undermined enforcement, and brought serious internal strife. Overall, it was a difficult decade for the Fort Worth police.

CHAPTER NINE

Booze, Drugs, Gambling, and Sex

In 1930, Prohibition remained the law of the land, but alcohol was never difficult to find in Fort Worth. Its presence can be seen in the 380 drunkenness arrests Fort Worth police made in December 1931, an average of more than 12 per day. The municipal court handled common drunkenness without much thought, usually assessing $10 fines, with more serious alcohol offenses, such as distributing, going to the county, district, or even federal courts, but even at higher levels, monetary punishments were common. The Depression actually brought some relief in the court of Federal Judge Robert T. Ervin, who reduced the standard fine for selling alcohol from $500 to $150, arguing that poor economic conditions made heftier amounts too burdensome. Ervin dealt even more leniently with mere possession cases, assessing Sam Graves only $30 for possessing several whiskey pints. Economics played a role in downsizing prosecutions but so did an obvious lack of widespread public support. Prohibition enforcement never enjoyed widespread popular backing; many law enforcement officials and solid members of society held deep reservations about the law. If that had not been the case, alcohol would not have been so readily available. A 1931 report from the Prohibition Bureau of North Texas admitted that moderately priced liquor and more expensive foreign brands were plentiful but still described enforcement as satisfactory, probably a comparative conclusion based on conditions in the Texas oil field towns or the Texas-Mexico border, where liquor flowed unabated, or to Galveston, Texas, where liquor, gambling, and prostitution flourished so openly that Galvestonians claimed the first they knew about Prohibition came when they were told it had been repealed.[1]

Local law enforcement made little effort at enforcing liquor laws before, during, or after Prohibition. A Tarrant County grand jury probe in 1930 described gambling as rampant, noting that slot machines were common in beer joints, one of many official reports that excoriated law enforcement for open access to gambling and booze. Fort Worth Police made the occasional raid or arrested a few low-level operators, accomplishing little other than generating favorable press. In 1930, police officers raided a 150-gallon still near Stop Six and another that was six times as large in the 3100 block of Glen Garden Drive, both on Fort Worth's east side and far removed from downtown clubs where the elite partied. Widespread and open vice could not have been possible without the knowledge and collusion of beat officers and police superiors. Federal District Attorney Clyde Eastus complained loudly about the lack of enforcement, suggesting that alcohol's availability at Fort Worth gas stations, barbershops, and garages could not have escaped the notice of beat officers. Eastus threatened to prosecute police officers protecting illicit businesses, a threat that posed little risk given the difficulties involved in building a case. One of the few cases to make it to the courts charged Sheriff J. L. Irvin of Lamb County, Texas (southwest of Amarillo); his son; and his chief deputy with taking bribes from bootleggers.[2]

State and federal agencies tried harder but were limited by the magnitude of the problem, by having few agents, and by local resistance. In July 1931, a gun battle in the alley of 1908 Henderson Street resulted in the death of both Robert Whitehead, a bootlegger, and Raymond Ezell, a federal Prohibition agent. Ezell's death, the first federal Prohibition agent killed in North Texas, brought calls for a war on bootleggers that led to a couple of raids on small operators and a major brewery in the 900 block of West Rosedale Street holding eleven thousand pints of beer. State forces, mostly the Texas Rangers, occasionally closed one or more Fort Worth joints, but they were stretched too thinly over a large state to have a sustained impact and tended to concentrate on larger alcohol distributors that also involved gambling.[3]

Prohibition began unraveling shortly after Franklin Roosevelt became president on March 4, 1933. Texas voted in favor of the Twenty-First Amendment repealing Prohibition on November 24, 1933, just two weeks before the thirty-sixth state made it official on December 5, but 130 Texas counties, including Tarrant and Dallas, had already approved 3.2 beer (beer containing no more than 3.2 percent alcohol) beginning September 15, 1933. Even that proved to be too long to wait for many shops and saloons, unbothered by legal niceties such as effective dates, that began selling beer that summer. Tarrant County District Attorney Jesse Martin became so upset at the malfeasance that he threatened mass padlocking of violators, although none was padlocked. In any case, preparations went forward for a grand celebration to begin at midnight, Friday morning, September 15. Fifteen local distributors prepared, bringing in fifty railcars of beer and loading one hundred trucks in anticipation of a huge demand, and many clubs planned parties lasting all night. The venues, both posh and not-so-posh, included the Texas Hotel's Rathskeller Room, located in its basement, and the nicer Colonial Room in the lobby that booked a nine-piece orchestra; the Blackstone Hotel offered Haynie Hall's Orchestra, Lake Worth Casino advertised the Jimmy Joy Orchestra, the Winter Garden on Magnolia Avenue promised a night of dancing, and the San Souci on the Dallas Pike scheduled big dances until the early hours on Thursday, Friday, and Saturday. As the final second hand ticked to midnight on September 14, a German band at the Rathskeller Room struck up "Nobody Knows How Dry I Am" before segueing into "Hail, Hail, the Gang's All Here" as the clock struck twelve.[4]

Legal beer proved to be not only popular but also an economic boost. The 1933 New Year's Eve celebration just a few months later again brought hordes downtown, packing streets with bumper-to-bumper traffic as revelers made the rounds, many clubs again offering dancing until dawn, including a Jewish community dance at the Texas Hotel. Most celebrants welcomed the end of Prohibition because they enjoyed alcohol, but others rejoiced at an estimated one thousand local jobs repeal created for waiters, bartenders, cooks, truck drivers, and musicians. Fort Worth, as a large, wet city, drew a large part of its alcohol sales from surrounding dry counties whose residents accounted for an estimated one-half of nightclub patronage. Still, not everyone welcomed beer, and resistance did not disappear. In September 1934, W. R. White, a leader of the Ministers Alliance and pastor of Broadway Baptist Church, complained that legalizing 3.2 beer had increased crime, drunkenness, and vehicular accidents.[5]

Liquor remained illegal but widely available; bartenders who served the hard stuff were said to speak "everybody's language." Like Prohibition laws in general, liquor violations were largely left to state and federal agents, who did their best while facing long odds. One raid by state agents in 1935 at the Tenth Street Bar, 101 West Tenth Street, netted forty-three arrests for liquor violations, including thirteen men on relief roles, a rather embarrassing result given the bar's location one block from police headquarters, but many other saloons were in easy walking distance. In 1935, Texas Rangers seized 385 cases of liquor from the Alamo Pharmacy at Main Street and Lancaster Avenue and from Moore's Drug at 1611 Main Street as well as confiscating $8,000 in liquor at the Hotel Texas, Siebold Hotel (Seventh and Commerce Streets), and Worth Hotel. The Fort Worth state-initiated seizures were part of a statewide coordinated effort targeting operators on the Mexican border and in Galveston designed to spur (embarrass) local police agencies into a more aggressive approach. Their effectiveness locally probably suffered when the grand jury repeatedly ruled the seized liquor inadmissible in the absence of search warrants, effectively ending prosecution.[6]

A September 1935 statewide referendum approved liquor sales in Tarrant and fourteen other counties and in parts of thirty-four others, but the return of full alcohol sales did not mean an end to violations. C. A. Paxton, chief supervisor of enforcement for the Texas Liquor Control Board (LCB), reported that alcohol-related problems declined statewide following legalization, except in Fort Worth and Dallas, the two cities he called Texas' worst. Many Fort Worth taverns operated twenty-four hours a day, seven days a week, some with legal supplemental permits permitting liquor, but many sold spirits without any pretense of authority. Three downtown bars within blocks of each other on Main Street became so egregious that, on November 20, 1937, the LCB, for the first time ever, assigned twenty-six agents to monitor the State Bar at 701 Main Street, the Crown at 501, and the Wayside Inn at 509, all operating, in the agency's description, without any semblance of respect for law. The agents, many brought in from other areas, earned $9.50 daily for eight-hour shifts working as two-man teams assigned both day night to each of the three bars. State officers also found time in December 1937 to arrest Tom Daly, the manager of the Ringside Inn, for serving liquor with only a beer and wine license. Close supervision brought a degree of compliance, allowing the removal of agents from the Crown after only ten days, contingent on the club demonstrating good intentions, and from the Wayside Inn in January 1938 after the owner, V. H. Osborn, dropped a challenging lawsuit and posted a $2,000 bond forfeitable on future violations. Teams eventually left the State Bar, also known as the State Café, but the club proved recalcitrant, leading to six arrests for running an open saloon and the confiscation of equipment, including chairs and tables, in July 1938. The State reopened within the week but closed permanently after another raid and seizure—the owner, Morris Antner, stating he had had enough and would get out of the business.[7]

The evidence is limited but indicates that illegal narcotics developed a new and expanded presence across Texas and in Fort Worth. Prior to the 1930s, few local newspaper reports mentioned drugs, and the few that did usually involved opium use among the local Asian community or morphine or cocaine, both commonly available in the past via prescription. In the 1930s, drug use and its trade seemed to expand dramatically, so much so that Texas and Fort Worth became widely known as major markets as well as supply routes. Of the 1,000 persons arrested in December 1936 during nationally coordinated drug raids, 149 were nabbed in Texas, the most of any state, and most of the Texas arrests were made in San Antonio, Fort Worth, and Houston. The drug problem became so powerful that in 1932, Texas passed a new narcotics code that, among other changes, criminalized marijuana. Most marijuana arrests receiving public notice involved Hispanics, although Anglos were common customers. North

Texas' first prosecution under the new code earned a two-year sentence for John Benavides of 1411 Calhoun Street, convicted of selling marijuana cigarettes to Anglos at a nickel each. At the trial, Officer L. M. Hukill testified that marijuana made users "a little crazy and drunk." Other incidents followed, including a 1935 arrest of a "tamale vendor" for being "drunk with marijuana." Marijuana demand created local producers. In 1937, Tarrant County sheriff's officers found fifty marijuana plants, some eight feet tall, worth $1,000 growing in Nazario Rodriguez's garden near Keller. For some reason, local users seemed to prefer imported grass. In 1940, federal agents filing charges against thirteen local marijuana "addicts" reported that "weed" from Kansas was the choice over the homegrown product.[8] Harder drugs, such as heroin and morphine, also appeared. In 1932, J. B. Burgess, arrested for selling heroin, claimed he had kicked the habit before but relapsed while in the Tarrant County Jail, where the supply was "continuous." Opiate use was often associated with other crimes—most notably, burglaries. In 1939, a narcotics "fiend" robbed the Elmwood Sanitarium on Denton Highway, getting away with one hundred opiate pills, and in 1935, Henry Schuessler, an escaped convict, was arrested for a string of burglaries committed to support his $7 daily opiate habit.[9]

Further evidence of an expanded drug trade appeared in the rise of a few large drug dealers. In 1938, five members of the Beland family and two associates received federal sentences ranging from two to five years for drug violations uncovered during six months of undercover investigation by Lonnie McIntosh, a federal agent posing as a morphine dealer. Those convicted included the matriarch, Lucy Beland, sixty-eight years old; her son Joe and her daughter Jacqueline; a married daughter, Mrs. Willie Beland James, and her husband, Leslie James; and Elizabeth Stonehocker and Lorine Taylor. Leslie James, also known as Lester James, was part of another family with a long drug history. Mr. James had been arrested in 1931, along with his wife and father, for possession and sale of seventy-three ounces of morphine worth $4,000. In 1939, a series of local raids on narcotics traffickers netted ten arrests, including Dewey O. Ross and his wife,

Marie Ross, of 410 Hawkins Street. Dewey also had a lengthy narcotics record, and Marie was the former wife of a local gangster, Floyd "Dago" Seay, who had recently been stabbed to death in prison.[10]

The largest bust of the pre–World War II period came in 1940, when authorities charged twenty-nine members and associates of the "Green Dragon" gang, the group's name a reference to an embossed dragon displayed on dope packages. The arrested included the leader, Phil Chadwick, who posed as Pete Sheridan, a farmer near Randol Mill; his wife and mother; and Nelson Harris, a syndicate deliveryman and enforcer who worked as a bouncer for a local club. Twenty-five associates were eventually arrested locally and in New York, Chicago, San Francisco, and Leavenworth Penitentiary, where a few were serving other charges. Three of the arrested fought extradition, and the mob killed Gerald Siegal after he turned informant; the rest faced trial in Fort Worth federal district court. During the trial, the government presented forty witnesses, including coconspirators who described a stratified operation that cut and distributed drugs with the help of post office and airline employees who facilitated shipments and the concordance of narcotic agents, all on the gang's payroll. The testimony revealed a flourishing national heroin ring operating from Randol Mill that depended on regular payoffs to authorities and otherwise legitimate citizens. The court convicted twenty-one of the twenty-two, handing out sentences. Two major subordinates: B. H. Schaffer, a federal narcotics officer on the take for hundreds of dollars monthly, received four years, and Nelson Harris, transporter and muscle man, was given two years. Phil Chadwick earned the longest sentence, twelve years, and his wife was given two, although both fled while out on bond.[11]

Gambling, which had always existed in Fort Worth, was considered by many to be a harmless vice deserving little to perfunctory notice by law enforcement. Grand juries and community groups like the Ministerial Alliance occasionally voiced loud complaints about rampant gambling, but any effect was ephemeral, while demand and supply remained constant. Gambling devices could be found in most bars and in many legitimate businesses, many of which set aside rooms in the back or upstairs. Tiffan Hall, founder of Mexican Inn Restaurants of Fort Worth (still in operation), leased the entire second floor of the Commercial Hotel for a casino. Like alcohol, gambling was too widely and openly present to have escaped police notice, but beat officers seldom took enforcement action, and state efforts were sporadic and usually limited to large operations, such as a February 1933 state raid at Top O' Hill Terrace that preceded the discharge of W. H. Hinkle and B. L. Seat, the head of the Fort Worth police vice squad and its sergeant, respectively, for gambling (see chapter 8).[12]

Some of the biggest gambling dens operated in nightclubs that featured bands and other entertainment. The most notable, Top O' Hill Terrace off Highway 80 just west of Arlington, began as a tea room until purchased by Fred Browning, a racehorse owner and associate of Benny Binion, a known gambler who later opened Binion's Horseshoe Casino in Las Vegas. Browning transformed Top O' Hill into a successful casino, complete with cozy dens for prostitution. As its fame spread, the scale of operations soared, with as much as $100,000 wagered on a night's play of dice, roulette, and blackjack. The cash and notoriety attracted celebrities, such as Howard Hughes; Hollywood stars, such as John Wayne, Mae West, and W. C. Fields; and gangsters, such as Bonnie and Clyde and Bugsy Siegel, who reportedly took notes on high-end casino management. The club survived for many reasons, but a major contributor to its longevity was the design that made raids difficult. The building sat in a remote open field accessible only by a long driveway, its entrance monitored by a guardhouse with an elaborate bell-and-telephone warning system to alert staff, giving them time to hide gambling equipment in secret rooms and allowing patrons to escape through long tunnels. Despite the precautions, a group of county, city, state, and federal officers successfully rushed in on February 21, 1933, seizing two large dice tables, poker chips, and dice. Fred Browning and Mary, his wife, maintained that the Terrace was their home and not a casino, but skeptical officers arrested them anyway. They were soon back in business and doing well in November 1935, when Texas Rangers, avoiding detection by plodding through woods to a rear entrance, surprised five men and seized $10,000 in gambling equipment. Those efforts proved fruitless when the grand jury refused to indict, citing the lack of a search warrant.[13]

Many other gambling joints of size and note carried on a lively trade. The 2222 Club at 2222 Northwest Highway (Jacksboro Highway) was a higher-class operation, attracting notables such as Gene Autry and Dick Kleberg of the King Ranch. Others further down the socioeconomic ladder included the Sylvan Club on the Dallas Pike and the Eighth Avenue Klub on the south side, where, in 1937, plainclothes officers viewed an open dice game before charging ten men and two women with gambling—all released after posting $10 bonds—and arresting owners James Taylor and Arthur Rone for keeping a gambling place. Enforcement intensified after the Fort Worth City Council passed a resolution calling for a war on gambling in October 1934. In response, officers raided the Oasis Club on White Settlement Road, known as much for its nickel-per-dance taxi dancers as gambling. At the Oasis, Tarrant County sheriff's deputies and Fort Worth police officers charged Frank Payne with keeping and exhibiting gaming equipment and confiscated a roulette wheel, dice table, playing cards, poker chips, and bookmaking equipment as evidence. Unfortunately, they left the equipment locked in the club while transporting the prisoners and, upon their return, found everything gone, destroying the case. That month, sheriff's officers also raided the Ringside Club on Northwest Highway, seizing five slot machines and twenty pints of liquor and arresting John Harrison, the manager. Gambling persisted throughout the 1930s and into the 1940s. In 1941, five masked men forced entry at gunpoint past a doorman at a "pleasure resort" (gambling den and/or prostitution house) on Exchange Avenue (stockyards area) that fronted as a pool hall. The robbers made off with $1,000 taken from the club and a dozen male patrons, but police reported the victims were reluctant to cooperate.[14]

The Ringside Night Club on Northwest Highway (now Jacksboro Highway) became one of the better-known operations. Co-owned and managed by former police lieutenant Claude Green, the Ringside opened formally on May 25, 1934, with an all-night show hosted by Durrell Alexander with two featured orchestras, the nationally known

Nordy Nordin Group and Billy Daniels and His Sweethearts (a local band), as well as two dance teams—Nita-Carlton, advertised as the most sensational dance team in vaudeville, and Gary and Lane—all available for a $0.75 cover charge on Saturdays and $0.50 the rest of the week. That small charge hardly seemed adequate to support such an impressive show, but other entertainment options surely abetted the profit margin. The October raid by sheriff's deputies, coming just five months after opening, was followed by a state raid in December in which agents detained several people and confiscated a roulette wheel as well as several dice and blackjack tables. Unfortunately, somehow the officers became so distracted that the five slot machines disappeared from under their noses and twenty-five men escaped while waiting for jail transportation (the women found on the premises were released), although they did manage to arrest and hold six persons, including Green, charged with maintaining a gambling premises. The unlikeness of that many slot machines and suspects disappearing suggests something more than incompetency was at work. The state moved forward anyway, receiving a temporary injunction that closed the club, but the co-owners—Lee Roberts, Dan Moody, and H. E. Williams—successfully sued to have the order overturned, returning the Ringside to full operation with an orchestra, an emcee, and several entertainers. This time, they either eliminated the gambling or became more discreet; a raid that March netted only arrests for selling liquor.[15]

Gamblers had to contend not only with law enforcement but with bitter rivals willing to use desperate measures. In August 1936, explosions damaged the Ringside and the Oasis on White Settlement Road on the same day, both blasts occurring ten minutes apart around 4:30 a.m. The timing and the use of identical fuses indicated both were the work of the same actor or actors, a supposition supported by Frank Payne, the owner of the Oasis, who blamed an unnamed business rival, and Fort Worth police, who suspected the bombers were associated with the Eighth Avenue Klub and Frontier Club and increased patrols around both to ward off retaliation. Instead, a third, stronger blast struck the Oasis at 3:40 a.m. on November 12, 1936, breaking twenty-five windows and destroying liquor worth $400 while leaving a hole in the bandstand floor but not injuring the Paynes, who were asleep in their upstairs quarters. Mr. Payne reported seeing a black sedan speeding away just before the explosion.[16]

Fort Worth also had a spate of non-gambling-related bombings in 1931 that was also likely the work of business competitors. That spring and early summer, explosions damaged two clothes cleaning plants (one at 2615 East Lancaster) operated by National Cleaning and Dryers, a local concern with several shops owned by M. E. Roberts. Roberts claimed that he had no idea why he was targeted but thought it could have been the work of other cleaners upset over recent price cuts. On June 13, 1931, an anonymous threat warned that Roberts's home and more of his plants would be hit; within days, an explosion damaged the home in the 1600 block of Humboldt Street, and twelve sticks of dynamite were found against an exterior wall of the cleaners at 901 Hemphill Street. The same month, a bomb destroyed the New Carlton Hotel at 1613½ Main Street, injuring eleven, but no identifying evidence or suspects were reported.[17]

Pari-mutuel wagering on horse races became legal in 1933, thanks in large degree to a few influential backers. Interest in horse racing and wagering developed rapidly after Arlington Downs opened in 1929 on W. T. Waggoner's Three-D Stock Farm fifteen miles east of downtown (near the site of Six Flags over Texas Amusement Park and Texas Rangers Stadium). Waggoner invested $4 million to build a grand facility, complete with two racing tracks, grandstands, and barns that could hold five hundred horses. The track opened with a fourteen-day racing schedule, but the run shortened in 1930 after the Texas legislature failed to legalize pari-mutuel wagering. Thereafter, it opened only one day each year for the Texas Futurity, leaving the clubhouse and stables largely unused, although the adjoining El Ranchito Polo Clubs drew crowds for weekend matches, but they were insufficient in themselves to justify the scale of facilities. Legislative intransience caused Waggoner to consider moving the track to Oklahoma, but that plan fell through when Oklahoma's governor vetoed gaming legislation. Arlington Downs revived in 1933 after the Texas legislature approved pari-mutuel wagering, making it legal for the first time since 1909. Racing and betting began on the first legal day, October 19, 1933, with Texas Governor Miriam Ferguson, Vice-President John Nance Garner, and Postmaster General James A. Farley in attendance. The successful first season ran for three weeks, followed with a successful twenty-one-day second run in 1934 that drew two hundred thousand, although marred somewhat by Waggoner's death at age eighty-two. All went well until 1937, when Texas repealed pari-mutuel gambling, putting Arlington Downs into an abject decline in which it served as a depot for military vehicles in World War II and as an automobile racetrack postwar before being razed in 1958.[18]

The 1933 legislation only legalized trackside wagering, but illegal bookie joints sprang up all around Fort Worth. In December 1933, just two months after pari-mutuel wagering became legal, Tarrant County District Attorney Jesse Martin promised an enforcement push after receiving complaints that at least seven bookie joints were in full operation. The initiative seemed to have little effect. In July 1934, Fort Worth City Councilman William Monnig warned that wide-open bookie and gambling joints would force the legislature to rescind legalized wagering. Still, city and police administrators had as much difficulty finding bookies as they did every other vice. Police Chief Henry Lewis and City Manager George Fairtrace denied "direct" knowledge of gambling houses, which must have been difficult for them to do and keep a straight face. During the outcry, the police hit a few small operations, raiding a south-side gasoline station, a hotel in the 1200 block of Main Street where officers found six men playing poker and dice while others watched, and the Oasis and Ringside Clubs (see previous paragraph), but bookie joints faced no existential threat. In 1941, five men were arrested at an operation on East Daggett Street brazenly broadcasting racing results via a loudspeaker (not very subtle), and Texas Rangers took down another joint at Seventh and Main Streets in the heart of downtown, filing felony charges against operators Andy Lore and George Wilkerson and misdemeanors against patrons.[19]

Gambling could be found at many places besides nightclubs, bookie joints, and casinos. Slot machines adorned country clubs, downtown hotels, shops, and even the local American Legion, becoming so numerous and profitable that operators began stealing the machines from each other. The thefts were not always reported and seldom prosecuted, although in 1932, the Cozy Lunchroom at 611 Lamar Street reported a machine's theft. The thefts grew to become a crime wave in Fort Worth, Dallas, Cleburne, and surrounding areas, causing Police Chief Lee to voice fear that gang warfare could break out. To forestall that, Lee ordered officers to seize machines, announcing the order one day in advance to allow businesses time for their removal. Lee was on firm, if recent, ground, the courts having recently affirmed the right of police to take illegal devices such as slots, but his order had little effect, as shop owners—seeing little effective difference between losing the slots to police or crooks—kept on operating but now quickly secreted the machines before officers arrived.[20]

Slots and other games of chance enticed a wide spectrum of players, including young people. In 1934, the Council of Parents and Teachers, led by Mrs. I. B. Broyles, charged that Central High students regularly lost lunch money at slot machines at eleven shops near the school. Chief Lewis reported that officers found only one true slot machine, suggesting that parents had confused "marble boards," which were legal, with slots. Marble boards were similar to Skee-Ball or pinball machines in that players scored points by rolling marbles or balls, requiring a degree of skill, which made them legal. The boards remained but continued to draw occasional complaints, including in 1937, when Lee responded to more complaints by saying his hands were tied until the state legislature classified the games as gambling devices. Still, the police made the occasional seizure, as in January 1937, when they removed a fourteen-foot board from the Alamo Tavern, 1628 Main Street. Ernest Walker, owner of several boards, sued the police and city over the confiscation.[21]

Other popular forms of gambling also came to public attention. Policy rackets, a lottery run twice daily in which numbers were chosen by spinning a wheel with winners receiving an $18 payoff, were popular among the working-class poor. In 1937, Councilman Hammond charged that the rackets victimized poor people, including hundreds of African Americans. Hammond pushed a resolution through city council calling on police to stop "big-time gambling, gambling devices, and the policy racket." Again, as they had in 1934, City Manager Fairtrace and Chief Lewis denied knowledge of all operations, bolstering their claims with a Texas Rangers report following their two-week investigation that did not discover any policy games in Fort Worth, a finding that Hammond claimed could only mean that the Rangers were either inefficient or naive. Hammond opposed gambling, arguing that, far from being harmless, it had pernicious effects that led to financial ruin and worse. He mentioned a recent incident in which Arthur Tyler jumped to his death from a downtown hotel after being fleeced by gamblers. The next day, vice officers arrested seven African Americans found with pencils, writing pads, and number slips, charging six with vagrancy and one with gambling. Still, the games continued, evidenced by an occasional arrest making the news. In 1938, police arrested Harold Hart, a lodger at the Milner Hotel, along with two other men for running a policy game out of their rooms.[22]

The other prevalent vice, prostitution, not only survived the Depression but benefited from enlightened perspectives. In the 1930s, Fort Worth had notorious prostitution centers around the east part of the downtown, an area bounded by First, Calhoun, Pecan, and Sixth Streets, where an estimated fifty prostitutes plied their trade as well as in the "Hill" around East Fourth Street and Rock Island Bottom east of the West Fork of the Trinity River and south of East Belknap Street. In 1936, the city council instituted progressive steps to protect prostitutes from systemic economic exploitation by lawyers. An analysis of twenty-eight women arrested (several arrested many times, one a total of nineteen times) in the thirty days prior to June 27, 1936, revealed interesting statistics: most were in their twenties but ranged in age from seventeen to forty-one, and they seldom faced jail when arrested but were usually released on bonds arranged by lawyers who waited at the police station like vultures. The system represented little more than a revolving door transferring money from poor women to lawyers without impeding prostitution at all. To the council's great credit, they tried to curtail the sham by ordering that police not arrest prostitutes not found soliciting on the streets or the subject of a complaint. The council also formed a committee to draft ordinances granting prostitutes legal standing, thereby protecting them from vice overlords and victimization through the bail bond system. Councilman Hammond, chair of the committee and a major critic of the existing system, recommended that police not bother prostitutes in known vice districts unless their conduct involved indecent exposure, drunkenness, or solicitation.[23]

In addition to monetary victimization, prostitutes also faced an occupational hazard from heightened exposure to venereal diseases. Fort Worth medical personnel familiar with the issue estimated that as many as 80 percent of local practitioners suffered or had suffered from some form of venereal infection, a number that seemed to be supported by the 1935 report that the City-County Hospital averaged treating 1,100 venereal cases monthly. Many of the afflicted suffered serious infections; a 1937 medical report listed five times as many cases of syphilis as gonorrhea. Councilman Hammond again took the lead, calling for a venereal disease treatment center for women as well as padlocking cribs at First and Calhoun, a center of cheap prostitution, as well as houses of prostitution operating around the Panther Boys Club and the Weatherford Street Methodist Church. He still recommended ignoring lone prostitutes who acted "properly," suggesting that completely closing all operations would just spread the problem citywide. The efforts may have had an effect; the 1936 annual health report listed just 206 cases of gonorrhea and 2,208 of syphilis, down considerably from 1935.[24]

Fort Worth expanded its concentration on fighting the spread of disease by requiring that women in the trade receive periodic medical examinations. After 1935, prostitutes, euphemistically called "street women," carried health cards indicating they were either disease-free or undergoing regular treatments. Most women followed the ordinance, although unaware newcomers occasionally offended. In April 1937, Chief Dowell reported that most of thirty-nine women recently arrested without health cards had recently arrived from out of town and were unfamiliar with the rules. They were released on a promise to be blood tested. The new tolerance and understanding did not eliminate raids, especially on larger operations. In September 1937, the largest vice operation in the city's history (to that point) hit several small downtown hotels and rooming houses, charging twenty-eight men and twenty-seven women for vagrancy and two others with pandering. In February 1938, another fifty men and thirty-five women were arrested at eleven downtown hotels, rooming houses, and taverns, all the women charged with vagrancy and released after being interviewed by an FBI agent investigating Mann Act violations (a federal law prohibiting the transport of women across state lines for immoral purposes). The federal agent charged James P. Clancy with bringing a woman from California, but the case was later dismissed in federal court, although Clancy did not escape punishment; the woman's father attacked him in the corridors as he walked out of court.[25]

Fort Worth's vice trade did not seem to diminish in the 1930s. The end of Prohibition may have removed one law enforcement issue prone to abuse, but local and state officers still faced rampant disobedience of vice laws. Gambling had never been hard to find in Fort Worth, and it continued to be accessible and, in the case of horse racing, actually became legal for a few years. Much the same could be said for prostitution's longevity, but it can also be added that Fort Worth displayed a new level of understanding and compassion that came with serious efforts at correcting some clear deficiencies and hazards. The other somewhat unique aspect of the decade was the expanded commerce in illegal narcotics, making illicit drugs a major law enforcement and social issue. Drug abuse had existed for some time but to a rather limited degree. That changed as Fort Worth's drug trade became a big business in the 1930s.

CHAPTER TEN

African Americans in the 1930s

The Ku Klux Klan survived in the 1930s, but not as the force it had been in the 1920s, when Klan power dominated local and state governments and members marched openly in massive parades. After 1930, only a few events drew press notice. In 1931, a large recruitment meeting in a field south of East Lancaster Avenue and two miles east of the Texas and Pacific Passenger Terminal made the news, as did the tarring and feathering of a man named Jones known to beat his wife and run with other women. In 1935, Mrs. Mae Stewart of 2908 South Jennings Street, leader of the local women's chapter and the Texas imperial wizard, officiated at a concave of Klan women, assisted by Mrs. Annie Bain of 1257 East Richmond Avenue, Stewart's second in command, and Mrs. Nita Wright of 901 Boland Street.[1]

The lower level of Klan activity did not imply great advances in civil rights; indeed, blatant racism continued to dominate prevailing perspectives, even within mainstream theology. A 1935 master's thesis at Southwestern Baptist Theological Seminary argued that blacks sprang from a "savage ancestry" that lacked restraint, honesty, and initiative; tended to give too much weight to parades and displays of office (gaudy uniforms); and were slow learners and thinkers. The silver lining, according to this religious scholar, was that African Americans were docile and childlike and therefore easily molded, making better candidates for conversion than Mexicans, who proved reluctant to abandon the Catholic faith. Similar attitudes underpinned all of a rigidly segregated society not far removed from the slave system that officially ended more than sixty years before. A 1931 federal court criminal case in Fort Worth illustrated the degree to which blacks in the 1930s still existed on the thin edge of bondage. Fred Lindsey, a farmer from Quanah, Texas, faced charges of peonage involving Joe Richbourg and four black women hired to pick cotton but left unpaid after Lindsey claimed all their wages had gone for room and board. The five, who had worked two weeks without salaries, tried to leave but were stopped by Lindsey and forcibly returned to work. The anomaly in this case may well have been the filing of charges, not Lindsey's egregious action.[2]

Racial ideas creating and justifying rigid segregation affected every aspect of life, even to the provision of basic municipal services. Fort Worth police set up a separate unit that handled offenses committed by African Americans, the Negro Crimes Unit, staffed by two detectives, Joe Defee and C. D. Bush, who were responsible for virtually every Fort Worth black person sent to prison from 1922 to 1937. Their exclusive partnership ended only when each was assigned to train a younger detective. John Peter Smith Hospital, the county medical provider, maintained segregated facilities, including a separate emergency room and wards, but most African Americans preferred black-only care facilities at the Negro Community Clinic, 1000 Missouri Avenue; the Asberry Clinic, 1162 Evans Avenue; or the Fort Worth Negro Hospital, 1200 East First Street. Fort Worth Negro Hospital, also known as Baptist Hospital, opened in 1918 at 509 Grove Street, becoming one of only three nationally accredited black-owned hospitals in the United States. In 1938, it moved to 1200 East First Street and was renamed Ethel Ransom Memorial for the mother of the founder, Dr. Riley Ransom. Despite the efforts of Dr. Ransom and others, health care for blacks remained inferior. A study by the Fort Worth Tarrant County Tuberculosis Society found substantially higher levels of infection and disease at the Negro Community Hospital, in students and faculty of Arlington Heights Negro School, and in residents of Mosier Valley, a community in eastern Tarrant County established by former slaves. Even welfare was segregated. In 1934, Fort Worth opened a relief center at 5315 Bonnell Street to handle "negro [*sic*] relief" for three hundred needy families in Como, a black neighborhood on Fort

Worth's west side. The center provided various forms of aid besides the monetary, such as distributing four hundred free mattresses to the indigent and employing fifty black women to make quilts and comforters.[3] Public education remained rigidly segregated. In the 1930–31 school year, black enrollment accounted for 4,789, or 13 percent of Fort Worth's total student body of 36,794. The district's 32,005 white and Hispanic students attended thirty-seven elementary, six junior high, and five high schools, while black students were limited to seven elementary, three junior highs, and one high school, I. M. Terrell. African American attendance rates surpassed those of whites in the elementary grades—71.2 percent to 62.1 percent, respectively—but lagged in junior high, 19.4 to 23.6 percent, and high school, 9.4 to 14.3 percent (note the low overall attendance percentages that became abysmal in higher grades). Inferior facilities and supplies may well have played a role in discouraging black participation in secondary education. A Colombia University study described Fort Worth school buildings designated for blacks as so bad as to warrant closure rather than repair and their supplies and furnishings so meager that "they make one wonder that they have developed and maintained the interest they have in their schools."[4]

African Americans successfully united to not only defend but expand their limited access to segregated city parks, achieving one of the few early civil rights victories. At the beginning of the 1930s, the only park space open to blacks was a set-aside section of Hillside Park. In 1932, even that small concession faced challenges from white residents of the Seventh Ward Civic League who petitioned the park board for closure, alleging that African Americans often spilled over into the white section, especially during Sunday baseball games. The Seventh Ward had a history of contentious racial relations displayed most blatantly in the bombings of several black-owned homes during the 1920s. Somewhat surprisingly, the park board denied the request, ruling the parks were public places from which citizens could not be excluded, an odd statement that ignored actual practice. During the 1930s, city administrators corrected some of the obvious imbalances by opening eight parks to African Americans and by establishing an office of "negro playgrounds" that oversaw facilities. During the annual Juneteenth Celebration in 1936, the two men in charge, Ruben Curtis and Mutelle Flint, produced *Dixie to Harlem*, a two-act play starring local children in a minstrel show that depicted Harlem nightlife. In 1940, white residents of Riverside, a neighborhood east of downtown and across the Trinity River, petitioned to change adjacent Greenway Park, located just south of Belknap Street, from blacks only to whites only, suggesting that the city compensate by converting two hundred acres along the Trinity River east of Chambers Hills, a black neighborhood, into parklands. Black residents and progressive whites united to defend Greenway Park, noting its use as a popular recreation center as well as the practice field for the I. M. Terrell High School football team. A delegation of black civic leaders that included William Coleman and Secretary J. W. Washington of the General Baptist Convention of Texas, as well as members of the Federated Women's Clubs and the Parent-Teacher Association (African American branches), were joined by white supporters Rabbi Samuel Soskin, Mrs. Alice B. Carson, and Texas Christian University (TCU) professors A. L. Porterfield and C. R. Sherer. The group stressed Greenway's convenient location and the lack of any other available sizable park space, noting that the set-aside at Hillside Park was too small to accommodate large gatherings while also mentioning that whites already enjoyed access to part of Greenway. The council kicked the matter to the park board, which ruled against changing Greenway Park until an equal or better facility became available.[5]

The two favorable rulings stood in stark contrast to the norm and did not extend to other facilities. Forest Park, Fort Worth's premier park, with the city zoo and midway-style rides, and the Botanical Gardens remained whites only except for the annual Juneteenth Celebration—also known as Negro Independence Day, Freedom Day, and Emancipation Day—commemorating the announcement of slavery's abolition on June 19, 1865, in Galveston, Texas (the holiday was sometimes celebrated on adjacent days depending on when it fell during the week). African Americans in Fort Worth observed the day with dances (sometimes featuring a big apple dancing contest), boxing,

Segregated water fountain in Mansfield, Texas, 1956. Courtesy Special Collections, the University of Texas at Arlington Libraries.

baseball, and women's softball as well as visiting Forest Park and the Botanical Gardens, reserved for blacks only until 4:00 p.m. One year (1938), a Gibbon ape escaped its zoo cage, biting two children about their hands and legs before being subdued. The 1936 Juneteenth party held at Lake Como was particularly grand, with a grand revue, *A Century of Negro Progress*, depicting four stages of African American development from Africa to the present; an address by William McDonald; the hypnotizing of a man on June 17 to be awakened on Emancipation Day; and a twenty-two-mile footrace from Arlington Downs to the lake. The expanded schedule was intended as compensation for the exclusion of "colored people" from the Frontier Centennial Exposition, running at the same time. Later, the exposition modified the racial ban to boost attendance and revenue, although it still restricted blacks to segregated seating and excluded them from the main show.

Segregation continued to be the practice for the following three years before the show ceased.[6]

Cinemas and vaudeville theaters were designated by race or were segregated by providing black seating in a separate area, often the balcony. For example, the Majestic Theater, a grand downtown venue at 1101 Commerce Street presenting both vaudeville stage shows and movies, advertised two hundred balcony seats available for "coloreds." Occasionally, a few all-white theaters set aside special nights when the whole house was reserved for African Americans, usually for black-themed shows. On February 24, 1934, for the first time, the Worth Theater scheduled the 11:30 p.m. performance of *Going to Town*, a "colored revue," for blacks only. The move must have proved successful; the theater followed with an exclusive performance by Cab Calloway and his Cotton Club Show on October 5, 1934. In a very few cases, the tables were turned, sending whites to separate seating in a largely black audience. In 1931, Will Rogers sold out his show at the Worth Theater, leaving many fans disappointed until parishioners of Mount Gilead Baptist Church offered separate seating for Rogers's appearance at their church. Such accommodations were rarer for performances by black entertainers, but one did occur in 1932, when the Negro Little Theater Company set aside a white section for its production of *The Mystery of the Third Gable*, directed by Mabel H. Spearman.[7]

Faced with widespread segregation, blacks developed their own entertainment facilities. In 1932, M. C. Embry converted the Owl Theater at Evans and Terrell Streets, which had maintained a small segregated section for whites, into a blacks-only theater—a minor step, since the Owl's clientele was 90 percent black. Embry promoted the theater as an asset for the African American community, available to host benefits for black schools and churches. He added that Fort Worth was overdue for a black theater—Dallas had four, Houston six, and even Tulsa, Oklahoma, boasted of two. Many whites opposed the plan, especially after Embry raised hackles by openly carrying firearms around the theater's premises, claiming he had a permit issued by the Tarrant County sheriff. Neighborhood whites also complained that the theater would lower property values, but the Fort Worth council refused to get involved, saying it could not prevent a business from opening, although Councilman William Monnig suggested they could "make it hot for them later." The Grand, the first complete theater for African Americans—opened May 12, 1938, at 1100 Fabons Street—was truly grand, costing $40,000 and seating 526 on the ground floor and 274 in the balcony. Opening day featured speeches by William McDonald and S. H. Fowler, secretary of the Colored YMCA, and music from the I. M. Terrell High School band. Ironically, the theater's manager, W. D. Hightower, and operator, J. E. Dodd, were white, but the floor manager, John Lee, and the rest of the staff were black.[8]

Many events offered segregated seating or designated special days reserved for blacks only. The Fort Worth Cats held their first Negro Appreciation Night on July 7, 1939, drawing a crowd of 5,000 that included 2,500 African Americans seated separately to enjoy the game and the music of Rubin Roddy and his Jim Hotel Cats playing "red hot jive." The band's name came from the Jim Hotel at 413 East First Street, advertised as "A First Class Hotel for Coloreds," which became a center of African American entertainment. A Holy Land traveling exhibit at 908 Main Street was whites only except for November 8, 1937, a Monday, when blacks, led by ministers from thirty-five black congregations, were admitted. A *Star Telegram*–sponsored cooking demonstration at the Municipal Auditorium turned the tables by being reserved for "Colored Men & Women Only."[9] Overall, segregation remained the standard, but a few isolated events played to mixed audiences, albeit in segregated seating.

Little to no progress developed in housing, where segregationists fought hard to maintain neighborhood boundaries defined by race. An academic study found well-defined geographic segregation lines for African American communities downtown, the south side around Morningside Drive, the southeast at Stop Six, Riverside east of downtown, Lake Como in the southwestern part of Arlington Heights, and between North Main Street and Azle Road. As Fort Worth's black population grew, the established neighborhoods proved inadequate to meet demand, forcing expansion into adjacent areas. That movement often sparked violent racial confrontations. An early conflagration point developed in the Seventh Ward, an area east and south of the main southbound railroad tracks, centered around Evans and Terrell Avenues, where several homes had been dynamited in 1926 after black families moved into historically white blocks. In the 1930s, white neighborhoods tended to rely less on bombing and more on civic leagues to fight integration. The Seventh Ward Civic League, formed during the bombings of the 1920s, remained active, becoming part of the protest movement against the Owl Theater in 1932. They were joined in 1938 by the Fifth Ward Civic League, which formed at the Missouri Avenue Methodist Church following reports that twenty-one adjacent blocks would be converted into a black residential area. Segregationists used direct political action, petitioning the city council, park board, and school board to stop integration, but failed. The initial failure had the effect of organizing opposition throughout the eastside white community and turning it into adopting more threatening postures. Signs warning "No negroes [*sic*] Wanted in This Addition" appeared around East Richmond Avenue and Duvall Street (east of the Seventh Ward near Polytechnic High School in the Graham Park Addition) after reports spread that blacks had purchased twenty-five lots. The Fort Worth council tried its best to avoid overt actions, preferring instead to pass on delicate matters, as it had in the dispute over Greenway Park. In 1938, the council, expressing its concern about the "encroachment of negroes [*sic*]" into the Union Depot area, ordered the housing authority to relocate blacks to neighborhoods where they would be unlikely to encounter objections. The agency's director, Homer Hunter, denied the request, stating he had no authority to direct or control relocation outcomes.[10]

When petitions and appeals failed, segregationists returned to direct, even violent action. In 1939, a gun battle broke out after Charles Stowe of 1456 East Morphy Street threatened to dynamite B. L. Manley's home at 1124 East Hattie Street if Manley sold to blacks. The two men exchanged thirteen shots without causing injury to either. On June 17, 1939, police dispersed white mobs at 940 East Annie Street protesting the home's sale to Otis Flake, an African American, but the rioters returned two days later and drove out Flake and his family after smashing most of their belongings. On May 3, 1940, dynamite damaged a home at 806 East Maddox Avenue owned by Douglas and Alberta Jones, a black couple who had moved in only two months earlier. The Jones had been warned by a newly formed civic league to leave and that Maddox Avenue had been designated the racial dividing line beyond which no blacks were allowed. The couple agreed but only on the condition that they were reimbursed for expenses, apparently souring the exchange.[11]

The courts made some very small, tentative steps recognizing basic legal rights. In 1932, Carter Rollins, a nineteen-year-old black man charged with killing a farmer near Crowley, was removed to the Dallas County Jail after mobs threatened a lynching, a not-uncommon outcome for African American prisoners. Rollins's trial was unusual in that it was the first in North Texas in which the defense successfully challenged the jury pool based on the exclusion of blacks, although that proved only a minor setback, as Rollins was convicted and sentenced to death shortly thereafter. Still, the idea that juries should represent the community gained judicial traction, going all the way to the US Supreme Court, where the justices mandated African American juror participation in communities with substantial black populations. In 1937, a Fort Worth district court order quashed three indictments, including two for murder, after John Swayne, Fort Worth's first city secretary, and others testified that no African Americans had ever served on grand juries despite the city's black population of fifteen thousand to twenty thousand. Other courts were not so progressive and ignored the ruling until February 1939, when an appeals court overturned a death penalty case based on black exclusion. In March 1939, Watson Barton of 1309 East Ninth Street appeared on the jury panel with his poll tax receipt, becoming the first black person to serve on a Fort Worth grand jury.[12]

Most African Americans never appeared on juror rolls simply because they were denied the right to vote. Blacks faced many obstacles to voter registration, ranging from outright, blatant denials backed with violence to impediments such as literacy tests and poll taxes, a tax paid on voting. Longtime residents could recall only one

African American on a jury panel, and he had been rejected for not having a poll tax receipt. Poor blacks and poor whites tended not to pay poll taxes, but blacks disproportionately faced additional obstacles that stymied all but a very few from registering. Indeed, the process was so demanding that only a few even bothered to try and even fewer were successful. The casting of approximately 1,500 black votes in the 1938 general election was so noteworthy that the *Star Telegram* reported it. In 1939, an estimated 3,000 African Americans were somehow registered, but few actually voted. Ironically, segregated housing concentrated black voters in a few precincts, helping them develop a degree of political clout. Centralization also helped organizations such as the Negro Voters League at 405 East Ninth Street, led by W. M. Coleman, organize black voters in support of progressive candidates. Unfortunately, an internal split between black progressives and mainstreamers such as Phil Register of 1058 Illinois Avenue, who supported more conservative candidates, weakened that effectiveness. Register, one of the most politically active black community leaders, served as a delegate to the Trades Assembly and state president of the Negro Democratic Club and ran for floterial representative in 1938, receiving the backing of five black Democratic clubs. The 1930s witnessed the growing political participation by blacks at the same time that blacks began to move away from the Republican and toward the Democratic Party. As late as 1938, the participation of a dozen black voters in the Lake Como precinct voting in the Democratic primary was enough to startle observers. The transition came about in part from affection for Franklin Roosevelt, earned largely by Franklin's wife, Eleanor. African Americans celebrated the president's birthday in January 1934 with six parties arranged by a planning committee chaired by Dr. Arthur B. Border, an obstetrician, who called FDR a president for all.[13]

Discrimination against blacks carried over into defense employment and even to military service. The outbreak of war in Europe in September 1939 brought an uptick in the defense budget, creating thousands of jobs, but black workers remained marginally affected, often bypassed or given only poorer-paying positions. Alton Blanton began work at Fort Worth's Consolidated Aircraft just four months after the plant opened in 1942. He recalled that Consolidated trained unskilled whites for high-paying jobs but hired blacks solely for janitorial work. Even wearing the nation's uniform counted for little under rigid Jim Crow racial guidelines. The USO Club in downtown Fort Worth admitted whites only, and donations were segregated as white or "negro," the latter going toward a black facility. Independence Day street dances were also segregated. A separate dance at Stephenson and Center Streets in the Butler Housing Project on July 3, 1941, was intended to compensate black soldiers for their exclusion from a huge downtown celebration the next day that drew twenty thousand.[14]

Confronted with overwhelming and widespread oppression, blacks struggled to survive. Shut out of most of white society, African Americans turned inward, forming a separate societal infrastructure that provided important community support, an option made possible by the presence of a critical population mass. In 1940, Tarrant County counted 39,060 black citizens, 12.6 percent of the total population, a sizable community able to form an alternative society capable of providing most services. Black charities united under the Council of Negro Charities to fund social causes such as child nurseries at 1000 West Humbolt Street and 619 Clifford Street, important to many working parents. The Colored YMCA was especially important in supporting social, cultural, political, and economic activities, providing facilities not readily available to blacks such as a cafeteria, restrooms, and meeting rooms for varied black organizations. One such group promoted aid for Ethiopia after the African country was attacked by Italy in 1935. The leader, Walter J. Davis of 2504 Clinton Avenue, a sergeant in the Great War, claimed he and many others were eager to join in the defense of their African brothers. The Y also funded legal challenges to civil rights cases or cases involving gross injustices. In 1937, it allocated $150 to fund a retrial motion for Earnest McCarty, a black man convicted and sentenced to death for assaulting Mrs. Irma Cain of 1213 Carlock Street in what the *Star Telegram* called a speedy trial, even by local standards. The Y's director, Ernest Fowler, announced he was prepared to take the matter to the NAACP if the appeal failed, but that became unnecessary after the court granted a new trial, although the outcome remained the same, leaving McCarthy's execution scheduled just one month later for June 11, 1937. By 1939, the Y moved into the old Como Hotel at Fifteenth and Jones Streets, purchased by Bill McDonald for their use.[15]

African American churches served important secular roles as community forums from which many African American leaders rose. Fort Worth's most influential black church, Mount Gilead, established by twelve former slaves in 1875, had grown by 1912 to occupy a remarkable neoclassical redbrick building at 600 Grove Street, complete with a library, orchestra, and pool. The Grove Street location sat at the northern end of a black economic zone known as the "Ninth Street Drag" that included, among many others, the Y, Jim Hotel, and Fraternal Bank and Trust Company, the last two owned by "Gooseneck" McDonald. Many Mount Gilead parishioners came from higher socioeconomic classes, but that did not insulate the church from controversy. The church's pastor, Reverend T. S. Boone, chosen "Most Useful Negro Citizen of 1933," was ousted just four years later under accusations that he annoyed the congregation by jingling coins during services and by displaying "gross extravagance" in owning twenty-eight suits, complemented by a matching dress for each for his wife. Boone saw the accusations as cover for a crass attempt to take control by a "silk-stocking group" who had also foreclosed on the Grand Lodge of the Colored Knights of Pythias. Boone left Mount Gilead, but he and his supporters formed a new church at a local funeral home.[16]

Many blacks turned to education as a means of advancement, although they found serious obstacles in their way. Channing Tobias, national senior secretary of the YMCA and later chairman of the NAACP, zeroed in on the problem, telling an audience at TCU that black progress correlated with educational budgets and that large gaps between expenditures for white and black students restrained black advancement. Fort Worth blacks certainly faced poor educational funding. In 1936, an independent survey of the ten black elementary schools and one high school found four—Lake Como, Valley View, Cooper Street, and Ninth Ward—in such bad condition that they recommended closing these schools, determining that repair was not cost-effective. Racial disparities in education can be seen clearly in teachers' salaries. The average annual wage for 101 black teachers serving 4,789 black students (an average of 48 students per teacher) was $1,111, one-third less than the $1,639 their white counterparts received. Blacks occasionally complained but to little or no avail. In 1934, some five hundred persons meeting at Mount Pisgah Baptist Church at Crump and Fifteenth Streets called for a new high school and improvements to other schools. Their lack of success was evident in the 1936 report.[17]

African Americans used various methods to fight discrimination despite ubiquitous opposition. In 1935, black customers boycotted Brandon's Grocery at 1301 Evans Avenue after store employees threatened Frank Nunn and his wife. The Nunns, like many of the store's customers, were African Americans, but a white man, Omar Brandon, owned the shop. Brandon complained to authorities that the action was illegal, citing a state law that made boycotts, defined by the Texas criminal code as an agreement between two or more persons not to trade with a person or business, a crime punishable by a prison term of two to ten years. The statute may have been the result of a similar trade action a few years earlier that had, according to Tarrant County Assistant District Attorney Dawson Davis, almost ruined a white merchant in the same neighborhood. Despite the legal jeopardy, many black leaders such as Smith Cary, pastor of Rising Star Baptist Church at Evans Avenue and Morphy Street (and father of Reby Cary, noted Fort Worth historian), supported the boycott, a display of courage that brought bomb threats to Cary's church. A grand jury investigation indicted Raymond Melton and C. R. Wise under the statute. During their trial, a suspicious explosion and resulting fire burned Brandon Furman and destroyed his home at 1003 East Elmwood Street; Brandon was a relative of Omar Brandon and a clerk at his grocery. The fire department could not determine the explosion's cause but reported the gas fixtures seemed to be in good working order.[18]

A few blacks took direct, physical exception to outlandish racial mores. In 1936, Detective R. L. Chaffin, dressed in plain clothes, was seated in a bus traveling from the north side to downtown when a forty-four-year-old African American man sat next to him, a violation of state Jim Crow laws requiring separate seating in public transit. Chaffin, without identifying himself as a police officer, told the gentleman to move, but he replied that he had paid his fare and had every right to sit there, although he later reluctantly moved to black seating. When Detective Chaffin left the bus at Ninth and Houston Streets, the gentleman accosted him, displaying a knife, which he surrendered when Chaffin drew his sidearm. Individual and mass resistance remained isolated and infrequent because both tended to draw severe reprisals and because local African American leaders rejected violence or even aggressively proactive measures, seeing them as provocative with little chance of success. Civil rights leadership frequently rose from African American churches, and no minister in Fort Worth advocated violence. In addition, Fort Worth blacks were more likely to be invested in their communities thanks to a high degree of homeownership. In the 1960s, more than half of Fort Worth African Americans owned the home in which they lived, a rate considerably higher than the national average. It also helped tamp down violence that the Fort Worth black community had a well-developed separate societal infrastructure that made assimilation less necessary and segregation somewhat less onerous.[19]

The history of Fort Worth's African American community in the 1930s reveals little progress. The Klan retracted, becoming less visible, less present, and less powerful, but its fall was more the result of its excesses tarnishing the organization than dissatisfaction with its philosophy. A few minor concessions appeared, although they were not of the level to represent noteworthy advances. For most African Americans, the victory lay in surviving, due in no small degree to supporting institutions within the black community.

CHAPTER ELEVEN

Neither Anglo nor Male

The historical record for non-Anglo males and women suffers from the neglect of contemporary sources that focused on Anglo males to the virtual exclusion of all others. Such a myopic view was congruent with a patriarchal society dominated by Anglos, while women and non-Anglos were relegated to serving important but hidden roles, receiving scant public attention. One of the great defining differences between the present and the past is cultural stratification, the degree to which society defined, and therefore limited, gender and racial boundaries. Much work may be left, but much has been accomplished in correcting the imbalance. For a historian, the failings of the past impede a broad analysis, since those left out of society's mainstream were also largely left out of its records. Fortunately, a few were able to leave an enduring mark.

Racial discrimination focused most intently and obviously on African Americans but also affected others. Hispanics, largely of Mexican descent, were Texas' third-largest ethnic group (after African Americans and Anglos). The 1920 US Census reported 3,785 Fort Worth residents had been born in Mexico, a huge increase from only 406 in 1910, although both numbers probably underrepresented the actual population. In 1930, when "Mexican" became a separate demographic category, the Census counted 3,955 in Fort Worth, but in 1940, that number declined to 1,329, an effect of the Depression driving many Mexican nationals from the city, including many who voluntarily returned to Mexico. The Fort Worth experience was part of a national trend that saw some 400,000 persons repatriate to Mexico between 1930 and 1934, some on their own accord but others receiving encouragement. Fort Worth assisted repatriation by arranging and funding transportation through its Welfare Department, although the travel accommodations left a lot to be desired. In November 1931, 25 persons from eight families crowded into a truck bed departing from the Mexican Presbyterian Mission at Bluff and Lexington Streets headed to the United States–Mexico border, where the Mexican government arranged interior transit. The journey covering hundreds of miles over poor roads requiring many hours must have been arduous. Those who remained tried to maintain contact with their cultural roots, especially during national holidays such as the 1933 Dieciséis Celebration, Mexican Independence Day, when six Mexican associations combined to present a day filled with speeches by City Manager George Fairtrace and the Mexican consul at Dallas as well as dancers under the direction of Mrs. Raul Lopez Guerre and a baseball game between teams from Fort Worth and Wichita Falls. Mexican nationals who remained and Americans identified as Mexicans had advantages denied African Americans, including the ability to send their children to the public schools with Anglos. In the 1930–31 school year, twenty-five of Fort Worth's forty-eight white public schools (thirty-seven elementary, six junior high, and five senior high schools) had at least some Mexican or Mexican American students, and nine had twenty or more enrolled. Many of those students had an additional burden of having to learn a new language. A study found that 524 families of Fort Worth school-age children spoke only Spanish at home, although the researchers admitted that an accurate count was difficult, so the number could have been higher. In addition, many of the 524 families could well have had multiple school-age children, making the number of students faced with learning in a second language much larger. Fort Worth offered English classes for Spanish-speaking students but only for the first and second grades and only at one school. In 1930–31, seventy-eight students enrolled in those two classes.[1]

Churches assisted in providing support for Fort Worth's Hispanic communities. Catholic churches were strategically located in the two largest Hispanic neighborhoods: the Immaculate Heart of Mary Catholic Church, dedicated on July 10, 1927, ministered to south siders, many of whom worked at Texas Steel, and San Jose Catholic Church at Fourteenth and North Commerce Streets, dedicated on October 26, 1930, did the same for the north side. San Jose also had a parochial school for the first six grades, all taught in three classrooms in a frame schoolhouse. The Presbyterian Church established a Mexican Center in 1925 on Henderson Street west of the courthouse, an area identified as having the city's worst incidence of poverty and mischief. The Reverend G. A. Walls headed the outreach from his home at 930 West First Street until the federal housing project forced a move two blocks west to Bluff and Lexington Streets, where a new, expanded center included a church and an education building with classes in basic life skills and crafts and hosted the Girl Reserves and Boy Scouts.[2]

Women in the 1920s and 1930s faced many hurdles but made some real, albeit limited, advances. Some thought women had achieved all they could reasonably expect to gain, including F. M. Brantley of Fort Worth, who wrote the *New York Times* in 1924 to laud Texas for recent legislation granting wives exclusive control of their earnings and separate property, save for real estate. Brantley deemed the advances so meaningful that he asked what more rights any progressive-minded women could want, adding that the law still required husbands to provide support on penalty of incarceration.[3] Still, a lot needed to be done, but developments in gender sensitivity tended to lag after the 1920 passage of the Nineteenth Amendment secured the right to vote. Many women continued the struggle, building upon their tenuous advances while facing difficult challenges. Some limited progress came in employment, bringing women close to a critical mass in the workplace. In 1930, the percentage of women employed in agriculture declined to 18.9 percent at the same time that women in the workplace increased to account for 8.9 percent of the Texas workforce. Women's entry into the nonagricultural workplace accelerated the shift of women from rural areas to cities, a major demographic change that, for the first time ever, showed women outnumbering men in Texas cities. Significant as the changes were, they had severe limitations in that women were generally confined to a few occupations deemed appropriate. Almost half of nonagriculturally employed women toiled in domestic service, and the few employed in business tended to work low-level jobs, 20 percent serving as clerks of some type and many others as telephone and telegraph operators. Education, the only professional occupation employing significant numbers of women, still paid female teachers substantially less than males, a condition true of most occupations, as unequal pay was the norm. In 1928, 93 percent of men made more than $15 weekly but only 47 percent of women. Both as a gateway into the business and professional world and as an occupation itself, education represented one of the few avenues open for women's advancement. In 1935, Fort Worth schools had two women principals, Amelia Deffenbach of 2614 Waits Avenue at Oakhurst Elementary and Eva Wall at B. H. Carroll Elementary. Mrs. Deffenbach earned a degree from Southwestern College and did graduate work at the University of Illinois. Sally B. Capps, wife of prominent attorney and businessman William Capps, was a leading figure supporting women's education, helping found the Fort Worth Kindergarten Association and serving as vice-president of the Texas Congress of Mothers and Parents-Teachers Association and as secretary of the Board of Regents of the College of Industrial Arts, now Texas Women's University. Very few women made remarkable advances within the business world. One exception was Dr. Minnie L. Massett of Fort Worth, who served on the board of the National Federation of Business and Professional Women's Clubs, an organization dedicated to advancing women in business and other professions. Dr. Masssett was an anomaly in an industry where few women attained professional status.[4]

Counterintuitively, the dire economic conditions of the Depression opened a few doors for women, but usually only because they could be paid less. In 1930, the Fort Worth police hired four female officers to deal with juveniles, primarily at dances. The women, who were trained by a woman from the East, were scheduled to be paid less than their male counterparts during their first two years, but the experiment ended after only a few months, long before they could have received equal pay. The program ended with one woman fired, another asked to resign, and the remaining two reassigned as jail matrons, all after one, Bobbie Childress, complained that Harry Scott, the police chief's secretary, tried to kiss her, dangling a promotion to sergeant in exchange for that and, presumably, future compliance. The matter was especially delicate given that Scott's wife served as the squad's sergeant and Childress's immediate supervisor, but the outcome was not surprising; the standard practice in the 1930s meant that such complaints usually resulted in the woman sacked and the man unaffected. In 1938, three twentysomething women—Mary Forbes, Fae Wolf, and Blanche Correll—became the first women call takers hired by the Fort Worth police. A newspaper article on their start reported that none "swooned" over a call on the first day. Three years later, the fire department employed its first woman secretary, Dorothy Card, but once again the motivation was more economy than progress, since Ms. Card, called a "firemanette," earned only $75 for the same month's work that paid a man $150.[5]

The Depression may have opened some opportunities, but it was a two-edged sword that cost others their livelihood. In 1932, Texas and Pacific Railway announced it would terminate approximately one hundred married women with husbands earning $50 or more monthly and replace them with men. Many of the affected workers appealed, but with little hope, since their union, citing the benefit of spreading jobs to more families, agreed to the dismissals. Eight women tried to circumvent the process by filing for divorce, but that extreme option proved unworkable when the company decided to use their marital status on May 16, 1932, the date the union signed off on the plan. The Fort Worth City Council also considered but decided against removing married women employees and banning their future employment, perhaps displaying some understanding of fairness. Women in the workplace caused family hardships, although some were less threatening than others. In 1933, twelve-year-old John E. Mathis wrote the Employment Service seeking a job for his father, explaining that his mother worked and he had a paper route but his father needed a job before they all died a horrible death from eating his cooking.[6]

With all the obstacles women faced in the Depression, it was remarkable that a few achieved remarkable advances in a masculine-dominated field such as aviation. In 1910, Baroness de la Roche, a Frenchwoman, became the first woman to earn a fixed-wing pilot's license, followed quickly in 1911 by an American, Harriet Quimby, who received license 37 from the Aero Club of America and achieved fame as the first woman to fly solo across the English Channel. Flight first came to Fort Worth in 1911, when Roland Garros, a French pilot later killed in World War I, took off in a field between White Settlement Road and West Seventh Street. Garros was also a well-known tennis player; Paris's Roland Garros Field, the site of the French Open Tennis Tournament, is named for him. Fort Worth women were in the air by the 1920s, and a few became professional pilots. Mary Owens of 1930 Rockridge Terrace was one of the first women anywhere to earn a full transit pilot's license, doing so at the young age of seventeen. Ms. Owens, who had been only the third local woman to earn a basic pilot's license, was a quick learner, soloing after only four hours of dual flight and quickly receiving a limited commercial transit pilot's license after logging the required minimum of sixty-five hours of flight time, adding the full rating in December 1932 after completing two hundred flight hours and passing a test. In June 1933, Edwyna Thro of 1509 Lagonda Avenue became the second Fort Worth woman transit pilot, celebrating afterward by taking her husband for a flight.[7]

African American women confronted biases against both race and gender, but a few still accomplished great strides. None was more remarkable than Manet Harrison Fowler. Mrs. Fowler was born in Fort Worth and graduated with the highest honors from I. M. Terrell High School before moving on to the Tuskegee Institute, the Chicago Musical College, the Art Institute of Chicago to study painting and the American Conservatory to train as a soprano. She also taught music at Prairie View State College before returning to Fort Worth as director of the Mt. Gilead Baptist Church Choir and cofounding the Texas Association of Negro Musicians. Her husband, Ernest Fowler, was also active, founding and serving as director of the Colored YMCA in Fort Worth. Around 1928, Mrs. Fowler, discontented with the racism that ignored and discredited black culture, established the Mwalimu ("the teacher" in Ugandan) movement, also known as the School of the Prophets, to promote appreciation of African heritage and culture through music and arts. In 1932, she followed her daughter, Maret Fowler, to New York City, where Maret had gone to study journalism after graduating in 1923 as valedictorian of sixty-five seniors at I. M. Terrell Negro High School. In New York, Mrs. Fowler reopened her institute in the Bronx but relocated to 76 Edgecomb Avenue in Harlem, where she taught some fifty students. The school, including its display of African art, survived thanks to support from many prominent black leaders. Fowler was ahead of her time in recommending that blacks be referred to as African rather than Negro, although she opposed the use of *black* due to its negative stigma.[8]

Other women contributed through more traditional means such as philanthropy or service to mainstream arts. Missouri Matilda Cook, wealthy from oil holdings in Shackleford County, donated $600,000 and the land for the first Cook's Hospital at 1212 West Lancaster Avenue. Lucille Manning Lyon, president of the National Federation of Music Clubs and a Fort Worth resident, promoted Fort Worth's music scene, writing an article for the *New York Times* in which she proudly credited an investment of more than $100,000 for bringing in many prominent musicians and vocalists. Ms. Lyon complimented most visiting celebrities as gracious but noted that two performers, who she did not name, had treated audiences with disdain, largely in reaction to the poor state of the Chamber of Commerce Hall used for performances. In contrast, she praised Enrico Caruso for his gracious appreciation for all the work required to make his appearance at Cowtown Coliseum such a great success, drawing eight thousand attendees and gathering $26,000 in receipts.[9]

A local woman brought considerable national attention to Fort Worth thanks to her marriage to Elliot Roosevelt, son of President Franklin Delano Roosevelt and Eleanor Roosevelt. Elliot first met Fort Worth's Ruth Googins at a Fort Worth rodeo, a meeting that began a whirlwind romance that four months later led to their marriage on July 22, 1933, just five days after Elliot's divorce was final.

Ruth's father, J. B. Googins, was a Swift executive who moved to Fort Worth from Chicago in 1902, settling into a home the family built at 1101 Penn Street. The newlyweds lived briefly in Los Angeles, where Elliot was an aviation editor, but relocated prior to their first daughter's birth in May 1934 to a 250-acre farm on Dutch Branch near Benbrook, southwest of Fort Worth. Both Franklin and Eleanor visited their son, daughter-in-law, and grandchildren, especially Eleanor, who came rather often, arriving first in 1935. The first lady was genial, taking time to visit schools and the botanical gardens, speak at the First Methodist Church, and patronize local shops, writing a $2 check for pickled peaches at the Farm Homemaker's Market, 4717 Camp Bowie Boulevard, during her eighth visit. FDR also visited, arriving the afternoon of June 12, 1936, at the Texas and Pacific Station, from which he was driven through a downtown crowd estimated at two hundred thousand to speak at Marine Park and then taken on a tour of the Frontier Centennial Grounds before arriving at Elliot's Benbrook ranch for the night, only to leave for Indiana the next day. The president would return twice more, on May 12, 1937, and July 9, 1938.[10]

Not all was harmony and glee in the Roosevelt households. A long-simmering split between the families of Republican Theodore Roosevelt and Democrat Franklin extended all the way to Texas. In 1936, Elliot canceled plans to introduce Mrs. Theodore Roosevelt Jr. at a Fort Worth Town Hall lecture after she wrote him that their "divergent political views" would make their meeting embarrassing for all concerned. Mrs. Roosevelt evaded press questions about the matter by simply stating she had not written Elliot any letter intended for publication. In addition, the honeymoon did not last long for Elliot and Ruth, who proved unable to make their marriage last. Elliot enjoyed some success in business, serving as southwest director of Hearst Radio for three years and becoming president in 1938 only to resign the next year to head the recently formed Texas State Network briefly before leaving for the Army Air Corps in 1940. Ruth filed for the divorce that was granted in March 1944 while Elliot was stationed in North Africa; three months later, she married Lt. Colonel Harry T. Edison of Indianapolis, who had been

Elliot's pilot in Africa. The two had met in 1942 at an Army Air Force gathering in Colorado Springs, Colorado.[11]

Women lived with a strict moral code that defined what was appropriate and inappropriate for almost every facet of life, including what they wore and did not wear. Fort Worth's 224 churches—approximately 1 church for every 750 residents, the number supplied by the Tarrant County Baptist Pastors' Conference in 1938—acted as moral guardians charged with protecting the very fabric of life. Baptist churches, particularly known for demanding moral standards, were some of the most active and were the most numerous denomination in town, accounting for 81 of the 224. Their numbers included 43 churches affiliated with the Southern Baptist convention, 12 unaffiliated, and 26 "colored." Ironically, the conference identified twenty-six Fort Worth neighborhoods as possible mission sites that lacked substantial church influence. The Women's Christian Temperance Union (WCTU), a religion-based women's organization, was also an active influence on moral standards. Mrs. Nellie Ryals, president of the local WCTU, wondered what would become of the younger generation after seeing young women on the streets "unclothed," her description of women in slacks with blouses and dresses with bare backs. Mrs. Ryals may have overreacted, but slacks were generally not accepted in the 1930s and could get a woman arrested, which happened to a woman in 1938 who appeared in slacks for jury duty. Things progressed during the decade to the extent that a survey of Tarrant judges indicated that most would accept slacks but not shorts.[12]

What women displayed on the streets seemed rather tame compared to what went on in other venues, especially theaters and saloons. A 1933 ad in the *Star Telegram* promoting a movie, *Virgins of Bali*, displayed women naked from the waist up but was probably permitted because the women were foreign and dark-skinned. Nightclubs aggressively pushed the envelope, stretching the moral code to its limits. In 1934, vice officers tried for over a week to close a show at the Buccaneer Club on Commerce Street but were stymied because the club varied performance times. Eventually, they were able to arrest Rita Carmen, her manager, and the master of ceremonies after observing Ms. Carmen dance wearing a bandeau (a narrow brassiere) and net panties stuck on with spirit gum. They charged the twenty-one-year-old dancer with indecent exposure, but Ms. Carmen was released and continued her performance, albeit with toned-down visuals. In April 1938, a new city ordinance struck at dance halls known as taxi dance clubs—places where men paid a nickel or a dime to dance with women who earned only tips. The clubs were thought to be a front for prostitution, and the new ordinance effectively put them out of business through stringent licensing requirements and a prohibition on employees dancing with patrons. Despite the churches and all the prohibitions and regulations, unmarried men and women still got together; in 1937, Fort Worth recorded 208 illegitimate births, exactly 4 per week.[13]

In the 1930s, non-Anglo males and women of all colors existed in a hostile environment. The Klan had declined substantially from its powerful position in the 1920s, but racism still dominated black lives, affecting their access to basics like city services, employment, health care, and housing. Shut out of most of white society, African Americans coped by developing a distinct and separate infrastructure fashioned to their needs. The situation for Hispanics deteriorated during the Depression as widespread unemployment curtailed labor demand, leading to sharpened racial distinctions in hiring to exclude all nonwhites. Many repatriated—some voluntarily, others involuntarily. The economy had varied effects on women. In some situations, their employment opportunities increased, largely because employers could pay them less, but in many cases, women faced dismissal simply to provide jobs for men. Overall, the record for the treatment of those outside of mainstream society was not good. A few exceptional people achieved great things despite major impediments, and a few minor concessions were granted, but most did well to just survive.

CHAPTER TWELVE

Signs of Recovery

The Depression dominated the 1930s. However, other important issues developed—most notably, the rise of Adolf Hitler and World War II, but they were far away in Europe and would not hit home for the average American until the 1940s. Meanwhile, the Depression plagued Americans throughout the 1930s, forcing millions of Americans into a daily struggle for survival that lasted years. Prolonged suffering tends to kill hope, and many did give up, but many others were buoyed by New Deal programs that brought some relief and by a sense of inevitability born of the conviction that things had to get better, an ungrounded hope that was completely reasonable given that the only alternative would have been perdition. Millions of Americans searched for signs that the recovery had arrived, not unlike farmers in a drought scanning the skies for rain clouds. Recovery would come, but it would take much longer than anyone hoped or feared.

Some saw the beginnings in New Deal programs such as the National Recovery Administration (NRA), the Civilian Conservation Corps (CCC), the Public Works Administration (PWA), and the Works Progress Administration (WPA). The NRA was a far-reaching agency designed to stimulate the economy through industry-defined standards to regulate prices, wages, and business practices. Thousands of shops proclaimed their commitment to the principles by displaying Blue Eagle placards, named for the blue eagle that symbolized the NRA, and consumers carried Blue Eagle pledge cards promising to patronize only NRA-compliant shops. Local resident and presidential son Elliot Roosevelt was one of the first to receive an NRA consumer card. On November 12, 1933, the agency head, General Hugh S. Johnson, told a Fort Worth crowd of seven thousand that the NRA had already alleviated 25 percent of the Depression, basing his figures on an independent study that estimated two thousand jobs, about one-fourth the local workforce, had been added since the Depression's nadir in the winter of 1932–33. The statistics may have represented something of a stretch, but little doubt existed that Roosevelt's programs had created jobs and paychecks, providing direct, palpable benefits that fed and housed many families and, in so doing, had blunted the Depression's worst effects. Many New Deal jobs were temporary, funded by one-time grants, making their effects ephemeral, but the CCC, operating from 1933 to 1942, was an exception. The CCC, one of the more popular New Deal agencies, employed young men between seventeen and twenty-eight on conservation projects such as planting trees and grasses to reduce wind erosion and cleaning and improving parks. On May 1, 1934, the CCC put two hundred men and boys to work clearing underbrush and doing general work on an underdeveloped area north of Nine Mile Bridge Road, housing them at Sunset Camp on the north shore of Lake Worth. In 1936, the CCC established a permanent presence, opening a Fort Worth regional office with one hundred well-paid jobs. The PWA and the WPA funded thousands of construction projects, producing tremendous short-term benefits in the form of paychecks for millions of workers as well as long-term value in the numerous roads, schools, hospitals, and local improvements to the national infrastructure that lasted decades. The PWA, the first great public works agency, contributed to a variety of local projects with funding for the new City-County Hospital that cost $500,000, providing $400,000 for a new library, $500,000 for a new city hall, and up to $175,000 for the Centennial Celebration, as well as the building of Arlington Heights High School and a home for orphans. After 1935, the WPA took over, spending $7,851,501 in the Fort Worth area in just four years, with most ($5,907,738) going for wages—a lot of money in an age when the annual city budget hovered around $2 million. Federal largesse, combined with funding secured from a large municipal bond program in 1935, helped sustain the local economy but was never sufficient to undo the Depression.[1]

Statistics indicate that the Fort Worth economy improved significantly after 1935, the year of the great bond package, but struggled to maintain those gains and never returned to pre-Depression levels until America's entry into World War II. General economic trends reflect steep declines after 1930 that continued until mid-decade, followed by a significant but limited recovery and stagnant growth thereafter. The chamber of commerce, always eager to proclaim good news, boasted in 1935 of the addition of twenty-seven manufacturers, forty-one wholesalers, and twenty-two oil companies, indicating an upswing from the worst but hardly a cause for grand celebrations. Despite chamber hoopla, most economic indicators show Fort Worth struggling but unable to return to 1930 production levels. Fort Worth bank clearings, a good barometer of economic activity, reached $520,254,095 in 1930 and then fell precipitously, declining by almost half by 1935 to $290,521,611 before rising to $412,281,830 in 1937 only to fall to $360,082,683 in 1938 and $355,864,499 in 1940—a more than 30 percent drop from 1930 to 1940, although up from the worst in 1935. Bank deposits reacted quicker than clearings but also recovered quicker. In 1929, deposits totaled $80.5 million but dropped to just $56.6 million in 1932 and then slowly rose to $95,095,731 in 1937 before dipping slightly in 1938 to $93.5 million before soaring to $116,550,987 in 1940, a 45 percent increase over 1930. The radically different outcomes between clearings and deposits may have been a reflection of a tendency to hoard money rather than spend, causing deposits to grow, while clearings stayed below their 1930 level. Building permits more closely resembled bank clearings, declining from $11.3 million in 1928—the most ever to that point—to $10,121,774 in 1930 before crashing 82 percent to $1.8 million in 1932 and then rising to $3,325,435 in 1935 and $5,723,695 in 1938, only to fall to $4,850,672 in 1940, recording a 52 percent drop from 1930. Even the good news concerning the 274 percent increase to $3,325,435 in building permits in 1935 over 1934 was muted in comparison to Houston, which recorded $4,232,625.[2]

Many Fort Worth businesses followed the same trends, faring poorly during the first half of the decade but recovering somewhat while still struggling after 1935. In 1938, Leonard's celebrated its twentieth anniversary, and Mrs. Baird's Bread did well enough to open a new $100,000 bakery at Summit Avenue and Vickery Boulevard, the largest in the South. Mrs. Baird's Bread began in 1908 with Mrs. Minnie Baird's baking bread at the family home, 1800 Washington Avenue, and grew into expanded facilities at 1410 West Terrell Street before moving to Summit Avenue. Baird's relocation was part of a wave of commercial concerns building in residential neighborhoods, creating quality-of-life issues that led Fort Worth in 1940 to adopt zoning regulations that established six regulated districts, the specifics presented during a series of public meetings.[3]

Business at two of Fort Worth's three major industries revived in the second half of the decade. The number of animals handled by the stockyards, a strict indicator of Fort Worth's packinghouse trade, declined almost 20 percent, from 2.1 million in 1929 to 1.7 million in 1934, but increased rapidly afterward, thanks in no small degree to a drought in 1933 and 1934 that forced thousands of head to market prematurely. The run to market glutted an already weakened economy, driving down prices dramatically. Eventually, the drought ended and cattle prices recovered, allowing the stockyards in 1935 to record a 25 percent increase in the total value of animals received over 1934, a jump of $10 million that helped make Fort Worth the South's largest livestock and grain center and second-largest national livestock market, trailing only Chicago, which maintained the top ranking by a wide margin. Livestock was big business not only in Fort Worth but also statewide; Texas was the nation's largest producer of both cattle and sheep. The stockyards economy also saw some early beneficial effects from the outbreak of war in Europe in September 1939. That same month, the Turkish government bought 1,500 mules for their war effort, perhaps the war's first direct economic impact on Fort Worth. All the inputs helped the Fort Worth stockyards handle 2.9 million animals in 1939, a 38 percent increase over 1929.[4]

Aerial view of Fort Worth Stockyards, ca. 1940s. Courtesy Special Collections, the University of Texas at Arlington Libraries.

The oil industry followed a similar path as demand and prices fell after 1930 but rose after mid-decade and continued to rise, especially after demand exceeded supply in 1939. In the week ending September 9, 1939, the average daily production for the United States—3,228,650 barrels (1,350,250, or 42 percent, produced in Texas)—fell 282,500 barrels short of the estimated demand of 3,510,700. Shortfalls continued thereafter, requiring daily imports that averaged 163,143 barrels. In 1941, a few months before America's entry into the war, a forum of petroleum retailers meeting in Fort Worth considered shortages so dire that they recommended a voluntary vehicle curfew between 7:00 p.m. and 7:00 a.m.[5]

General financial statistics track similar trends, with uniform declines after 1930 continuing until mid-decade, followed by a slight recovery but remaining below 1930 production. Fort Worth city tax property values totaled $188,308,600 in the 1931–32 fiscal year but declined steadily to $162,380,793 in 1936–37, and the outlook for 1938–39 reflected little change, with an estimated total of only

$163 million. Tax collections followed a similar pattern but reacted sooner, declining from 85.81 percent of total assessments in 1929–30 to just 71.79 percent in 1933–34 followed by a slow rise afterward. The number of employed showed little overall change in the decade, declining 6 percent from 8,600 in 1929 to 8,122 in 1939, but soaring to 13,955 in 1940, an almost 72 percent increase in just one year. The cost of relief in Fort Worth increased steadily each year after 1932 before dropping to just $180,625 for the first six months of 1939, followed by another 10 percent decline to $163,568 for the same period in 1940. Not surprisingly, the number on relief rolls also declined, dropping 22 percent from 1,559 in October 1939 to 1,201 in April 1940. The contemporaneous rise in employment and decline in relief suggests a significant transition of people from relief rolls to work rolls after 1939. Indeed, after 1939, all the signs seemed to point to recovery. In the first six months of 1940, fifty-three new businesses employing 1,200 opened in Fort Worth, driving tax revenue upswings that allowed the city council to present its largest budget ever, $5,352,098 for 1941, or $562,000 more than in 1940. Despite all the good news, the Depression was not over in 1940; the Census reported 5,110,270 unemployed Americans that March, still remarkably high but significantly down from the worst.[6]

An early effect of the employment surge was seen in a housing crunch made worse by a heavy reliance on single-family homes. In 1940, most Fort Worthians, 87.1 percent, lived in single-family dwellings, while only 4.6 percent and 3.2 percent resided in apartments and duplexes, respectively. A 1940 zoning study showed a housing market dominated by single-family options, counting 35,585 single-family dwellings, 945 duplexes, and 573 apartment houses with 2,754 dwellings. The same report listed 128 hotels and 157 boarding and rooming houses as well as 4,161 commercial establishments, including 381 garages and automobile repair shops, 743 light industries, 285 heavy industries, 67 public schools, and 294 semipublic buildings such as churches and private schools. Single-family dwellings occupied the most land (5,583 acres), followed by industries with 846 acres, semipublic structures covering 810 acres, and public

Queue at Pioneer Palace to collect surplus food, 1940. Courtesy Special Collections, the University of Texas at Arlington Libraries.

schools covering 459 acres, leaving 39 percent unoccupied.[7] A 1941 housing survey estimated 43,000 dwelling units reserved for whites and 7,000 for blacks (with an average monthly rent of $25) and a vacancy rate of only 2.8 percent in white housing and 8 percent in black housing, suggesting a total of 1,764 unoccupied habitations, but the effective vacancy was much lower, since only 700 of the 1,764 empty units were considered habitable, leaving only 1.4 percent of habitable housing unoccupied. Some hope for housing relief came in the summer of 1941, when work began on 600 middle-class homes costing $3,750 to $12,000 in an area four blocks north of 6100 Camp Bowie Boulevard. Those at the lower end of the economic scale looked toward two subsidized-rent apartment complexes that opened in 1940, two of fifty-two such complexes funded nationally through the WPA. Each Fort Worth facility housed 250 families in apartments furnished with modern features like gas ranges and a "mechanical refrigerator." A 20-acre development at Chambers Hill near I. M. Terrell High School was reserved for black families who paid $15.50

to $16.75 monthly, while whites at Belknap and Henderson paid between $17.25 and $18.50 (all rates included gas, electric, and water). The apartments were open to anyone who had lived in Fort Worth for at least three years and met income restrictions that allowed $1,020 annually for a family of six. In September 1940, the first 60 families at Belknap and Henderson Streets and the first 25 families at Chambers Hill began settling into their new homes.[8]

The marked economic improvement responsible for the housing crisis was, at least in part, a product of increased military spending. In 1940, Hicks Field became one of twenty-eight civilian-operated facilities the Army Air Corp leased for military-supervised pilot training. The army also spent $250,000 updating existing facilities to accommodate and house 500 flight staff and 500 support personnel needed for the first group of 120 trainees who began their studies on August 1, followed by another 95 cadets arriving every five weeks to spend ten weeks learning to fly Fairchild PT-19s. The course was so demanding that 40 percent washed out, but the stricter guidelines and training requirements significantly reduced training fatalities compared to World War I, when Hicks and two other Fort Worth military air training bases experienced fatality rates approaching one per day, an insanely high rate that the new director of Hicks Aviation School, Major B. S. Graham, blamed on unqualified instructors who knew little more than their students. Major Graham expressed confidence that the state of the art had improved substantially in the intervening twenty years, and history proved him right. Hicks Airfield operated for almost a year and accrued forty thousand flying hours before the first death, Cadet Trainee Robert Whitford of Tennessee. A few months later, an instructor and cadet perished in a crash near Boyd, Texas, but accident rates remained a fraction of what they had been in the Great War. Hicks represented another link tying Fort Worth to aviation, an industry that would arguably become Fort Worth's most important.[9]

Meacham Airport was another link. By 1930, Meacham was firmly established as a mail and package carrier and had developed a solid base of passenger service, offering twelve daily arrivals and departures capable of carrying up to 216 passengers on direct flights to and from Houston and El Paso, Texas; Oklahoma City, Oklahoma; New Orleans, Louisiana; and Kansas City and St. Louis, Missouri, all with connections to other points. Civilian commercial air passenger travel began in 1929, when Mrs. Temple Bowen presented ticket number 1 for a departure flight out of Meacham. Mrs. Bowen's husband, Temple Bowen, was a bus line owner and founder of Bowen Air Lines, with connecting service all the way from Meacham to Washington, DC, and New York City. Bowen Air used Lockheed Sirius monoplanes, the world's fastest passenger airplanes, capable of flying from Fort Worth to Washington in just seven hours. Passenger service expanded rapidly throughout the 1930s despite being out of the financial reach of most Americans; a ticket to New York City cost $400 in 1929, more than an average worker earned in three months. On April 1, 1932, Meacham added direct service to Chicago, Illinois, on flights departing at 8:30 p.m. and arriving at 7:30 a.m., with returns departing an hour later. Passengers on eleven-hour northbound flights enjoyed coffee, sweet rolls, and cheese with wafers. Travel became easier in 1939 with the introduction of the American Airlines "Skysleeper" service offering sleeping berths on flights to New York via Washington, DC, that departed at 10:45 p.m. and arrived at 9:25 a.m. By 1934, Meacham had an impressive thirty-four daily arrivals and departures, almost triple the total in 1930, but passenger traffic grew at an even faster rate, rising from 5,446 in 1929 to 73,179 in 1936, a 1,243 percent increase. The numbers declined slightly to 72,968 in 1938 but took off in 1941, when five airlines carried 150,000 passengers on twenty thousand flights, an average of fifty-four a day, making Meacham America's third-busiest airport behind only Chicago and Newark, New Jersey. Meacham led in the installation of new technologies to make flying safer and easier, with beacon and ground lighting added in 1937, twenty-four-hour radio service for air traffic control in January 1939, and—along with New York City, Chicago, Cleveland, Kansas City, and Los Angeles—the nation's first "blind," or instrument-controlled, landing systems in 1940. In 1939, the *Star Telegram* celebrated ten years of aviation progress with a special section highlighting Meacham's transition from humble beginnings to a dynamic industry employing three hundred workers providing reliable air transportation to most major American cities.[10]

The growth in air service demand brought several airlines to Meacham. In 1932, American Airlines relocated four hundred employees of its southern division headquarters, lured in part by Amon Carter's influence in securing favorable rents on a thirty-three-year lease. American would become a major player in Meacham's physical development, building a $150,000 hangar and terminal in 1933, the largest in the Southwest, with offices and radio operations as well as rooms for pilots. To keep its fifty planes in the air, American built a repair shop that employed ninety mechanics, one of only three in the United States able to do major overhauls (the others were in Pontiac, Michigan, and Chicago). Braniff Airlines also opened an office in Fort Worth, and in 1938, Delta made Fort Worth its western terminus, building a communications center and bringing in eight mechanics to serve its two daily departures to Atlanta, a six-hour flight in Lockheed Electras. The city of Fort Worth contributed to Meacham's growth, spending $113,400 in 1935 for an administration building, the cost partially funded by the PWA.[11]

Dallas and Fort Worth came close to a joint airport almost thirty years before 1974 (the year Dallas–Fort Worth International Airport opened), but partisan bickering killed the opportunity. The two had considered a regional concept as early as 1920, but the discussion turned serious at the end of the 1930s, when the Dallas Chamber of Commerce suggested expanding the Curtiss-Wright Corporation Airfield in Grand Prairie. The Fort Worth Chamber rejected the plan, saying that the location was too favorable to Dallas and that a regional operation would harm Meacham. The joint venture revived in a petition seeking a $2 million WPA grant for a military air base near Grapevine, Texas (located on the Tarrant and Dallas border), that would be converted into a regional commercial airport when international relations stabilized. Dallas aggressively backed the proposal, arguing that the time was ripe for federal funding but that the window would soon close, while the airlines stressed that a regional airport would be more cost-efficient as well as provide longer and stronger runways needed for bigger aircraft. Supporters from all sides cautioned that Fort Worth's withdrawal would force Dallas to go forward alone, leaving its western neighbor entirely out of the regional aviation future. Opponents countered that no hard assurances had been made on the total cost or of Washington's contribution, leaving each city's financial responsibility unclear, and that the use of public money to subsidize private airlines was questionable.[12] Fort Worth civic leaders had their own concerns about the viability of a single airport serving two cities more than thirty miles apart and the lack of clearly defined administrative roles on airport operation. (Who would manage the airport, Fort Worth or Dallas?) Perhaps most importantly, they objected that, once again, the proposed site favored Dallas, being only fourteen miles distant, while Fort Worth lay twenty-two miles to the west. Don Johnson of the Fort Worth Chamber of Commerce stood in staunch opposition, saying he would not support the plan even with Washington funds, adding that a "midway airport" was simply a ruse to keep Braniff Airlines headquarters in Dallas (Fort Worth tried for years to lure Braniff west). Eventually, and after a lot of discussions, the antis prevailed, ending hope for a regional airport for thirty years, although the Civilian Aviation Board (CAB), ignoring both Fort Worth and Dallas, turned its attention to an Arlington site. The CAB moved quickly, announcing its plans in August 1941, backed by a $400,000 appropriation for construction slated to begin within ninety days on 640 acres, land that Braniff and America had deeded to the city of Arlington, which immediately granted the companies a fifty-year lease. The city of Arlington joined with American and Braniff airlines to form Midway Airport Corporation (MAC) to run the airport operations. Eventually, Dallas's opposition crashed the plan, although a small facility was built. Regional bickering continued, killing a 1943 Midway Airport proposal for Euless, Texas, in northeast Tarrant County. Fort Worth expanded the smaller Midway in Arlington into Carter Field, named in honor of Amon G. Carter, then renamed Greater Fort Worth International Airport in 1953 and Greater Southwest International Airport in 1962. Greater Southwest closed in 1974 after Dallas–Fort Worth Airport opened.[13]

A regional airport failed in the 1930s for many reasons, but one of the more important contributing issues was a shift in interest from commercial to military aviation, as Fort Worth turned its attention to a unilateral effort to secure a military air base and factory. Fort Worth had been mentioned as a potential military aircraft factory as early as 1935, when federal officials inspected potential locations locally as well as in Dallas, Houston, and New Orleans, Louisiana. Rumors of a big project persisted thereafter, reaching a crescendo in August 1939, when reports circulated widely that Amon Carter's intense lobbying had finally been rewarded and reappearing in 1940, when Army Air Corp leased Hicks Field. The rumors were all but confirmed when Fort Worth applied for a $434,000 WPA grant to build an airfield capable of accommodating both land and seaplanes on 840 acres south of Lake Worth. The base prospectus showed that it would be linked to one of seven aircraft factories planned for the Midwest and Southwest by the Defense Plant Corporation, an entity formed by Congress in August 1940 charged with constructing inland military factories less susceptible to attack.[14]

On January 3, 1941, the War Department made it official, announcing the construction of a $10 million bomber plant on 1,200 acres near Lake Worth. The scale was of a degree unseen in Fort Worth or even Texas, involving a single workplace that would employ fourteen thousand and produce fifty B-24 bombers monthly. Civic leaders rejoiced, boasting that the factory would make Fort Worth an aviation center and act as a magnet attracting auxiliary factories. The construction schedule seemed incredible, calling for breaking ground in just thirty days and actual aircraft assembly in just fifteen to eighteen months. To cement the deal, Fort Worth passed a $4,250,000 bond issue on March 4, 1941, that would fund an adjacent airfield and infrastructure improvements such as extending utilities and roads, installing a new garbage incinerator, and expanding the sewage plant. Two weeks later, condemnation proceedings began on 1,022 acres of the 1,450 needed. A three-person committee appointed by Tarrant County Court Judge J. F. Barcroft set land values that averaged just more than $150 per acre but with some wide variations. In one case, the committee paid

$34,937 for one 86-acre plot, or more than $406 an acre, and one of the largest sections, 526 acres owned by Mrs. Genevieve Tillar, sold for $99,750, almost $190 an acre. The actual cost for both land and machinery, which some suspected was heavily inflated, reached $22.4 million.[15]

Construction got a late start but quickly made up for the lost time. Austin Company, the contractor, waited to confirm the bond issue had passed before opening their construction site offices on March 28, pushing back groundbreaking ceremonies to April 19, two months later than expected. From that point on, the pace quickened. Hiring began the following Monday, drawing eager jobseekers seeking well-paying construction jobs and jamming roads. Just four months later, 3,200 workers were earning a $200,000 combined weekly payroll, an average wage of $62.50. Before the end of the month, another 500 were added, pushing the workforce to 3,700. They were all needed to handle all material required, including twenty-six thousand tons of steel costing $2,838,160. Construction went at a furious pace, seven days a week, twenty-four hours a day, to meet stage goals, including having the floor and roof, which covered 29 acres, completed by December 8, 1941 (the day after the Pearl Harbor bombing). By the end of 1941, machine tools began being installed, one of the final preoperational hurdles before production, slated to begin just two weeks later. The official opening of Consolidated Aircraft came in April 1942, the same month that the first B-24 Liberator rolled off the assembly line (three months ahead of schedule), a mere year after breaking ground. During the war, employment grew to 35,000, and production rose to an average of 175 bombers monthly, almost 6 per day. The plant continues operation today, with Lockheed Martin building the F-35 and other aircraft.[16]

As the aircraft plant neared completion in 1941, a $200,000 army depot for material storage was being built adjacent to Hemphill Street in far south Fort Worth. Although not as massive, the depot was a major project requiring 1,100 people working two shifts, not counting those toiling to build an eight-mile road connecting Hemphill Street with Camp Bowie Boulevard, which would provide access from the depot to Highways 377, 13, and 80 (the route to the army's Camp Bowie in Brownwood, Texas) without going through downtown. All the defense work had a massive and early economic impact, driving the North Texas economy past the rest of Texas. A 1941 report showed department store sales down 3 percent statewide, 11 percent in San Antonio and 18 percent in Houston, but up 3 percent in Dallas and 15 percent in Fort Worth.[17]

The transition from a nation at peace to a nation preparing for war after 1939 marked a clear turning point for the United States that ushered in wide-ranging manifestations besides the economic. Americans became rather rigid in dealing with dissent or even practices outside the norm. In 1940, the Fort Worth City Council rejected an application from Jehovah's Witnesses to hold a meeting at the city auditorium, citing their congregants' refusal to salute the flag or participate in national defense. Bohemian Hall on Roberts Cutoff also refused to accommodate the church. Fort Worth had a history of dealing harshly with labor organizers, and that predilection had not altered. Fort Worth detectives found communist literature in the hotel room of Ruel Stanfield, a labor organizer and suspected communist who described himself as a marine firefighter and a labor organizer. Stanfield had a criminal history, having served thirty-seven months in prison for possessing an explosive device during the Standard Oil Strike of 1935. He was in Dallas at the time of the search but arrested after Fort Worth wired an arrest warrant to Dallas police. Stanfield was released after five days only to be rearrested at Seventh and Houston Streets and released again on a writ of habeas corpus for lack of charges.[18]

Militarization also brought an increased awareness and appreciation for America's military, an effect evident in celebrations and considerations honoring soldiers. In June 1941, Fort Worth granted a five-year lease for a tent facility in Sycamore Park open to military personnel at no cost, and a USO Club opened in the Colonial Room of the Texas Hotel, providing military personnel a lounge, game tables, telephones, and stationery every Thursday through Sunday from 9:00 a.m. until the last soldier left. The operational cost, an estimated

$60,000, came from private donations, including money raised during a mock ten-minute air raid drill on June 30, 1941, which began at 12:30 p.m. with strategically placed sirens blaring, joined by factory and train whistles as well as ambulances and fire trucks racing about while twelve bombers from Hensley Naval Field in Dallas flew low over downtown, dropping USO pamphlets. The following week, on July 4, 1941, the city closed Main, Houston, Seventh, and Sixth Streets for a massive street dance honoring servicemen that drew twenty thousand, including five thousand men in uniform and one thousand women who volunteered as dance partners. In November 1941, the mayor spoke and the Paschal High School Band played before the first contingent of draftees left on buses, each of the forty-one whites and fifteen blacks receiving a box of Pangburn's chocolates.[19]

In 1941, Fort Worthians also began to take the possibility of war seriously and to make some tentative preparatory steps. In May 1941, seven months before Pearl Harbor, Fort Worth filed a blackout plan with the War Department to counter aerial bombardment, and the Water Department began placing guards around the Lake Worth dam and the Holly Water Pumping Station. Also in 1941, local officials selected twenty-eight locations around Tarrant County for aircraft observation stations, where spotters would search the skies for enemy aircraft. Of course, most went about their lives relatively unaffected. On December 6, 1941, the *Star Telegram* featured the usual local news and tidbits: the Hollywood Theater advertised *Suspicion*; an Alfred Hitchcock thriller, while the Worth Theater offered a live show, *Abe and Pappy's All Colored Revue* featuring Danny and Edith along with "Dusky Dancing Stars from Europe"; and North Fort Worth Baptist Church on West Fifteenth Street announced the first services in their new $70,000 building would be the next day, December 7, 1941. The front page reported that "Britain Goes on Alert in Far East" but did not elaborate.[20]

The next day, Sunday, December 7, 1941, everything changed for Americans everywhere. In the next few days, approximately one thousand men reported to local recruitment offices, most vying for the Coast Guard; organizers rushed to begin immediate staffing at eight aircraft observation stations; and Fort Worth police, faced with an impossible task of protecting 240 local plants with Defense Department contracts, dispatched officers to guard Double Seal Piston Ring on Montgomery Street and Crown Machine and Tool on Foch Street, but not to the Consolidated Aircraft Plant or army quartermaster depot, both still under construction and both with private guards. Police also cracked down on deserters and malingers, arresting a man who had walked away from military duty in Louisiana, a transient who spoke abusively of the president, and two men who violated Selective Service (the military draft law), one for simply not having a draft card. All seemed rushed in those first few days, an understandable reaction. Given the shock that America had endured, alacrity and even a bit of panic were understandable.[21]

After 1935, Fort Worth's economy recovered from the worst of the Depression but lost much of the gains in 1937 before regaining some momentum as the 1930s closed. The general upward trend after 1935 stemmed from market issues, including the stabilization of Fort Worth's livestock trade and the growth of oil demand. The evidence also suggests that economic growth, uneven as it was, had at least an association with government expenditures, most notably New Deal programs and the 1935 municipal bond package funding varied construction projects. The federal government's economic stimulus intensified after 1939, with defense dollars reopening Hicks Field and building an aircraft plant and an army depot. As 1939 turned to 1940, Fort Worthians were able, for the first time in years, to see a light at the end of the economic tunnel.

Conclusion

Between 1919 and 1941, Fort Worth lost the great economic momentum it had gained in the first two decades of the twentieth century. The transformation of Fort Worth from just another medium-sized town into a city with Texas' largest industrial production began with the great packinghouses in 1903 and was sustained and increased by oil and by federal spending related to World War I, the two great post-1914 economic drivers. After 1920, the stockyards remained vibrant, although certainly affected, but Fort Worth's petroleum and defense economies waned; the latter all but totally erased by peace and the former diminished by the rise of other cities, most notably Houston. That decline and Houston's rise were the major defining economic issues for Fort Worth in the years separating the two world wars.

Fort Worth's problems remained partially hidden by raw population statistics that seemed to reflect respectable population increases. Between 1920 and 1940, Fort Worth added 71,266 people, or 67 percent, to reach 177,721, becoming the nation's forty-sixth largest city, while maintaining its relative standing among Texas cities: fourth behind San Antonio (253,854), Dallas (293,306), and Houston (386,150). In the same period, Houston rose from Texas' third to its largest city, San Antonio fell from first to third, and Dallas remained second. Most of Fort Worth's increase occurred during the 1920s, when the city added 56,965, an impressive 53.5 percent, compared to only 14,301, or only 8.7 percent, in the 1930s. Slower growth in the 1930s was true of most cities as urban growth slowed during the Depression. Fort Worth's population increase in the 1930s was not only reduced but also more concentrated in the suburbs than the central city. From 1930 to 1940, Arlington Heights experienced the largest percentage increase of any neighborhood, adding 37.8 percent to reach 17,864, followed by Riverside (a 32.9 percent increase) and Sycamore Heights (a 19.1 percent rise to 6,398), while the south side, the most populous region with 77,156 residents, experienced just 5.3 percent growth, only slightly below the overall increase, suggesting that downtown and the north side decreased in population.[1] The rise of suburbia was a major change affecting many American cities, but more crucial for Fort Worth was what the raw data did not reveal—namely, that virtually all Fort Worth's population gain in the 1920s (56,965) came from an estimated 50,000 achieved via annexation. That meant that very little actual growth occurred from 1920 to 1940, adding fewer than 22,000 people, or only 20.7 percent, to Fort Worth's population, a 1 percent annual growth rate. (See table C.1.)

Fort Worth's slow to nonexistent growth stood in stark contrast to that of Dallas and more so to that of Houston. From 1920 to 1930, Fort Worth's published rate of increase outpaced San Antonio but lagged behind that of Dallas and fell remarkably short of Houston, which outperformed all other Texas cities. In that ten-year period, Fort Worth added 56,965 people, an almost 54 percent rise that bested San Antonio's 32 percent rate, but ranked significantly below Dallas's 70 percent and was less than half of Houston's 111 percent. In the 1930s, all four cities added population at much lower rates. Fort Worth and Dallas recorded approximately 9 percent increases and San Antonio 19 percent, but Houston, although down from the 1920s, outperformed everyone once again, adding 32 percent. Cumulative figures for the two decades from 1920 to 1940 show that Fort Worth rose 67 percent, slightly more than San Antonio's 59 percent but behind Dallas's 85 percent and well behind Houston's whopping 178 percent increase. In actual numbers, between 1920 and 1940, Houston added more people, 247,238, than Fort Worth's total population in 1940, almost equal to San Antonio's population and 84 percent of Dallas's. The statistics show clearly that between 1920 and 1940, Fort Worth and San Antonio grew slightly and Dallas experienced steady growth, but Houston boomed, experiencing a triple-digit increase almost three times as large as that of Fort Worth and San

Table C.1. Population growth of Texas' four largest cities, 1920–40

	Absolute populations			Percentage increases		
	1920	1930	1940	1920–30	1930–40	1920–40
Houston	138,276	292,352	384,514	111	32	178
Dallas	158,976	269,475	294,734	70	9	85
San Antonio	161,379	213,542	253,854	32	19	59
Fort Worth	106,482	163,447	177,447	53	9	67

Source: "Fort Worth, Texas," Wikipedia, last modified January 8, 2020, 21:29, https://en.wikipedia.org/wiki/Fort_Worth,_Texas; "Dallas," Wikipedia, last modified January 23, 2020, 04:27, https://en.wikipedia.org/wiki/Dallas; "San Antonio," Wikipedia, last modified January 23, 08:52, https://en.wikipedia.org/wiki/San_Antonio; "Houston," Wikipedia, last modified January 23, 2020, 12:02, https://en.wikipedia.org/wiki/Houston.

Antonio and more than twice that of Dallas. From 1920 to 1940, both Houston's and Fort Worth's growth separated them from the other two large Texas cities, but each went in different directions. (See table C.1.)

Tarrant County experienced similar but slightly slower growth. Fort Worth's home county added 72,221 residents between 1920 and 1940, a 47.6 percent overall increase that largely happened in the 1920s, when Tarrant grew 29.3 percent, the same trend as in Fort Worth that was also seen in Bexar, Dallas, and Harris Counties. Like Fort Worth, Tarrant remained fourth largest in the state behind Bexar (338,176), Dallas (398,564), and Harris (528,961), but all three other counties changed positions. Harris climbed from third to first, while Bexar fell from second to third, and Dallas fell from first to second. The statistics reveal some clear growth trends: downward for Tarrant County, which experienced the smallest growth rate, and upward for Harris County, which exploded, growing at a rate almost four times that of Tarrant and twice that of second-place Dallas County. (See table C.2.)

Economic statistics show a similar pattern in which Houston outdistanced Fort Worth, Dallas, and San Antonio to become Texas' largest industrial producer. To broaden the results and control for variations

Table C.2. Population growth in Texas' four largest counties, 1920–40

	Absolute populations			Percentage increases		
	1920	1930	1940	1920–30	1930–40	1920–40
Harris	186,667	359,328	528,961	92.5	47.2	183.4
Dallas	210,551	325,691	398,564	54.7	54.7	89.3
Bexar	202,096	292,533	338,176	44.7	44.7	67.3
Tarrant	152,800	197,553	225,521	29.3	29.3	47.6

Source: *Fourteenth Census of the United States* (Washington, DC: Government Printing Office, 1922), pp. 9:1449–50; *Fifteenth Census of the United States* (Washington, DC: Government Printing Office, 1930), pp. 3:507–9; *Sixteenth Census of the United States* (Washington, DC: Government Printing Office, 1940), pp. 3:982–84.

created by annexations, the analysis uses county rather than municipal statistics. An illustration of vagaries in local statistics is seen in an increase between 1919 and 1929 in Fort Worth's value added by manufacturing from $15.3 million to $27.7 million, a rise of $12.4 million, or 81.1 percent—an extreme rise that was almost entirely an effect of annexing Niles City with the Swift and Armour packinghouses. The annexation effect becomes obvious by comparing Tarrant County statistics (which included Fort Worth), which decreased 1.5 percent during the same period. Annexation also explains an anomaly between Fort Worth's population growth of 53.3 percent in the 1920s, while Tarrant County's value of manufacturing declined 1.5 percent and value of manufactures declined 15.4 percent (see table C.2), widely divergent results that can be explained by Fort Worth's aggressive annexations in the 1920s.[2]

In 1920, Tarrant County had the largest manufacturing economy in Texas, registering the most value added by manufacturing and value of manufacturing and the second greatest number of wage earners and total wages despite having the fewest business establishments. By 1940, Fort Worth ranked third in all categories, ahead of only Bexar (San Antonio), except in the number of establishments, where it remained last, while Harris (Houston) was first in every category except in establishments, where Dallas led. (See table C.3.)

Table C.3. Economic statistics of Texas' four largest cities, 1920–40

	Establish-ments	Wage earners	Wages	Value added	Value of manufactures
Tarrant County					
1920	257	9,196	$10,563,346	$33,706,350	$155,299,159
1930	246	8,600	$10,607,560	$33,181,626	$131,336,433
1940	312	8,122	$8,555,913	$30,319,695	$106,431,481
1920–40	+21.4%	–11.7%	–19.0%	–10.0%	–31.5%
Dallas County					
	Establish-ments	Wage earners	Wages	Value added	Value of manufactures
1920	492	8,708	$8,752,025	$32,671,541	$116,160,150
1930	572	13,853	$15,516,780	$65,348,733	$168,211,802
1940	716	16,339	$15,522,683	$61,653,398	$155,945,064
1920–40	+45.5%	+87.6%	+77.4%	+88.7%	+34.3%
Harris County					
	Establish-ments	Wage earners	Wages	Value added	Value of manufactures
1920	422	11,411	$12,173,174	$31,913,784	$104,776,719
1930	475	22,131	$28,096,678	$93,497,836	$285,227,185
1940	655	22,765	$30,655,880	$107,138,268	$337,130,303
1920–40	+55.2%	+99.5%	+151.8%	+235.7%	+221.8%
Bexar County					
	Establish-ments	Wage earners	Wages	Value added	Value of manufactures
1920	328	6,869	$5,977,625	$13,903,017	$37,045,241
1930	412	9,395	$8,946,800	$26,067,818	$60,804,038
1940	356	6,827	$6,023,169	$22,547,283	$54,528,055
1920–40	+8.5%	–.6.1%	+7.6%	+62.2%	+47.2%

Source: *Fourteenth Census of the United States* (Washington, DC: Government Printing Office, 1922), pp. 9:1449–50; *Fifteenth Census of the United States* (Washington, DC: Government Printing Office, 1930), pp. 3:507–9; *Sixteenth Census of the United States* (Washington, DC: Government Printing Office, 1940), pp. 3:982–84.

A comparison of the percentage change in each region's manufacturing economy between 1920 and 1940 provides conclusive evidence that Tarrant County was the big loser, declining in every category, except for a 21.4 percent increase in establishments, while Dallas, Harris, and Bexar all increased in every manufacturing category, except that Bexar declined 6.1 percent in number of wage earners. Tarrant's (Fort Worth's) fall was clear and remarkable. Between 1920 and 1940, Fort Worth lost 10 percent in value added in manufacturing and 31.5 percent in value of manufacturing, while Dallas increased 88.7 percent and 34.3 percent, respectively; Bexar increased 62.2 percent and 47.2 percent; and Harris increased 235.7 percent and 221.8 percent. In the process, Tarrant County fell from first to third in both categories, ahead of only Bexar County, while Harris County climbed from third to first. The economic story of those twenty years was one of Fort Worth's decline and Houston's ascendancy.

Most of the gap between Fort Worth and Houston and, to a lesser extent, Dallas developed during the 1920s. Between 1920 and 1930, Tarrant County declined in every category except wages, which increased 0.4 percent, while the other three counties increased across the board. Fort Worth's value of manufacturing declined 15.4 percent, while Dallas increased 44.8 percent, Bexar 64.1 percent, and Harris an amazing 172.2 percent. Put in general terms, between 1920 and 1930, Harris and Tarrant underwent significant but opposite economic trends, while Dallas and Bexar experienced moderate upswings. In the process, Harris County emerged as the big winner, climbing in just ten years from the third-largest Texas economy to first by a wide margin, while Tarrant County lost big, declining from first to third, ahead of only Bexar County.

The 1930s continued and augmented the growing gap between Fort Worth and its competitors, especially Houston. During the Depression, Tarrant County and Bexar County declined in every measure except that Tarrant slightly increased in the number of establishments at the same time that Dallas County increased in establishments, wage earners, and wages but declined in value added by manufacturing and value of manufacturing. In contrast,

Houston experienced growth in every sector. In raw statistical terms, between 1930 and 1940, the value of manufacturing declined 19.0 percent in Tarrant County, 7.3 percent in Dallas, and 10.3 percent in Bexar but rose 18.2 percent in Harris County, a tremendous achievement during the nation's worst depression.

A big factor driving Houston's growth was a shift in Texas' oil production away from North Texas to East Texas and the Gulf Coast. In 1920, Fort Worth was the center of Texas' fledgling oil trade thanks to its proximity to oil fields in Ranger, Burkburnett, and West Texas, but by 1935, Houston and Midland-Odessa had supplanted Fort Worth as the centers of Texas oil commerce. Like Fort Worth, between 1900 and 1920, Houston's rise as an oil center after 1920 owed a lot to geography. Houston sat adjacent to Texas' largest oil-producing region, East Texas, which pumped 14,628,950 barrels annually, as well as to the Gulf Coast, with another 6,919,800 barrels of production, while production in the West Texas region slipped in the 1930s to Texas' third largest, although it still recorded a respectable 5,603,100 barrels. In addition, increasing amounts of the West Texas oil trade had begun to shift from Fort Worth to Midland-Odessa as their commercial and financial development caught up with production, leaving Fort Worth with only the North Texas region producing a mere 3,550,850 barrels. Fort Worth's economy had taken off during World War I thanks in large part to oil production, especially at Ranger, but by the end of the 1920s, Fort Worth's oil boom was over and Houston's was just beginning. Fort Worth's other big industry, meat packing, remained steady in the long run, continuing in 1941 to employ around five thousand and pump $6.25 million in wages into the local economy, but the packinghouses had reached maturity, becoming more a sustaining force than a growth industry.[3]

Houston's dominance of the oil trade was timely, occurring as oil developed into Texas' most important industry. At the start of the twentieth century, the Texas economy rested on cotton, cattle, corn, and lumber—all, except corn, well integrated into the national market economy. The 1901 discovery at Spindletop, ninety miles east of Houston, started the Texas oil boom that would, for the first time, drive manufacturing to overtake agriculture as the state's main economy and in 1921 make petroleum refining Texas' third economic pillar, joining lumber and food processing. In the 1930s, the development of pulp and paper industries adjacent to Houston and of heavy chemical industries centered in Houston enhanced the region's already stimulated economy. At this early stage, Texas was largely a colonial economy, exporting raw materials and importing finished goods, but the rise of oil represented the beginning of a dramatic shift away from agriculture to industry. The industrialization of Texas did not mean that agriculture slumped; in fact, cotton production increased to the extent that in 1920, Texas produced 42 percent of American cotton and 30 percent of the world crop. It did mean that petroleum, as the state's dominant economic force, was the catalyst that drove Texas' manufacturing to multiply by a factor of three between 1920 and 1940. In the course of that journey, Houston became Texas' largest city, while Fort Worth stagnated and dreamed of better days.[4]

Notes

Introduction

1. *Fort Worth Star Telegram,* January 1, 1920, p. 1; September 24, 1920, p. 1; July 19, 1921, p. 12; April 6, 1923, p. 1; July 22, 1923, p. 11; May 24, 2017, p. 9DD; Fort Worth Chamber of Commerce, *Fort Worth in Brief* (n.p.: Fort Worth Chamber of Commerce, 1925), p. 15, Briscoe Center for American History, University of Texas at Austin; City of Fort Worth Records, Mayor and Council Proceedings, box 1, folder January 1920, Local History Section, Fort Worth Public Library; Roscoe Ady, "Our City Fort Worth" (unpublished manuscript), chap. 8, p. 8, Roscoe Ady Papers, box GA 18, Special Collections, University of Texas at Arlington Library.
2. *Fort Worth Star Telegram,* June 17, 1920, pp. 1, 2; June 20, 1920, part 2, p. 10; June 15, 1921, p. 13; Julia Kathryn Garrett, *Fort Worth: A Frontier Triumph* (Fort Worth: Texas Christian University Press, 1996), pp. 125–28.
3. *Fort Worth Star Telegram,* April 18, 1929, p. 1; January 9, 1922, pp. 1, 4; *Fort Worth Press,* January 9, 1922, p. 1; January 10, 1922, p. 1. And see the following sources from the Paddock Papers, Special Collections, University of Texas at Arlington Library: Mary Paddock, sister of B. B. Paddock, "What I Learned about the Paddocks," n.d., box GA 195, folder 20; Family Register of Boardman Paddock drafted by Aaron D. Rolfe, June 11, 1854, box GA 195, folder 20; Genealogical Data gathered by W. V. Burnell, March 22, 1945, box GA 195, file 20; Boardman B. Paddock to Emmie Harper, April 29, 1863, box GA 194, folder 3; Boardman B. Paddock to Emmie Harper, April 30, 1863, box GA 194, folder 1; Boardman B. Paddock to Emmie Harper, March 16, 1865, box GA 194, folder 3; Boardman B. Paddock to Emmie Harper, March 28, 1865, box GA 194, folder 3.
4. *Fort Worth Star Telegram,* March 24, 1926, p. 5; Boardman B. Paddock to Emmie Paddock, November 4, 1872, box GA 195, folder 3, Paddock Papers, Special Collections, University of Texas at Arlington Library, Local History Collection; Boardman B. Paddock to Emmie Harper, January 4, 1872, box GA 194, folder 3, Paddock Papers, Special Collections, University of Texas at Arlington Library; Boardman B. Paddock to Emmie Harper, February 24, 1873, box GA 194, folder 4, Paddock Papers, Special Collections, University of Texas at Arlington Library; Ady, "Our City," chap. 5, p. 3.
5. *New York Times,* June 28, 1922, p. 12; September 6, 1922, p. 12; September 17, 1922, p. 28; December 14, 1923, p. 22; *Fort Worth Star Telegram,* November 17, 1928, p. 13; February 24, 2016, p. 5A; Gary Cartwright, "Showdown at Waggoner Ranch," *Texas Monthly*

Magazine, January 2004, pp. 1–21, http://texasmonthly.com/articles/showdown-at-waggoner-ranch; Bill Porterfield, *A Loose Herd of Texans* (College Station: Texas A&M University Press, 1978), p. 87.

6. *Fort Worth Star Telegram*, March 19, 1930, pp. 1, 4, 6; March 20, 1930, p. 1; July 27, 1932, pp. 1, 4.
7. Brian Cervantez, "Lone Star Booster: The Life of Amon Carter" (PhD diss., University of North Texas, 2011), pp. 53–54; *Fort Worth Star Telegram*, May 6, 1920, p. 1; May 29, 1921, Souvenir section; May 31, 1921, p. 1; September 17, 1922, pp. 12–13; September 27, 1922, p. 7; January 1, 2018, p. 3A.
8. *Fort Worth Star Telegram*, March 28, 1929, p. 19; January 11, 2015, p. 4A; Harold Rich, *Fort Worth: Outpost, Cowtown, Boomtown* (Norman: University of Oklahoma Press, 2014), pp. 155–56.
9. J. Frank Norris, *Inside the Cup: Or My 21 Years in Fort Worth* (Fort Worth: n.p., 1939), pp. 22–23, 26, 71–77; David R. Stokes, *The Shooting Salvationist: J. Frank Norris and the Murder Trial That Captivated America* (Hanover, NH: Steerforth, 2011), pp. 275–79; *New York Times*, July 8, 1925, pp. 1, 6; May 26, 1926, p. 29; July 24, 1926, p. 9; September 7, 1928, p. 3; January 13, 1929, p. 9; January 14, 1929, p. 16; Lynn Ray Musselwhite, "Texas in the 1920s: A History of Social Change" (PhD diss., Texas Technological University, 1975), p. 377; Irvin Farman, *The Fort Worth Club: A Centennial Story* (Fort Worth: Fort Worth Club, 1985), pp. 95–97.
10. *New York Times*, July 18, 1926, pp. 1, 3; July 24, 1926, p. 9; October 31, 1926, p. 16; November 1, 1926, p. 23; *Fort Worth Star Telegram*, October 12, 2016, p. 7DD; Farman, *Fort Worth Club*, pp. 95–97.
11. *New York Times*, October 19, 1926, p. 31; October 31, 1926, p. 16; November 1, 1926, p. 23; November 3, 1926, p. 14; December 19, 1926, p. 10; January 27, 1927, pp. 1, 2; *Fort Worth Star Telegram*, October 12, 2016, p. 7DD.
12. *Fort Worth Star Telegram*, July 17, 1936, p. 1; September 17, 1938, p. 10; October 6, 1939, p. 2; *New York Times*, June 19, 1938, p. 2.

Chapter One

1. *Fort Worth City Council Minutes*, vol. A1, April 15, 1919; vol. A1, April 12, 1921; vol. A1, April 10, 1923, Local History Section, Fort Worth Public Library; *Fort Worth Star Telegram*, February 11, 1921, p. 14; April 4, 1923, p. 10; October 8, 1924, p. 1.
2. *Fort Worth Star Telegram*, January 9, 1924, p. 5; April 8, 1925, p. 1; April 14, 1925, p. 1; April 25, 1925, p. 1; April 12, 1927, p. 1; May 24, 2017, p. 7DD; Fort Worth Chamber of Commerce, *Fort Worth* (Fort Worth: Fort Worth Chamber of Commerce, 1934), p. 3, Briscoe Center for American History, University of Texas at Austin; Eric Wake, "A Study in Conservative Politics: The Fort Worth City Council, 1925–1938" (MA thesis, Texas Christian University, 1967), pp. 2, 7–8; *Fort Worth City Council Minutes*, vol. B1, April 12, 1927; vol. C1, April 19, 1927.
3. *Fort Worth Star Telegram*, January 9, 1924, p. 5; December 12, 1924, pp. 1, 8; June 2, 1925, p. 1; June 21, 1928, p. 1; June 28, 1928, p. 1; February 6, 1929, p. 1; May 19, 1929, p. 47; *New York Times*, May 19, 1929, p. E2; *Fort Worth City Council Minutes*, vol. A1, April 22, 1924; vol. A1, November 24, 1924; vol. A1, December 17, 1924; vol. A1, April 14, 1925; *The Charter of the City of Fort Worth* (Fort Worth: Stafford-Lowdon, 1928; adopted April 1925), pp. 3, 37, Special Collections, University of Texas at Arlington Library.

4. *Fort Worth Star Telegram*, January 25, 1920, p. 4; February 15, 1920, part 3, p. 1; August 20, 1920, p. 9; March 10, 1921, p. 1; July 20, 1922, p. 1; Mary A. Keavney, "The Depression Era in Fort Worth 1929–1934" (MA thesis, University of Texas at Austin, 1974), p. 12.
5. *Fort Worth Press*, January 31, 1922, p. 1; *Fort Worth Star Telegram*, August 18, 1920, p. 1; January 31, 1922, pp. 1–2.
6. *Fort Worth Star Telegram*, August 10, 1920, p. 17; August 15, 1920, part 6, p. 2; March 10, 1921, p. 1; April 26, 1921, pp. 1, 4; August 16, 1921, p. 1; January 30, 1922, p. 1; January 31, 1922, p. 1; May 4, 1922, p. 1; July 5, 1922, p. 1; July 29, 1922, p. 1; November 12, 1922, p. 1; March 5, 1923, p. 1; March 29, 1923, p. 1; July 24, 1923, p. 1; August 1, 1923, p. 1; October 6, 1923, p. 1; May 24, 2017, p. 7DD.
7. *Fort Worth Star Telegram*, July 23, 1922, p. 1; July 29, 1922, p. 1; August 14, 1922, p. 9; November 22, 1922, p. 1; October 6, 1923, p. 1; July 11, 1924, p. 1; July 14, 1924, p. 1.
8. *Fort Worth Star Telegram*, February 1, 1920, p. 1; August 9, 1920, p. 1; November 9, 1924, p. 1; November 10, 1924, p. 18; November 13, 1924, p. 1; January 8, 1920, p. 6; June 17, 1922, p. 1; Ady, "Our City," chap. 9, p. 6; Wake, "Study in Conservative Politics," p. 10.
9. *Fort Worth Star Telegram*, August 9, 1924, p. 1; January 26, 1926, p. 1; May 10, 1926, p. 13.
10. *Fort Worth Star Telegram*, July 20, 1922, p. 1; March 9, 1921, p. 18; September 29, 1921, p. 1; September 15, 1924, p. 1; October 20, 1924, p. 1; Fort Worth Chamber of Commerce, *The Statistical Handbook of Fort Worth, Texas* (Fort Worth: Fort Worth Chamber of Commerce, 1930), p. 88, Briscoe Center for American History, University of Texas at Austin.
11. *Fort Worth Star Telegram*, January 29, 1922, p. 2; September 14, 1923, p. 1; December 7, 1923, p. 1; January 1, 1924, p. 4. See also "History of Fort Worth's Water System," *Fort Worth Star Telegram*, January 1–3, 1916.
12. *Fort Worth Star Telegram*, January 21, 1920, p. 9; October 4, 1920, p. 1; October 12, 1920, p. 1; January 29, 1922, p. 2; October 18, 1921, p. 1; October 19, 1921, p. 1; October 28, 1921, p. 6; November 15, 1921, p. 1.
13. *Fort Worth Star Telegram*, May 19, 1924, p. 4; July 10, 1924, p. 8; December 23, 1923, p. 1; December 30, 1923, p. 1; January 1, 1924, pp. 1, 4; February 3, 1924, p. 2; May 2, 1924, p. 26; March 21, 1925, p. 1; March 5, 2017, p. 11B.
14. *Fort Worth Star Telegram*, April 25, 1922, pp. 1, 2; April 26, 1922, pp. 1, 2; April 27, 1922, p. 1; April 28, 1922, p. 1; *Fort Worth Press*, April 26, 1922, n.p.; Research Data, Federal Writer's Project, Fort Worth and Tarrant County Texas, Local History Section, Fort Worth Public Library, 1941, pp. 4278–79; "TRWD History," Tarrant Regional Water District, http://www.trwd.com/about-trwd/history; *New York Times*, April 27, 1922, p. 15; April 28, 1922, p. 16; Ady, "Our City," chap. 10, p. 1.
15. *New York Times*, April 26, 1922, p. 1; *Fort Worth Star Telegram*, January 10, 1926, p. 1; Ady, "Our City," chap. 9, p. 6, and chap. 10, pp. 3–4.
16. "Diamond Jubilee of 1923," box Fort Worth, file Events: Diamond Jubilee 1923, Tarrant County Archives, Fort Worth; Rita Cook, *A Brief History of Fort Worth: Cowtown through the Years* (Charleston, SC: History Press, 2011), p. 53; *Fort Worth Star Telegram*, September 28, 1923; November 10, 1923, pp. 1, 4; November 11, 1923, pp. 1, 4; November 13, 1923, pp. 1, 4; November 14, 1923, pp. 1, 4; November 10, 1923, pp. 1, 4; Fort Worth, *Historical Pageant of Fort Worth: Diamond Jubilee, November 11-12-13-14, 1923* (Fort Worth: Marvin D. Evans, 1923), p. 11, box Fort Worth, file Events: Diamond Jubilee 1923, Tarrant County Archives, Fort Worth; *Dallas Morning News*, November 11, 1923;

November 14, 1923; Undated clipping, *Fort Worth News Tribune*, William E. Jary Papers, box 21, file 21, Special Collections, University of Texas at Arlington Library.

17. *Fort Worth Star Telegram*, June 17, 1922, p. 1; December 22, 1926, p. 4; August 7, 1927, part 2, p. 1; March 21, 1926, p. 1; December 21, 1932, p. 1; J'Nell Pate, *North of the River: A Brief History of North Fort Worth*, Chisholm Trail Series 11 (Fort Worth: Texas Christian University Press, 1994), pp. 38–47.
18. *Fort Worth Star Telegram*, April 6, 1923, p. 1; July 22, 1923, p. 11; November 29, 1923, p. 1; December 17, 1922, p. 1; September 4, 1928, p. 6; October 28, 1926, p. 9. Also see "A History of Trinity Park," *Fort Worth Star Telegram*, April 7, 1929, Oil and Automobile section, p. 12.
19. *Fort Worth Star Telegram*, January 25, 1927, p. 1; June 13, 1927, p. 1; July 10, 1927, part 2, p. 17; August 24, 2014, p. 16A; February 12, 1928, Auto Classifieds section, p. 16; May 10, 1928, p. 2; July 29, 1928, part 2, p. 1; August 21, 1928, p. 17; January 1, 2018, p. 3A.
20. *Fort Worth Star Telegram*, September 17, 1922, pp. 12–13; September 27, 1922, p. 7; *New York Times*, June 18, 1922, p. 38; February 1, 1925, p. 181; April 19, 1923, p. 22; Bill C. Malone, *Country Music, U.S.A.* (Austin: University of Texas Press, 1985), pp. 32–34.
21. *New York Times*, January 22, 1922, p. 77; March 16, 1932, p. 17; November 7, 1932; *Fort Worth Star Telegram*, April 2, 1935, p. 11; January 10, 1926, part 2, p. 7.
22. Quentin McGown, *Fort Worth in Vintage Postcards*, Postcard History Series (Charleston, SC: Arcadia, 2003), p. 70; *Fort Worth Star Telegram*, November 27, 1927, part 2, p. 1; February 23, 1927, p. 2; March 4, 1927, p. 2; August 15, 1929, p. 21; October 27, 1929, Society and Club section, p. 10.
23. Jan Jones, *Renegades, Showmen and Angels: A Theatrical History of Fort Worth from 1873–2001*, Chisholm Trails Series (Fort Worth: Texas Christian University Press, 1999), p. 145; *Fort Worth Star Telegram*, August 16, 1925, p. 4; April 11, 1926, part 2, p. 3; October 9, 2017, p. 10A.
24. *Fort Worth Star Telegram*, October 19, 1920, p. 1; October 20, 1920, p. 1; January 7, 1924, p. 1; January 11, 1924, p. 12; April 21, 1926, pp. 4, 14; October 17, 2016, p. 4A; *New York Times*, April 20, 1926, p. 30; April 21, 1926, p. 30.
25. *New York Times*, June 22, 1928, p. 25; May 27, 1929, p. 1; *Fort Worth Star Telegram*, September 26, 1927, pp. 1, 4; September 7, 1938, p. 1; September 14, 2015, p. 7A; May 24, 2017, p. 9DD; Barry Schiff, "Pilot Briefing," *AOPA Pilot Magazine* 61, no. 4 (April 2018): p. 48.
26. *New York Times*, April 9, 1923, p. 20; *Fort Worth Star Telegram*, February 24, 1925, p. 1; August 23, 1925, p. 2; January 21, 1929, p. 1; April 14, 2014, p. 6B; Pate, *North of the River*, p. 128.
27. *Fort Worth Star Telegram*, November 4, 1919, p. 8; November 14, 1919, p. 8; February 1, 1920, p. 6; February 20, 1920, p. 1; February 23, 1920, p. 1; February 27, 1920, p. 1; February 28, 1920, p. 1; February 29, 1920, p. 11.
28. *Fort Worth Star Telegram*, January 28, 1924, p. 5; September 13, 1928, p. 6; December 16, 1929, p. 5.
29. *Fort Worth Star Telegram*, December 28, 1924, p. 1; February 29, 1920, part 3, p. 11; February 12, 1920, p. 1; July 7, 1921, p. 4; July 13, 1921, p. 1; October 31, 1921, p. 1; April 22, 1923, pp. 1, 6; November 19, 1921, p. 1.
30. *Fort Worth Star Telegram*, August 2, 1922, p. 1; May 20, 1928, p. 4; *Fort Worth Press*, February 21, 1926, Research Data, Federal Writers' Research Project, Fort Worth and Tarrant County Texas, Local History Section, Fort Worth Public Library, 1941, p. 11947.

31. *Fort Worth Star Telegram*, November 4, 1919, p. 8; August 17, 1922, p. 18; Jerry Flemmons, *Amon: The Life of Amon Carter, Sr., of Texas* (Austin: Jenkins, 1978), p. 179–80.
32. *Fort Worth Press*, January 26, 1922, p. 1; January 27, 1922, p. 1; *Fort Worth Star Telegram*, June 24, 1923, p. 1; June 27, 1923, p. 4; July 30, 1923, p. 19; March 28, 1924, p. 1; January 5, 1926, p. 1; September 7, 1926, p. 1.
33. *Fort Worth Star Telegram*, January 6, 1922, pp. 1, 4; January 5, 1926, p. 1; September 7, 1926, p. 1; December 28, 1926, p. 1; *New York Times*, January 10, 1924, p. 23; December 29, 1926, p. 10; December 28, 1926, p. 1.

Chapter Two

1. *Fort Worth Star Telegram*, October 19, 1919, p. 1; January 16, 1920, p. 11; March 26, 1921, p. 11; November 29, 1924, p. 4; July 17, 1921, p. 55; January 16, 1920, p. 11; December 20, 1920, pp. 1, 2; February 21, 1921, p. 7; June 17, 1923, p. 10; November 18, 1929, p. 4.
2. *Fort Worth City Council Minutes*, vol. A1, April 16, 1921; *Fort Worth Star Telegram*, January 16, 1920, p. 11; April 11, 1921, pp. 1, 2; April 30, 1921, p. 1; July 17, 1921, p. 3; October 25, 1921, pp. 3, part 3, p. 1; December 31, 1928, p. 1.
3. *Fort Worth Star Telegram*, February 18, 1923, p. 14; April 11, 1921, pp. 1, 2.
4. *Fort Worth Star Telegram*, January 4, 1924, p. 18; January 13, 1926, p. 22; September 11, 1927, part 2, p. 1; November 13, 1926, p. 1; June 27, 1924, p. 2; February 23, 1929, p. 9; October 23, 1927, p. 10.
5. *Fort Worth Star Telegram*, October 1, 1926, p. 8; October 2, 1926, p. 2; August 30, 1927, p. 20; January 23, 1928, p. 4; December 26, 1929, p. 1; August 15, 1929, pp. 1, 4; September 4, 1929, pp. 1, 4; December 20, 1929, p. 1; *New York Times*, June 10, 1926, p. 52.
6. *Fort Worth Star Telegram*, May 27, 1919, p. 13; September 13, 1919, p. 1; September 26, 1919, p. 3; August 1, 1921, p. 3.
7. *Fort Worth Star Telegram*, October 25, 1919, p. 3; May 9, 1921, p. 14; May 4, 1924, p. 1; July 29, 1920, p. 20.
8. *New York Times*, September 16, 1921, p. 15; November 11, 1928, p. 10.
9. *New York Times*, December 24, 1920, p. 8; *Fort Worth Star Telegram*, April 9, 1920, p. 1; December 21, 1920, p. 1; December 23, 1920, pp. 1, 2; December 24, 1920, pp. 1, 2; December 27, 1920, p. 1; August 14, 1921, p. 1; August 15, 1921, p. 2; December 23, 1926, p. 1; December 24, 1926, p. 1.
10. *Fort Worth Star Telegram*, May 20, 1928, p. 1; May 21, 1928, p. 1; May 29, 1928, p. 1; July 16, 1928, p. 1; June 18, 1929, p. 1; August 2, 1929, p. 1; August 4, 1929, part 2, p. 1; August 5, 1929, p. 1.
11. *Fort Worth Star Telegram*, October 21, 1920, p. 1; June 2, 1921, p. 1; July 10, 1921, p. 1; August 5, 1921, p. 1; November 16, 1920, p. 1; November 17, 1921, p. 1.
12. *Fort Worth City Council Minutes*, vol. A1, April 16, 1919; *Fort Worth Star Telegram*, April 11, 1921, pp. 1, 2; April 30, 1921, p. 1; July 14, 1922, p. 1.
13. *Fort Worth City Council Minutes*, vol. A1, November 8, 1922; vol. A1, November 10, 1922; vol. A1, November 14, 1922; vol. A1, November 21, 1922; vol. A1, November 28, 1922; vol. A1, November 29, 1922; vol. A1, January 2, 1923; *Fort Worth Star Telegram*, November 8, 1922, pp. 1, 4; November 9, 1922, pp. 1, 4; November 10, 1922, pp. 1, 4; November 15, 1922, p. 10; November 16, 1922, p. 4; November 17, 1922, p. 4; November 21, 1922, pp. 1, 4; November 26, 1922, p. 4; November 27, 1922, pp. 1, 4; November 28, 1922, pp. 1, 4; November 29, 1922, p. 1; January 16, 1922, p. 4; May 23, 1923, p. 1.

14. *Fort Worth Star Telegram*, August 15, 1922, p. 18; May 10, 1923, p. 3; September 29, 1920, p. 18; *Fort Worth Record*, February 3, 1921, Research Data, Federal Writer's Project, Fort Worth and Tarrant County Texas, Local History Section, Fort Worth Public Library, 1941, p. 14682; *Fort Worth Press*, January 28, 1922, p. 1.
15. *Fort Worth Star Telegram*, June 25, 1925, p. 1; June 27, 1925, p. 1; September 14, 1925, p. 1; November 16, 1925, pp. 1, 4; November 17, 1925, pp. 1, 4; April 17, 1926, p. 1; December 15, 1926, p. 1; May 28, 1924, p. 1; October 10, 1924, p. 2.
16. *New York Times*, July 31, 1920, p. 2; *Fort Worth Star Telegram*, October 20, 1920, p. 1.
17. Flemmons, *Amon*, p. 268; *Fort Worth Star Telegram*, May 26, 1920, p. 3; January 4, 1920, p. 8; March 12, 1920, p. 12; May 24, 2017, p. 9DD.
18. Chester T. Crowdell, "Strange News from Texas," *Tom Hickey's Magazine* 1, no. 7 (April 1925): p. 7, T. A. Hickey Papers, box 3K423, Briscoe Center for American History, University of Texas at Austin; *Fort Worth Press*, October 20, 1921, p. 1.
19. *Fort Worth Star Telegram*, May 1, 1921, Fort Worth Magazine section; February 6, 1921, p. 8; July 21, 1921, p. 1; August 14, 1921, p. 1; September 1, 1921, p. 1.
20. *Fort Worth Star Telegram*, January 8, 1924, p. 1; February 3, 1924, p. 1; July 4, 1924, p. 13; January 19, 1926, p. 20; June 5, 1926, p. 1; July 6, 1926, p. 1; October 30, 2017, p. 4A.
21. *Fort Worth Star Telegram*, May 10, 1923, p. 3; June 2, 1922, pp. 1, 4; June 3, 1922, p. 1; June 6, 1922, p. 1; June 10, 1922, p. 1; June 11, 1922, p. 1; July 6, 1923, p. 1; September 25, 1921, p. 1A; July 19, 1922, p. 1.
22. *Fort Worth Star Telegram*, September 15, 1925, pp. 1, 2; November 8, 1925, p. 1; May 27, 1926, p. 4.
23. *Fort Worth Star Telegram*, December 14, 1920, p. 3; July 21, 1921, p. 1; August 2, 1923, p. 1; August 22, 1923, p. 2; November 12, 1924, p. 1; January 10, 1926, p. 2; Rich, *Fort Worth*, pp. 189–90.
24. Rita Cook and Jeffrey Yarborough, *Prohibition in Dallas and Fort Worth: Blind Tigers, Bootleggers and Bathtub Gin* (Charleston, SC: American Palate, 2013), pp. 10–12; Vickie Bryant and Camille Hess, *Top O'Hill Terrace*, Images of America Series (Charleston, SC: Arcadia, 2012), pp. 9–54.
25. *Fort Worth Star Telegram*, March 31, 1920, pp. 1, 2; July 31, 1923, p. 1; August 1, 1923, p. 11; August 2, 1923, p. 1; August 22, 1923, p. 2.
26. *New York Times*, January 15, 1922, pp. 14 and 37; January 31, 1922, p. 14; *Fort Worth Star Telegram*, March 5, 1922, p. 11; February 27, 1921, p. 3; February 1, 1922, p. 14; February 8, 1922, p. 1.
27. *Fort Worth Star Telegram*, March 5, 1922, p. 11; August 17, 1921, p. 1; September 18, 1921, p. 1; August 6, 1921, p. 1; October 27, 1924, p. 1; *Fort Worth Press*, January 21, 1921, p. 1.
28. *Fort Worth Star Telegram*, March 5, 1922, p. 11; January 7, 1920, p. 1; February 11, 1922, p. 1; May 20, 1928, p. 4; July 6, 1926, p. 1.

Chapter Three

1. *Fort Worth Star Telegram*, July 19, 1921, p. 12; January 29, 1922, p. 2; August 6, 1924, p. 5; November 8, 2017, pp. 1A and 3A; Fort Worth Chamber of Commerce, *Fort Worth* (Fort Worth: Fort Worth Chamber of Commerce, 1924), p. 21, Briscoe Center for American History, University of Texas at Austin.
2. *New York Times*, April 27, 1921, p. 17; *Fort Worth Star Telegram*, February 25, 1990, section 1, pp. 1, 4, box Fort Worth, file Ku Klux Klan, Tarrant County Archives, Fort Worth; November 2, 1926, p. 12.

3. *Fort Worth Star Telegram*, July 19, 1921, p. 17; *New York Times*, February 25, 1928, p. 33.
4. *Fort Worth Press*, September 15, 1924, Research Data, Federal Writer's Project, Fort Worth and Tarrant County Texas, Local History Section, Fort Worth Public Library, 1941, p. 5129; *New York Times*, November 11, 1929, p. 93; *Fort Worth Star Telegram*, April 22, 1923, p. 6; May 25, 1928, p. 25.
5. *Fort Worth Star Telegram*, November 21, 1921, p. 14; October 17, 1926, Oil, Automobile, and Classified section, p. 2; October 29, 1926, p. 9; March 28, 1920, Picture Press Gravure section, p. 1; April 18, 1920, part 4, p. 11; June 28, 1920, p. 3; Christopher Connolly, "Meet the Man Believed to be the First Black Millionaire in Texas," Kera News, December 19, 2016, http://keranews.org/post/meet-man-believed-be-first-black-millionaire-texas.
6. *Fort Worth Star Telegram*, Real Estate and Classified section, p. 1; July 20, 1922, p. 11; *Fort Worth Press*, October 15, 1921, p. 1.
7. *Fort Worth Star Telegram*, May 16, 1922, p. 1; May 10, 1923, p. 1; May 11, 1923, p. 1; May 15, 1923, p. 8; June 1, 1924, p. 6; November 19, 1924, p. 20.
8. *Fort Worth Star Telegram*, April 30, 1926, p. 1; May 21, 1926, p. 1; August 23, 1932, pp. 1, 4; Richard Selcer, *A History of Fort Worth in Black and White: 165 Years of African-American Life* (Denton: University of North Texas Press, 2015), pp. 146–47. Selcer reported inaccurately that the *Star Telegram* did not report the bombing.
9. *Fort Worth Star Telegram*, June 5, 1920, p. 8; February 3, 1921, p. 4; February 4, 1921, p. 6; February 5, 1921, p. 1; February 21, 1921, p. 1; October 11, 1921, pp. 1, 4; *New York Times*, November 26, 1920, p. 14; October 8, 1921, p. 19; *Fort Worth Press*, October 7, 1921, p. 1.
10. *Fort Worth Star Telegram*, January 2, 1921, p. 6; October 9, 2002, section F, pp. 1, 4–6; *New York Times*, December 24, 1920, p. 8.
11. Barry T. Sandlin, "The 1921 Butcher Workmen Strike in Fort Worth, Texas" (MA thesis, University of Texas at Arlington, 1988), pp. 57–58, 67; *New York Times*, December 12, 1921, p. 21; February 14, 1922, p. 18; *Fort Worth Star Telegram*, October 9, 2002, section F, pp. 1, 4–6; December 7, 1921, p. 1; December 12, 1921, pp. 1, 2; February 13, 1922, pp. 1, 2; April 10, 1922, p. 1; October 1, 1922, p. 1; *Fort Worth Press*, December 12, 1921, p. 1.
12. *Fort Worth Star Telegram*, October 26, 1921, p. 1; June 30, 1923, p. 2; July 27, 1921, p. 1.
13. *New York Times*, July 24, 1922, p. 1; November 1, 1923, p. 1; November 29, 1923, p. 15; June 4, 1922, p. 2; January 10, 1924, p. 2; May 14, 1924, p. 3; Darwin Payne, *Big D: Triumphs and Troubles of an American Supercity in the 20th Century* (Dallas: Three Forks, 1994), p. 87.
14. *Fort Worth Star Telegram*, October 2, 1921, p. 1; October 4, 1921, p. 6; October 16, 1921, p. 1; *New York Times*, October 18, 1923, pp. 1, 3; May 24, 2017, p. 8DD.
15. Kevin G. Portz, "Political Turmoil in Dallas: The Electoral Whipping of the Dallas County Citizens League by the Ku Klux Klan," *Southwestern Historical Quarterly* 99, no. 2 (October 2015): p. 150–51; Payne, *Big D*, p. 74–77, 87; *New York Times*, July 24, 1922, p. 1; November 1, 1923, pp. 1, 3; *Fort Worth Star Telegram*, April 4, 1921, p. 1; May 24, 2017, p. 8DD.
16. Keavney, "Depression Era," p. 16; *Fort Worth Star Telegram*, September 23, 1922, p. 2; April 4, 1925, p. 1; August 20, 2014, p. 4B; May 24, 2017, p. 8DD. See *Fort Worth Star Telegram*, October 25, 1990, section 1, pp. 1, 4; February 25, 1990, section 1, pp. 1, 4–5, box Fort Worth, file Ku Klux Klan, Tarrant County Archives, Fort Worth.
17. George Kellam, "A Guide to the George W. Armstrong Papers" (Arlington: University of Texas Press, 2008), pp. 1–3, 9, 14, Special Collections, University of Texas at Arlington

Library; George W. Armstrong to A. R. Crawford, October 19, 1921, George W. Armstrong Papers, box 24, file KL, Special Collections, University of Texas at Arlington; Hollace Ava Weiner, *Jewish Junior League: The Rise and Demise of the Fort Worth Council of Jewish Women* (College Station: Texas A&M University Press, 2008), p. 48.

18. *Fort Worth Star Telegram*, February 25, 1990, section 1, pp. 1, 4–5, box Fort Worth, file Ku Klux Klan, Tarrant County Archives, Fort Worth; *Fort Worth Star Telegram*, October 18, 1921, p. 1. The author's grandfather was a Fort Worth Klansman.
19. *Fort Worth Star Telegram*, January 18, 1921, p. 1; February 17, 1922, pp. 1, 4, 6; June 9, 1923, pp. 1–2; December 3, 1924, p. 7; May 24, 2017, p. 8DD; Portz, "Political Turmoil in Dallas," p. 151; Ty Cashion, *The New Frontier: A Contemporary History of Fort Worth and Tarrant County* (San Antonio: Historical Publishing Network, 2006), pp. 65–66; Weiner, *Jewish Junior League*, p. 146n52.
20. *Fort Worth Star Telegram*, February 9, 1923, p. 6; May 5, 1924, p. 11, box Fort Worth, file Ku Klux Klan, Tarrant County Archives, Fort Worth; March 11, 1924, p. 13; Victoria Buenger and Walter Buenger, *Texas Merchant: Marvin Leonard and Fort Worth*, Kenneth E. Montague Series in Oil and Business History (College Station: Texas A&M University Press, 1998), pp. 63–64; Payne, *Big D*, p. 93.
21. *Fort Worth Star Telegram*, July 22, 2012, section B, pp. 1–3, box Fort Worth, file Ku Klux Klan, Tarrant County Archives, Fort Worth; April 24, 1922, p. 15; May 25, 1923, p. 20; October 26, 1921, p. 1; May 9, 1922, p. 7; April 23, 1922, p. 8; December 7, 1924, p. 1; August 8, 1921, p. 1; August 14, 1921, pp. 1, 6; August 15, 1921, p. 5; Payne, *Big D*, p. 80.
22. *Fort Worth Star Telegram*, February 25, 1990, section 1, pp. 1, 4–5, box Fort Worth, file Ku Klux Klan, Tarrant County Archives, Fort Worth; June 30, 1923, p. 2; October 20, 1923, p. 2; September 7, 1923, p. 1; March 11, 1924, p. 13; May 18, 1924, p. 1; November 6, 1924, p. 1; July 22, 2012, section B, pp. 1–3, box Fort Worth, file Ku Klux Klan file, Tarrant County Archives, Fort Worth; July 9, 1997, section B, p. 6, box Fort Worth, file Ku Klux Klan, Tarrant County Archives, Fort Worth; *Fort Worth Press*, May 19, 1924, box Fort Worth, file Ku Klux Klan, Tarrant County Archives, Fort Worth; Jones, *Renegades, Showmen and Angels*, p. 141; *New York Times*, November 7, 1924, p. 3; Buenger and Buenger, *Texas Merchant*, pp. 63–64; *Fort Worth Business Directory of 1928*, box Fort Worth, file Ku Klux Klan, Tarrant County Archives, Fort Worth.
23. *Fort Worth Star Telegram*, July 2, 1921, p. 1; July 6, 1921, pp. 1–2; August 7, 1921, p. 1; August 8, 1921, p. 1; August 11, 1921, p. 16; November 27, 1921, p. 1; September 13, 1922, p. 1; July 8, 1921, p. 4.
24. *Fort Worth Star Telegram*, July 27, 1921, p. 1; August 26, 1921, p. 4; April 21, 1922, p. 26; May 9, 1922, p. 7; Payne, *Big D*, pp. 83–86.
25. *New York Times*, November 1, 1923, pp. 1, 3; October 9, 1924, p. 26; August 24, 1924, pp. 1, 2; July 19, 1926, p. 15; August 3, 1926, p. 35; August 26, 1926, p. 3; Payne, *Big D*, p. 96; *Fort Worth Star Telegram*, May 24, 2017, p. 8DD.
26. Buenger and Buenger, *Texas Merchant*, pp. 63–64; Cashion, *New Frontier*, p. 66; Cervantez, "Lone Star Booster," p. 79; *Fort Worth Star Telegram*, August 3, 1925, pp. 1, 3.
27. *Fort Worth Star Telegram*, March 16, 1924, p. 8; September 8, 1924, p. 13; October 11, 1924, p. 1; January 29, 1922, p. 10; *New York Times*, August 2, 1926, p. 8.
28. *Fort Worth Star Telegram*, November 21, 1921, p. 14; September 1, 1929, p. 1; June 29, 1928, p. 14; McGown, *Fort Worth in Vintage Postcards*, p. 63; Selcer, *History of Fort Worth*, p. 170. For William McDonald, see Alwyn Barr and Robert A. Calvert, eds., *Black Leaders: Texans for Their Times* (Austin: Texas State Historical Association, 1981); William Oliver Bundy, *Life of William Madison McDonald, Ph.D.* (Fort Worth: Bunker, 1925).

29. *Fort Worth Star Telegram*, February 2, 2015, p. 6A; January 2, 1925, p. 5; July 3, 1920, p. 2; October 7, 1921, p. 24; July 4, 1928, p. 14; Young Men's Christian Association, *Fort Worth and Its Young Men's Christian Association: A Survey* (Fort Worth: Young Men's Christian Association, 1947), p. 43.
30. *Fort Worth City Council Minutes*, vol. A1, April 17, 1923; vol. A1, April 24, 1923; vol. A1, May 8, 1923; *Fort Worth Star Telegram*, May 16, 1925, p. 7.
31. Cheryl L. Simon, "Jim Hotel," Handbook of Texas Online, https://tshaonline.org/handbook/online/articles/xdj01.
32. *Fort Worth Star Telegram*, October 20, 1925, p. 19; April 1, 1928, p. 6; February 12, 1928, p. 6; April 2, 1929, p. 19; Reby Cary, *How We Got Over! Second Update on a Backward Look; A History of Blacks in Fort Worth* (Fort Worth: n.p., 2006), p. 59; Selcer, *History of Fort Worth*, pp. 183–84.

Chapter Four

1. *Fort Worth Star Telegram*, January 9, 1921, p. 8; August 6, 1922, p. 12; January 31, 1926, p. 14; May 17, 1929, p. 1; January 25, 1921, p. 1.
2. *Fourteenth Census of the United States* (Washington, DC: Government Printing Office, 1922), pp. 9:1447–48.
3. *Fort Worth Star Telegram*, July 16, 1921, p. 1; *Fourteenth Census*, p. 9:1447.
4. *Fort Worth Star Telegram*, November 8, 1923, p. 22; May 17, 1925, p. 1; May 18, 1925, p. 1; May 27, 1925, p. 1.
5. *Fort Worth Star Telegram*, June 28, 1925, p. 1; July 4, 1925, p. 8; July 2, 1926, p. 1; July 16, 1927, p. 1; July 17, 1927, p. 1; October 23, 1928, p. 4; May 8, 1926, p. 1; October 18, 2015, pp. 1, 5–6; Ady, "Our City," chap. 9, pp. 1–3; Richard Selcer, *Fort Worth: A Texas Original*, Fred Rider Cotton Popular History Series (Austin: Texas State Historical Association, 2004), p. 64; *New York Times*, May 15, 1926, p. 14.
6. *Fort Worth Star Telegram*, July 2, 1926, p. 1; November 28, 1926, p. 4; October 18, 2015, p. 5A; April 10, 1927, p. 6; May 5, 1929, p. 1; May 7, 1929, p. 11; June 10, 1929, p. 1; June 9, 1929, Auto section, p. 9; July 2, 1929, p. 23; August 23, 1929, p. 1; September 15, 1929, p. 1; June 29, 1937, p. 13; May 24, 2017, p. 7DD; Flemmons, *Amon*, p. 245. Texas Air Transport is listed as Texas Air Transit in some sources.
7. *Fort Worth Star Telegram*, March 24, 1929, p. 6; April 3, 1929, p. 1.
8. *Fort Worth Star Telegram*, December 31, 1921, p. 5; August 23, 1925, p. 2; May 2, 1920, part 2, p. 8; May 29, 1921, Manufacturers and Jobbers section, p. 2; December 30, 1923, pp. 1–2; February 13, 1924, p. 1; *New York Times*, February 27, 1921, p. 12; Fort Worth Chamber of Commerce, *Fort Worth in Brief*, p. 15.
9. *Fort Worth Star Telegram*, August 10, 1924, p. 11; November 21, 1920, part 5, pp. 3, 12; November 4, 1920, p. 5; January 4, 1920, part 4, p. 1; *Fort Worth City Council Minutes*, vol. A1, August 2, 1921.
10. *Fort Worth Star Telegram*, June 28, 1925, Oil and Auto Classified section, p. 16; October 11, 1925, p. 10; January 4, 1920, part 4, p. 1; December 11, 1921, p. 1; October 2, 1921, pp. 8, 10, 12; January 4, 1920, part 4, p. 1; December 5, 1920, p. 3; February 1, 1920, part 4, p. 1; February 3, 1920, p. 1; June 24, 1920, p. 20; December 1, 1920, p. 18; May 29, 1921, Souvenir section; May 31, 1921, p. 1; May 24, 2017, p. 6DD; *Fort Worth Press*, December 3, 1921, p. 1.
11. *Fort Worth Star Telegram*, December 30, 1923, p. 1; February 13, 1924, p. 1; December 30, 1923, p. 1; March 9, 1924, p. 1; April 1, 1924, p. 1; April 13, 1924, p. 7; May 4, 1924, p. 1;

August 16, 1924, p. 2; December 26, 1924, p. 19; McGown, *Fort Worth in Vintage Postcards*, p. 65.

12. *Fort Worth Star Telegram*, October 25, 1925, p. 1; November 3, 1925, p. 1; November 8, 1925, p. 1; April 24, 1927, Medical Arts section, p. 1; November 20, 1927, p. 1.
13. Fort Worth Chamber of Commerce, *Fort Worth in Brief*, p. 4; *Fort Worth Star Telegram*, February 20, 1924, p. 18; January 3, 1926, Finance and Business section, p. 2.
14. Keavney, "Depression Era," pp. 3–5; *New York Times*, July 23, 1922, p. 37; Liz Oliphant, *Ben E. Keith Company: The First One Hundred Years, 1906–2006* (Austin: Eakin, 2006), p. 23; *Fort Worth Star Telegram*, Twenty Years of Progress section, June 28, 1925, pp. 1–14.
15. Fort Worth Chamber of Commerce, *Fort Worth: The Capital City of a New Empire* (Fort Worth: Fort Worth Chamber of Commerce, 1927), pp. 1, 11; Historical Committee of the Fort Worth Petroleum Club, *Oil Legends of Fort Worth* (Fort Worth: Taylor, 1993), pp. 11–13, 23; Ady, "Our City," chap. 9, p. 2; *Fort Worth Star Telegram*, May 24, 2017, p. 3DD; June 25, 2017, pp. 1A and 5A; November 13, 2017, p. 5A.
16. *Fort Worth Star Telegram*, May 29, 1921, Oil and Gas section, p. 4; Manufacturers and Jobbers section, p. 2; June 28, 1925, Twenty Years of Progress section, pp. 1–14; Historical Committee of the Fort Worth Petroleum Club, *Oil Legends of Fort Worth*, pp. 11–13, 23; Fort Worth Chamber of Commerce, *Fort Worth in Brief*, pp. 4, 13; J'Nell Pate, *Livestock Legacy: The Fort Worth Stockyards, 1887–1987*, Centennial Series of the Association of Former Students, Texas A&M University (College Station: Texas A&M University Press, 1988), p. 121; Oliver Knight, *Fort Worth: Outpost on the Trinity* (Fort Worth: Texas Christian University Press, 1990), pp. 187–92.
17. Fort Worth Chamber of Commerce, *Fort Worth: Capital City*, pp. 1, 11; Ady, "Our City," chap. 9, p. 2; *Fort Worth Star Telegram*, June 25, 1928, Twenty Years of Progress section, pp. 1–14; *Fifteenth Census of the United States* (Washington, DC: Government Printing Office, 1933), p. 1:30.
18. Knight, *Fort Worth*, pp. 187–92; *Fort Worth Star Telegram*, February 6, 2017, p. 6A; June 25, 2017, pp. 1A and 5A; *New York Times*, June 7, 1921, p. 6; April 7, 1923, p. 15; January 6, 1924, p. 185; October 25, 1923, p. 4; October 9, 1924, p. 16; May 24, 2017, p. 3DD; Selcer, *Fort Worth*, p. 174.
19. Knight, *Fort Worth*, p. 198; Keavney, "Depression Era," p. 7; *New York Times*, April 6, 1923, p. 8; February 2, 1923, p. 17; July 11, 1923, p. 40; February 16, 1923, p. 7; November 22, 1923, pp. 1, 4; October 9, 1924, p. 16.
20. *Fort Worth Press*, November 23, 1921, pp. 1, 8; City of Fort Worth Records, Mayor and Council Proceedings, box 1, folder January 1920, Local History Section, Fort Worth Public Library; *Fort Worth Star Telegram*, January 19, 1921, p. 4; May 24, 2017, p. 7DD; *Fort Worth News Tribune*, January 11, 1980, William E. Jary Papers, box 22, Special Collections, University of Texas at Arlington Library.
21. Undated clipping from *Fort Worth Star Telegram*, William E. Jary Papers, box 21, Special Collections, University of Texas at Arlington Library; *Fort Worth Star Telegram*, January 24, 1922, p. 1; August 24, 1920, p. 1; December 19, 1923, p. 1; December 20, 1923, p. 1; December 22, 1923, p. 1; December 23, 1923, p. 1; December 31, 1923, p. 1; January 5, 1924, p. 1; January 23, 1924, p. 1; January 26, 1924, p. 1; February 1, 1924, p. 1; February 23, 1924, p. 1; March 22, 1924, p. 1; June 7, 1924, p. 2; December 5, 1926, p. 5; February 20, 1931, pp. 1, 8.
22. *Fort Worth Press*, December 10, 1921, p. 1; *Fort Worth Star Telegram*, April 6, 1922, p. 10; March 3, 1922, p. 15; Edward Henry Manwarring, "A Brief History the Union Gospel

Mission" (MA thesis, Southwestern Baptist Theological Seminary, 1928), pp. 10–12, 26–27.

23. *Fort Worth Star Telegram*, April 3, 1921, p. 11; May 21, 1921, p. 1; May 1, 1921, pp. 1, 6; May 6, 1921, p. 1; May 7, 1921, p. 1; May 10, 1921, p. 2; May 14, 1921, p. 1; June 18, 1921, p. 10; October 10, 1921, p. 2.
24. *Fort Worth Star Telegram*, March 4, 1918, p. 1; May 29, 1921, section 2, p. 4; October 22, 1921, p. 5; January 19, 1921, p. 4; Fort Worth Chamber of Commerce, *Fort Worth: Capital City*, pp. 9–10.
25. *New York Times*, April 11, 1920, p. 2; November 10, 1921, p. 21; November 19, 1921, p. 8; November 19, 1921, pp. 1, 6; *Fort Worth Press*, December 5, 1921, p. 1; December 7, 1921, p. 1; Sandlin, "1921 Butcher Workmen Strike," pp. 54, 62; *Fort Worth Star Telegram*, March 8, 1921, p. 11; March 14, 1921, p. 10; March 17, 1921, p. 1; May 3, 1921, p. 1; November 10, 1921, p. 6; November 25, 1921, p. 1; December 5, 1921, p. 1; December 6, 1921, p. 1; December 7, 1921, p. 1; January 5, 1922, p. 1; January 2, 1922, p. 12; December 1, 1922, p. 1.
26. *Fort Worth Star Telegram*, July 27, 1922, p. 5; July 28, 1922, p. 1; August 19, 1922, p. 1; September 25, 1922, p. 1; August 23, 1922, pp. 2, 4; August 25, 1922, p. 1; August 20, 1922, p. 1; May 21, 1921, p. 1; July 23, 1921, p. 1; July 19, 1921, p. 12; July 24, 1923, p. 18.
27. *Fort Worth Star Telegram*, December 26, 1923, p. 1; January 5, 1924, p. 1; March 20, 1923, p. 1; March 21, 1923, p. 1; March 22, 1923, p. 1; March 23, 1923, p. 1; March 3, 1922, p. 15; March 30, 1921, p. 3.
28. *Fort Worth Star Telegram*, July 20, 1923, p. 19; July 21, 1923, p. 1; September 12, 1922, pp. 1, 4.
29. *Fort Worth Star Telegram*, December 5, 1926, p. 5; May 24, 2017, p. 6DD; December 20, 2017, p. 5A; Buenger and Buenger, *Texas Merchant*, pp. 57–58, 67–68, 73, 78.
30. Buenger and Buenger, *Texas Merchant*, pp. 32–34; Fort Worth Chamber of Commerce, *Statistical Handbook*.
31. *New York Times*, September 28, 1925, p. 21; *Fort Worth Star Telegram*, April 6, 1925, p. 5; January 8, 1930, p. 1; February 16, 1930, Oil and Auto Classified section, p. 5.
32. Keavney, "Depression Era," pp. 3, 5; *Fort Worth Star Telegram*, January 1, 1928, p. 1; January 23, 1927, pp. 1, 6; June 10, 1928, part 2, p. 1; September 29, 2014, p. 5B. As a sixteen-year-old, the author worked for one week as an usher at the Worth Theater.
33. Fort Worth Chamber of Commerce, *Statistical Handbook*; *Fort Worth Star Telegram*, November 3, 1928, p. 1; May 5, 1929, part 2, p. 1; January 21, 1929, p. 13.
34. *Fort Worth Star Telegram*, June 10, 1928, part 2, p. 1; September 28, 1928, pp. 24–25; September 28, 1928, Montgomery Ward's section, pp. 1–16; September 30, 1928, pp. 1, 4; February 26, 1929, p. 4; October 5, 2015, p. 4A; October 6, 1929, Blackstone Hotel section, pp. 1–14; McGown, *Fort Worth in Vintage Postcards*, pp. 65–78.
35. *Fort Worth Star Telegram*, July 21, 1929, pp. 1, 2.
36. *Fort Worth Star Telegram*, July 2, 1924, p. 9; August 8, 1926, Oil and Auto Classified section, p. 6; April 1, 1927, p. 1; December 16, 1928, Oil and Auto Classified section, p. 13; April 22, 1928, Better Homes section, p. 3; Fort Worth Chamber of Commerce, *Statistical Handbook*.
37. *Fort Worth Star Telegram*, December 29, 1929, part 2, p. 1; December 11, 1929, p. 10; December 12, 1929, p. 1.
38. Fort Worth Chamber of Commerce, *Statistical Handbook*; George Strayer, *Survey of Schools of Fort Worth, Texas* (New York: Teachers College, Colombia University, 1931), p. 88, Briscoe Center for American History, University of Texas at Austin; Keavney,

"Depression Era," pp. 3, 5; *Fort Worth Star Telegram*, August 9, 1927, p. 26; January 1, 1928, p. 1.

Chapter Six

1. *New York Times*, May 29, 1930, p. 48; July 17, 1930, p. 4.
2. *Fort Worth Star Telegram*, June 12, 1930, p. 1; June 17, 1930, p. 7; August 18, 1930, p. 1; August 28, 1941, p. 8; Strayer, *Survey of Schools*, pp. 87–92.
3. Buenger and Buenger, *Texas Merchant*, pp. 73, 78, 85; *Fort Worth Star Telegram*, December 28, 1930, part 2, p. 1; January 1, 1937, p. 7; January 26, 1930, p. 7; January 29, 1930, pp. 1, 4; March 29, 1930, p. 1; October 1, 1930, pp. 1–2; October 23, 1930, p. 1; August 31, 1930, Fair Building section, p. 1; November 16, 1930, part 2, p. 1; May 24, 2017, p. 8DD; McGown, *Fort Worth in Vintage Postcards*, p. 77; Fort Worth Chamber of Commerce, *This Month in Fort Worth* 13, no. 3 (March 1939): p. 15.
4. David Alvin Henderson, "Fort Worth and the Depression, 1929–1933" (MA thesis, Texas Christian University, 1964) pp. 30, 32, 34; Keavney, "Depression Era," p. 180; Richard Kenneth Horner, "Fort Worth during the Depression, September 1, 1932, to August 31, 1933" (MA thesis, University of Texas at Austin, 1974), pp. 5–7; *Fort Worth Star Telegram*, December 28, 1930, part 2, p. 1; January 1, 1931, p. 7; September 17, 1931, p. 1; May 4, 2016, pp. 1A and 5A; June 2, 1933, p. 1; December 27, 1934, p. 1; December 27, 1934, p. 1; Wake, "Study in Conservative Politics," p. 19; Cashion, *New Frontier*, p. 68; Fort Worth Chamber of Commerce, "Five Years of Progress," *Fort Worth Chamber of Commerce News* 5, no. 1 (January 1932): pp. preface, foreword, 2–5, 19; Fort Worth Chamber of Commerce, *This Month in Fort Worth* 13, no. 3 (March 1939): p. 15.
5. Henderson, "Fort Worth," pp. 24 and 26; Cashion, *New Frontier*, p. 68; "Five Years of Progress," pp. preface, foreword, 2–5, 19; "TRWD History"; *Fort Worth Star Telegram*, October 23, 1930, p. 1; January 16, 1932, p. 31; June 1, 1931, p. 1; March 4, 1932, p. 25; April 19, 1932, p. 1; April 21, 1932, pp. 1, 4; November 8, 1938, p. 10; *New York Times*, June 2, 1931, p. 60; Fort Worth Chamber of Commerce, *This Month in Fort Worth* 12, no. 7 (July 1938): pp. 4–5.
6. *Fort Worth Star Telegram*, September 30, 1930, p. 24; November 23, 1930, p. 4; March 12, 1931, p. 10; September 6, 2016, p. 4A; November 15, 2016, p. 4A; Undated clipping from *Fort Worth Star Telegram*, William E. Jary Papers, box 21, Special Collections, University of Texas at Arlington Library; Keavney, "Depression Era," p. 76; Letter, Alvin H. Scaff to Mr. Coney [Librarian at University of Texas at Austin], November 18, 1936, Woodman Papers, box 2, file 163-2-16, Special Collections, University of Texas at Arlington Library.
7. *Fort Worth Star Telegram*, April 3, 1931, p. 14; October 4, 1937, p. 1; Fort Worth Chamber of Commerce, *Fort Worth* (1934), p. 14; *New York Times*, July 24, 1934, p. 9.
8. Buenger and Buenger, *Texas Merchant*, pp. 73 and 78; Farman, *Fort Worth Club*, p. 104.
9. *New York Times*, February 2, 1930, p. 14; February 3, 1930, p. 17; *Fort Worth Star Telegram*, March 9, 1930, pp. 1, 6; April 22, 1930, p. 1; June 18, 1931, p. 1; December 4, 1934, p. 1; Keavney, "Depression Era," p. 57–59, 64, 67.
10. George V. Schmidt, interviewed by W. A. Schmidt, March 2, 1975, transcript, Ruby Schmidt Collection of Bicentennial Interviews, Oral History of Fort Worth, Inc., Tarrant County Archives, Fort Worth; Cervantez, "Lone Star Booster," p. 102; J'Nell Pate, *Hazel Vaughn Leigh and the Fort Worth Boys Club* (Fort Worth: Texas Christian University Press, 2000), p. 23; *Fort Worth Star Telegram*, February 19, 1930, pp. 1, 4; May 24, 2017,

p. 8DD; Flemmons, *Amon*, pp. 294–95; Keavney, "Depression Era," pp. 53, 59–60; *New York Times*, March 13, 1932, p. 85.

11. *New York Times*, July 17, 1930, p. 31; April 9, 1932, p. 23; *Fort Worth Star Telegram*, March 1, 1931, p. 1; *Fort Worth Chamber of Commerce 1936*, file Fort Worth 1930, Business Organizations: Chamber of Commerce-Fort Worth-Industrial, Tarrant County Archives, Fort Worth; Fort Worth Chamber of Commerce, "Fort Worth: Where the West Begins," *Fort Worth Chamber of Commerce News*, March 1936, file Fort Worth, Business Organizations: Chamber of Commerce, Tarrant County Archives, Fort Worth; Fort Worth Chamber of Commerce, *Industrial Fort Worth* (Fort Worth: Fort Worth Chamber of Commerce, [1940?]), p. 9; Fort Worth Chamber of Commerce, *This Month in Fort Worth* 12, no. 2 (February 1938): p. 8; Fort Worth Chamber of Commerce, *This Month in Fort Worth* 13, no. 6 (June 1929): p. 6.
12. *Fort Worth Star Telegram*, February 24, 1932, p. 34; March 4, 1932, p. 25; April 19, 1932, pp. 1, 4; April 21, 1932, pp. 1, 4; *New York Times*, July 24, 1934, p. 9; Buenger and Buenger, *Texas Merchant*, pp. 73 and 78.
13. Harris Methodist Fort Worth Hospital, *The History of Harris Methodist Fort Worth Hospital* (Fort Worth: Harris Methodist Fort Worth Hospital, 2006), pp. 17–19; McGown, *Fort Worth in Vintage Postcards*, pp. 63 and 84.
14. *Monthly Business Record of the Federal Reserve Bank of Dallas* 20, no. 10 (December 1, 1935): p. 7, National Recovery Administration (NRA) Papers, HM 2008, E9NRF-1, Group Nine, Records, box 3, National Archives at Fort Worth; Horner, "Fort Worth," pp. 2–3; *New York Times*, November 12, 1933, p. 17.
15. *Fort Worth Star Telegram*, April 4, 1934, p. 22; October 28, 1937, p. 1; March 10, 1936, p. 1; October 23, 1939, p. 8; April 10, 2017, p. 6A; Fort Worth Chamber of Commerce, *Fort Worth Chamber of Commerce News* 9, no. 1 (January 1936): p. 6. We are left to wonder where the other $1 million went.
16. *Fort Worth Star Telegram*, November 10, 1931, p. 1; November 25, 1941, p. 1; *New York Times*, November 3, 1938, p. 15; Fort Worth Chamber of Commerce, "Them as Has, Gits," *This Month in Fort Worth* 12, no. 7 (July 1938): p. 8; Marvin Lee Downing, "The P. W. A. and the Effort to Secure the Fort Worth Public Library Building" (MA thesis, Texas Christian University, 1963), p. 11; Carrie Taylor, "Texas Highways by the Number," *Houston Chronicle*, August 28, 2013, https://www.chron.com/news/houston-traffic/slideshow/Texas-highways-By-the-numbers-69108.php.
17. Statement dated January 20, 1927, C. W. Woodman Papers, box 2, file 163-2-13, Special Collections, University of Texas at Arlington Library; Leslie T. Smith, interviewed by J. A. Burgess, transcript, Ruby Schmidt Collection of Bicentennial Interviews, Oral History of Fort Worth, Inc., Tarrant County Archives, Fort Worth; Wake, "Study in Conservative Politics," p. 30; *Fort Worth Star Telegram*, March 12, 1931, p. 10; February 24, 1932, pp. 1, 4; December 23, 1933, p. 1; May 1, 1940, pp. 1, 4; September 26, 2016, p. 4A; Horner, "Fort Worth," pp. 21–25; Keavney, "Depression Era," pp. 100, 140–41; Downing, "P. W. A.," p. 9; A. H. Flickwir, *Annual Report of the Department of Health* (Fort Worth: n.p., 1937), p. 1; Young Men's Christian Association, *Fort Worth*, p. 32; Fort Worth Chamber of Commerce, *This Month in Fort Worth* 13, no. 3 (March 1939): p. 15.
18. *New York Times*, November 17, 1935, p. 107.
19. Sadye Hailey Rippy, interviewed by Jo Buck Jones, February 21, 1975, transcript, Ruby Schmidt Collection of Bicentennial Interviews, Oral History of Fort Worth, Inc., Tarrant County Archives, Fort Worth; Gail A. Clement, "Politics of Dissent: W. J. Hammond, City Councilman and Mayor, 1935–1938" (MA thesis, Texas Christian University, 1967),

p. 13; *Fort Worth Star Telegram*, December 29, 1933, pp. 1, 4; August 20, 1934, p. 1; February 24, 1932, pp. 1, 4; March 3, 1932, pp. 1, 4; March 18, 1932, p. 1; December 23, 1933, p. 1; September 26, 2016, p. 4A; Keavney, "Depression Era," p. 102; Henderson, "Fort Worth," p. 79; Flickwir, *Annual Report*, p. 1.

20. *Fort Worth Star Telegram*, June 1, 1932, p. 18; Interview, June 14, 1972, Rail Yards Folder, Alice Leavy interview transcript of October 1973, pp. 3–5, Oral History Project: The Depression, box 1, file Alice Leavy, Oral History Project, Local History Section, Fort Worth Public Library; *Fort Worth Press*, October 9, 1923; December 1, 1923, p. 10, file Depression 1929–40, Tarrant County Archives, Fort Worth; Keavney, "Depression Era," p. 110.
21. Pate, *Hazel Vaughn Leigh*, p. 37; Flickwir, *Annual Report*, p. 1; *Fort Worth Star Telegram*, December 24, 1932, p. 1–2; December 23, 1933, p. 1; *New York Times*, March 16, 1941, p. 206; September 26, 2016, p. 4A; December 19, 2016, p. 4A.
22. Henderson, "Fort Worth," pp. 67–68; Sherrie S. McElroy, "In the Interests of the Children," in *Grace and Gumption: Stories of Fort Worth Women*, ed. Katie Sherrod (Fort Worth: Texas Christian University Press, 2007), pp. 109–10; Cashion, *New Frontier*, p. 71; *Fort Worth Star Telegram*, May 24, 2017, p. 10DD.
23. *Fort Worth Star Telegram*, August 21, 1939, pp. 1, 4; October 26, 1939, pp. 1, 6; October 27, 1939, pp. 1, 10; November 1, 1939, pp. 1, 4.
24. *Fort Worth Star Telegram*, February 7, 1933, p. 1; July 8, 1936, pp. 1, 4; Arthur Randell interview transcript conducted June 6, 1972, pp. 3–5, Oral History Project: The Depression, box 1, file Arthur Randell, Local History Section, Fort Worth Public Library.
25. *Fort Worth Star Telegram*, April 7, 1932, p. 20; June 2, 1932, p. 19.
26. *Fort Worth Star Telegram*, November 15, 1934, p. 4; December 19, 1934, p. 1; May 23, 1935, p. 1; September 9, 1936, pp. 1, 4.
27. *Fort Worth Star Telegram*, March 22, 1931, part 1, p. 1; August 14, 1935, pp. 1, 4; January 1, 1936, p. 5; *New York Times*, November 10, 1938, p. 56.
28. *Fort Worth Star Telegram*, June 1, 1932, p. 18; June 26, 1933, p. 1; September 7, 1933, p. 1; September 8, 1933, pp. 1, 4; September 11, 1933, pp. 1, 4; Horner, "Fort Worth," p. 39; Dick J. Reavis, "Fort Worth's Red Scare," *Texas Observer*, September 2, 2011, https://www.texasobserver.org/fort-worths-red-scare/.
29. *Fort Worth Star Telegram*, June 12, 1937, p. 1; June 24, 1937, pp. 1, 4; June 15, 1938, p. 5.
30. *Fort Worth Star Telegram*, March 20, 1940, p. 1; March 21, 1940, p. 1; March 22, 1940, pp. 1, 6.
31. *Fort Worth Star Telegram*, January 6, 1941, p. 18; February 2, 1939, p. 1; January 8, 1940, pp. 1–2.
32. *Fort Worth Star Telegram*, January 25, 1940, pp. 1, 6; November 27, 1940, p. 1.

Chapter Seven

1. *Fort Worth Star Telegram*, September 15, 1937, pp. 1, 4; April 16, 1938, p. 1; April 5, 1937, p. 1; April 7, 1937, pp. 1, 3; Clement, "Politics of Dissent," pp. 25–26.
2. *Fort Worth Star Telegram*, July 8, 1937, p. 1; September 28, 1937, pp. 1, 4; October 29, 1937, p. 1; December 4, 1937, pp. 1–2; May 11, 1938, p. 1; May 12, 1938, p. 6; June 21, 1938, p. 1; June 22, 1938, p. 1; June 28, 1938, p. 1; July 15, 1938, p. 1; July 25, 1938, pp. 1, 4; July 27, 1938, pp. 1, 4.
3. *Fort Worth Star Telegram*, May 13, 1937, p. 1; May 20, 1937, p. 1; May 21, 1937, pp. 1, 4, 19; February 14, 1940, pp. 1, 4; July 17, 1940, p. 1.

4. *Fort Worth Star Telegram*, June 28, 1939, p. 1; June 30, 1939, pp. 1, 6; July 3, 1939, pp. 1, 4; June 23, 1931, p. 1.
5. *Fort Worth Star Telegram*, April 28, 1937, p. 1; May 4, 1937, p. 1; May 15, 1937, p. 1; June 1, 1937, pp. 1, 4; June 8, 1937, p. 1; June 9, 1937, pp. 1, 4; September 16, 1937, p. 28; Angie Smith, "More Than a Settlement: The Condensed History of White Settlement, Texas" (student paper for History 4970, Texas Christian University, n.d.), p. 5, Local History Section, Fort Worth Public Library.
6. *Fort Worth Star Telegram*, May 3, 1941, pp. 1–2; May 23, 1941, p. 10; Texas History Class of Miss Clare Head, "History of White Settlement," Fort Worth, Brewer High School, 1952, Local History Section, Fort Worth Public Library.
7. Wake, "Study in Conservative Politics," p. 29; City of Fort Worth, *City of Fort Worth Municipal Life: 1931–1937* (Fort Worth: Bureau of Management Research, 1937), pp. 41–42; *Fort Worth Star Telegram*, November 10, 1930, p. 1; July 27, 1931, pp. 1, 4; September 2, 1931, pp. 1, 6; February 12, 1935, p. 7; May 24, 2017, p. 10DD.
8. *Fort Worth Star Telegram*, April 5, 1932, p. 4; June 22, 1932, p. 18; October 13, 1932, pp. 1, 6; May 24, 2017, p. 10DD.
9. *Fort Worth Star Telegram*, June 7, 1934, p. 1; January 30, 1935, p. 6; June 6, 1935, p. 1; June 5, 1935, p. 1; May 24, 1933, p. 1; July 27, 1931, pp. 1, 4; Keavney, "Depression Era," p. 127.
10. Strayer, *Survey of Schools*, pp. 39, 99, 312; *Fort Worth Star Telegram*, September 12, 1931, p. 1; July 14, 1939, p. 1; July 19, 1937, p. 18; April 1, 1938, p. 21; Wake, "Study in Conservative Politics," p. 29.
11. Cashion, *New Frontier*, p. 69; Marcel D. Ezell, "Progressivism in Fort Worth Politics, 1935–1938" (MA thesis, Texas Christian University, 1963), pp. 3–4; *Fort Worth Star Telegram*, February 1, 1933, p. 8; Flickwir, *Annual Report*, p. 1.
12. *Fort Worth Star Telegram*, April 3, 1937, p. 10; September 3, 1937, pp. 1, 4; August 24, 1937, p. 1; July 5, 1938, p. 20; July 15, 1939, pp. 1–2; December 20, 1939, p. 1.
13. *New York Times*, April 28, 1931, p. 29; *Fort Worth Star Telegram*, July 20, 1934, p. 1.
14. *Fort Worth Star Telegram*, July 30, 1934, p. 1; August 8, 1934, pp. 1, 4; August 15, 1934, p. 4; Lewis (engineer) to Fairtrace (city manager), December 1, 1935; Superseding Grant Agreement, PWA Docket Number 507, April 1, 1936; Specifications and Contract Documents for Improvements to Present Sewage Treatment Plant filed with PWA, February 18, 1936, pp. 13–15; City of Fort Worth Records, Mayor and Council Proceedings, Transportation and Public Works, Series I, PWA Projects, Water and Sewer Projects, 1936–50, box I, D. L. Local History Section, Fort Worth Public Library.
15. *Fort Worth Star Telegram*, July 20, 1934, p. 1; March 10, 1936, pp. 1, 4; November 9, 1937, p. 1; November 10, 1937, p. 9; January 20, 1938, p. 2.
16. *Fort Worth Star Telegram*, March 10, 1936, pp. 1, 4; October 22, 1937, p. 1; January 3, 1939, p. 1; March 24, 1939, pp. 1, 8–9; March 10, 1936, p. 1; October 28, 1937, p. 1; December 31, 1937, p. 1; January 15, 1938, pp. 1–2; January 17, 1938, pp. 1–2; February 24, 1938, p. 1; March 19, 1938, p. 1; March 21, 1938, p. 1; June 23, 2014, p. 4B; June 20, 2011, box Buildings: Fort Worth Post Office, file 1930, Tarrant County Archives, Fort Worth.
17. *New York Times*, June 30, 1932, p. 16; August 2, 1936, p. 147; Clay Reynolds and Marie-Madeleine Schein, *A Hundred Years of Heroes: A History of the Southwestern Exposition and Livestock Show* (Fort Worth: Texas Christian University Press, 1995), pp. 173–76; Jan Jones, *Billy Rose Presents . . . Casa Mañana* (Fort Worth: Texas Christian University Press, 1999), p. 7; *Fort Worth Star Telegram*, July 8, 1935, pp. 1–2; July 18, 2016, p. 4A; August 28, 1935, pp. 1, 4; September 11, 1935, p. 1; November 14, 1935, pp. 1, 4. Also

see Jacob W. Olmstead, "From Old South to Modern West: Fort Worth's Celebration of the Texas State Centennial and the Shaping of an Urban Identity and Image" (PhD diss., Texas Christian University, 2011).

18. *Fort Worth Star Telegram*, March 10, 1936, p. 1; March 4, 1937, p. 6; March 5, 1937, p. 21; March 6, 1937, p. 1; June 20, 2011, box Buildings: Fort Worth Post Office, file 1930, Tarrant County Archives, Fort Worth; Olmstead, "From Old South."
19. Reynolds and Schein, *Hundred Years of Heroes*, pp. 173–76; Cervantez, "Lone Star Booster," pp. 97 and 133–36; *Fort Worth Star Telegram*, July 20, 1935, p. 1; March 10, 1936, p. 1; December 7, 1935, p. 1; December 13, 1935, p. 1; March 9, 1937, p. 6; Debbie M. Liles, *Will Rogers Coliseum*, Images of America Series (Charleston, SC: Arcadia, 2012), p. 39; Ann Arnold, *Gamblers and Gangsters: Fort Worth's Jacksboro Highway in the 1940s and 1950s* (Austin: Eakin, 1998), pp. 4–7; Jones, *Billy Rose Presents*, pp. 5, 7; City of Fort Worth, *City of Fort Worth*, p. 7; *New York Times*, August 2, 1936, p. 147.
20. *Fort Worth Star Telegram*, March 17, 1936, p. 1; March 9, 1936, p. 1; March 26, 1936, p. 24; May 11, 2016, p. 3A; March 14, 1936, p. 1; July 1, 1936, p. 1; July 3, 1936, p. 8; July 9, 1936, p. 1; May 8, 1936, p. 1; May 24, 2017, p. 10DD; Jones, *Billy Rose Presents*, pp. xi–xiii, 2, 25; Liles, *Will Rogers Coliseum*, pp. 23, 43–44; Arnold, *Gamblers and Gangsters*, pp. 4–8; Porterfield, *Loose Herd of Texans*, p. 80; Brian Cervantez, "For the Exclusive Benefit of Fort Worth," *Southwestern Historical Quarterly* 99, no. 2 (October 2015): p. 135; Cook, *Brief History*, p. 55; *New York Times*, July 19, 1936, p. 1.
21. Jones, *Billy Rose Presents*, pp. xi–xiii, 2, 25; McGown, *Fort Worth in Vintage Postcards*, pp. 87–88; *Fort Worth Star Telegram*, March 26, 1936, p. 24; July 18, 2016, p. 4A; September 6, 1936, p. 1; July 17, 1936, p. 1; July 18, 1936, pp. 1–2; July 10, 1936, p. 26; November 3, 1936, p. 1; Liles, *Will Rogers Coliseum*, p. 29.
22. Arnold, *Gamblers and Gangsters*, pp. 4–6; *Fort Worth Star Telegram*, March 23, 1936, p. 7; May 11, 1936, p. 11; May 25, 1936, p. 8; July 22, 2013, p. 4B; November 2, 1936, p. 6; *New York Times*, May 24, 1936, p. 166; July 20, 1936, p. 1; August 10, 1936, p. 5; August 7, 1936, p. 22; September 22, 1936, pp. 1–2; Jones, *Billy Rose Presents*, pp. 89–94.
23. *Fort Worth Star Telegram*, July 18, 2016, p. 4A; December 10, 1936, p. 5; March 9, 1937, p. 6; *New York Times*, July 30, 1936, p. 22; Jones, *Billy Rose Presents*, pp. 99, 101–3; Cook, *Brief History*, p. 55.
24. *Fort Worth Star Telegram*, June 25, 1937, pp. 1, 19; April 15, 1937, p. 2; April 24, 1937, p. 1; August 6, 1937, p. 26; July 29, 1938, pp. 1, 4; September 27, 1937, pp. 1, 4; August 22, 1939, p. 5; July 21, 1939, pp. 1, 4, 16; August 4, 1939, p. 1; *New York Times*, September 9, 1937, p. 21; June 5, 2017, p. 5A; Jones, *Billy Rose Presents*, pp. xi–xiii, p. 25; *This Week in Fort Worth* 12, no. 9 (September 1939): p. 3.
25. *Fort Worth Star Telegram*, January 10, 1930, p. 1; January 22, 1930, pp. 1, 4; May 4, 1930, p. 1; January 24, 1936, p. 23; Fort Worth Chamber of Commerce, *Fort Worth* (1934), pp. 6–7; Fort Worth Chamber of Commerce, *This Month in Fort Worth* 12, no. 8 (August 1938); Malone, *Country Music*, pp. 160–64.
26. *Fort Worth Star Telegram*, April 13, 1930, part 2, p. 1; July 9, 2018, p. 4A; *New York Times*, September 29, 1940, p. 122; July 14, 1941, p. 7; July 19, 1941, p. 7; July 21, 1941, p. 5; October 31, 2016, p. 4A.
27. *Fort Worth Star Telegram*, April 30, 1934, p. 1; May 1, 1934, p. 20; August 23, 1938, p. 1; March 14, 1941, pp. 1, 4.
28. *Fort Worth Star Telegram*, April 6, 1938, p. 31; January 24, 1936, p. 23; *New York Times*, March 8, 1934, p. 28; July 13, 1940, p. 15; April 2, 1935, p. 11.

Chapter Eight

1. Horner, "Fort Worth," p. 9; *Fort Worth Star Telegram*, March 24, 1931, pp. 1, 4; January 19, 1937, p. 7; March 29, 1935, p. 4; January 18, 1939, p. 4; January 2, 1939, p. 1; November 1, 1931, p. 1; November 26, 1931, p. 1; *Annual Report of the Police Department of the City of Fort Worth* (Fort Worth: n.p., 1932), pp. 6–9, Briscoe Center for American History, University of Texas at Austin.
2. *Fort Worth Star Telegram*, December 31, 1932, pp. 1–2; March 24, 1931, pp. 1, 4; January 1, 1934, p. 11; January 5, 1934, p. 18; January 1, 1936, p. 1; *New York Times*, March 30, 1933, p. 8; *Annual Report of the Police Department* (1932), pp. 6–9, Briscoe Center for American History, University of Texas at Austin; Flickwir, *Annual Report*, p. 1, Briscoe Center for American History, University of Texas at Austin; *Annual Report of the Police Department of the City of Fort Worth* (Fort Worth: n.p., 1938), p. 7, Briscoe Center for American History, University of Texas at Austin.
3. *New York Times*, March 30, 1938, p. 8; *Fort Worth Star Telegram*, June 29, 1934, p. 25.
4. *Fort Worth Star Telegram*, September 25, 1930, pp. 1, 4; January 8, 1934, pp. 1, 4; January 12, 1934, p. 1; January 26, 1934, p. 1.
5. Keavney, "Depression Era," p. 46; *Annual Report of the Police Department* (1932), pp. 6–9; *Fort Worth Star Telegram*, March 24, 1931, pp. 1, 4; January 14, 1935, p. 1; January 15, 1935, p. 13; March 19, 1940, p. 1; January 18, 1939, p. 4.
6. *New York Times*, April 11, 1930, p. 34; April 18, 1930, p. 18; Blanche Caldwell Barrow, *My Life with Bonnie and Clyde*, ed. John Neal Phillips (Norman: University of Oklahoma Press, 2004), pp. 254–55n22; *Dallas Times Herald*, April 17, 1930; *Fort Worth Star Telegram*, April 10, 1930, pp. 1, 6; April 17, 1930, pp. 1, 4; April 18, 1930, p. 1; April 20, 1930, pp. 1, 6; April 21, 1930, p. 1; June 4, 1930, p. 1; October 16, 1930, p. 1; December 5, 1930, pp. 1, 4; June 3, 1931, p. 1; September 28, 1931, p. 1; April 27, 1932, p. 1.
7. *Fort Worth Star Telegram*, January 3, 1935, p. 1; *New York Times*, April 18, 1930, p. 30.
8. *Fort Worth Star Telegram*, August 9, 1930, pp. 1–2; August 10, 1930, pp. 1, 6; October 3, 1930, p. 1; *New York Times*, August 10, 1930, p. 1; Pate, *Livestock Legacy*, pp. 157–58; Barrow, *My Life with Bonnie and Clyde*, p. 255n22.
9. Percy Wyly, "Memo on Robberies Using Nitroglycerin in Fort Worth and Dallas," FBI Memorandum on Dallas and Fort Worth, Texas, Bank Robberies, July 26, 1946, box GA 212, Special Collections, University of Texas at Arlington Library.
10. *Fort Worth Star Telegram*, June 20, 2011, file Buildings: Fort Worth Post Office, Tarrant County Archives, Fort Worth; July 10, 1933, pp. 1, 5; July 11, 1933, pp. 1, 4; July 13, 1933, pp. 1, 4; July 2, 1933, p. 1; February 24, 1934, p. 1; April 3, 1934, p. 1; June 16, 1934, pp. 1–2; September 23, 1936, pp. 1, 4; October 12, 2016, p. 4DD; Cashion, *New Frontier*, pp. 71–72; Cook and Yarborough, *Prohibition in Dallas*, pp. 35–36.
11. *Fort Worth Star Telegram*, January 19, 1933, pp. 1, 4; September 26, 1933, p. 1; December 23, 1933, p. 1; April 2, 1934, pp. 1, 4; May 21, 1934, p. 20; May 22, 1934, pp. 1, 5; May 24, 1934, pp. 1, 6; May 26, 1934, pp. 1–2; May 31, 1934, pp. 1, 4; October 12, 2016, p. 5DD; *New York Times*, April 2, 1934, p. 5; May 22, 1934, p. 16; May 24, 1934, p. 3; "Clyde Champion Barrow Fingerprint Chart, 01/22/1928- Fort Worth, Texas Police Department," Portal to Texas History, https://texashistory.unt.edu/ark:/67531/metapth78876/; Barrow, *My Life with Bonnie and Clyde*, pp. 186–89, 221–22.
12. *Fort Worth Star Telegram*, May 21, 1934, p. 20; May 22, 1934, pp. 1, 5; May 24, 1934, pp. 1, 6; May 26, 1934, pp. 1, 2; May 31, 1934, pp. 1, 4; October 12, 2016, p. 5DD; *New York Times*, May 22, 1934, p. 16.

13. *Fort Worth Star Telegram*, January 19, 1933, pp. 1, 4; August 18, 1933, p. 1; May 24, 2017, p. 10DD. For the Charles Urschel kidnapping, see Stanley Hamilton, *Machine Gun Kelly's Last Stand* (Lawrence: University Press of Kansas, 2003).
14. *Fort Worth Star Telegram*, March 29, 1935, p. 4; January 19, 1937, p. 7; January 21, 1938, p. 1; January 2, 1939, p. 1; January 18, 1939, p. 4; *New York Times*, January 30, 1937, p. 173; Fort Worth Chamber of Commerce, *This Month in Fort Worth* 12, no. 7 (July 1938): p. 12.
15. *Fort Worth Star Telegram*, January 24, 1938, p. 1.
16. *Fort Worth Star Telegram*, March 24, 1931, pp. 1, 4; January 2, 1939, p. 1; November 12, 1935, p. 9; November 15, 1937, p. 1; January 18, 1939, p. 4; Flickwir, *Annual Report*, p. 1.
17. *Fort Worth Star Telegram*, January 3, 1933, p. 1; October 1, 1936, p. 27.
18. *Fort Worth Star Telegram*, December 3, 1937, p. 5; December 31, 1937, p. 1; *New York Times*, December 19, 1937, p. 49.
19. *Fort Worth Star Telegram*, October 4, 1932, p. 1; August 1, 1933, p. 1; October 17, 1933, p. 2; September 19, 1933, p. 1; March 8, 1934, p. 6; March 29, 1935, p. 4; January 21, 1938, p. 1; January 19, 1937, p. 7.
20. *Fort Worth Star Telegram*, November 13, 1933, p. 1; January 2, 1934, p. 1; January 3, 1934, p. 1; January 3, 1934, p. 1; January 4, 1931, p. 1; January 18, 1939, p. 4.
21. *Annual Report of the Police Department* (1932), pp. 6–9; *Fort Worth Star Telegram*, January 30, 1937, p. 2; October 20, 1938, p. 1; October 27, 1938, p. 14; January 10, 1939, p. 4.
22. *Fort Worth Star Telegram*, September 3, 1931, p. 1; May 6, 1932, p. 1; May 9, 1932, p. 1; June 11, 1932, pp. 1–2.
23. *New York Times*, July 24, 1931, p. 5; *Fort Worth Star Telegram*, June 23, 1934, pp. 1–2; June 25, 1934, p. 14; June 29, 1934, p. 1.
24. *Fort Worth Star Telegram*, February 14, 1933, pp. 1, 4; February 21, 1933, pp. 1, 4; February 22, 1933, pp. 1, 4.
25. *Fort Worth Star Telegram*, February 21, 1933, pp. 1, 4; February 23, 1933, p. 1; February 28, 1933, pp. 1, 4.
26. *Fort Worth Star Telegram*, March 1, 1933, pp. 1, 4; March 2, 1933, pp. 1, 4; March 15, 1933, pp. 1, 6.
27. *Fort Worth Star Telegram*, March 1, 1933, pp. 1, 4; March 2, 1933, pp. 1, 4; March 7, 1933, pp. 1, 4; March 9, 1933, p. 1; March 10, 1933, p. 1; March 30, 1933, p. 20; March 29, 1933, p. 1.
28. *Fort Worth Star Telegram*, May 25, 1933, pp. 1, 4.
29. *Fort Worth Star Telegram*, February 27, 1933, pp. 1, 4; March 1, 1933, pp. 1, 4; March 13, 1933, p. 1; May 1, 1933, p. 4; April 10, 1937, p. 1; October 6, 1938, p. 1; October 13, 1938, p. 1.
30. *Fort Worth Star Telegram*, May 10, 1935, pp. 1, 8, and 11; May 11, 1935, p. 1.
31. *Fort Worth Star Telegram*, October 12, 1932, p. 1; September 2, 1938, pp. 1, 6; September 3, 1938, pp. 1–2; *New York Times*, October 31, 1932, p. 1.
32. *Fort Worth Star Telegram*, January 16, 1034, p. 1; November 16, 1939, p. 4; April 12, 1932, p. 1; June 29, 1938, pp. 1, 4; October 12, 1932, p. 1; July 19, 1939, pp. 1, 4; August 28, 1941, p. 13; *New York Times*, November 29, 1935, p. 40.

Chapter Nine

1. *Fort Worth Star Telegram*, March 24, 1931, pp. 1, 4; January 26, 1933, p. 1; February 21, 1931, p. 1; *New York Times*, March 24, 1935, p. 72.

2. *Fort Worth Star Telegram*, December 18, 1930, p. 1; March 7, 1930, p. 32; May 27, 1933, pp. 1–2; July 5, 1933, p. 1; *New York Times*, April 23, 1935, p. 6.
3. *Fort Worth Star Telegram*, July 28, 1931, pp. 1, 4; August 1, 1931, p. 1.
4. *Fort Worth Star Telegram*, May 27, 1933, pp. 1–2; July 5, 1933, p. 1; September 13, 1933, pp. 1, 4; September 14, 1933, pp. 1, 4; September 15, 1933, pp. 1, 4.
5. *Fort Worth Star Telegram*, January 1, 1934, p. 4; September 13, 1933, pp. 1, 4; September 14, 1933, pp. 1, 4; September 15, 1933, pp. 1, 4; September 24, 1934, pp. 1, 4; "Fort Worth: Where the West Begins," *Fort Worth Chamber of Commerce Magazine*, April 1936, file Fort Worth, folder Business Organizations; Chamber of Commerce, Tarrant County Archives, Fort Worth.
6. *Fort Worth Star Telegram*, January 1, 1934, p. 4; April 10, 1935, p. 1; April 3, 1935, p. 1; *New York Times*, March 24, 1935, p. 72.
7. *Fort Worth Star Telegram*, September 10, 1935, p. 1; November 20, 1937, p. 1; January 7, 1938, p. 4; November 22, 1937, pp. 1, 4; December 3, 1937, p. 1; December 1, 1937, pp. 1, 4; December 24, 1937, p. 3; January 5, 1938, p. 1; July 9, 1938, p. 1; July 12, 1938, p. 1.
8. Rich, *Fort Worth*, pp. 8, 99, 153; *New York Times*, September 30, 1936, p. 52; *Fort Worth Star Telegram*, June 3, 1932, p. 22; November 14, 1936, p. 4; August 18, 1937, p. 1; August 10, 1940, p. 7.
9. *Fort Worth Star Telegram*, June 4, 1932, pp. 1–2; December 3, 1939, p. 1; July 27, 1935, p. 1.
10. *Fort Worth Star Telegram*, April 11, 1938, pp. 1, 4; September 15, 1931, pp. 1, 4; March 9, 1939, p. 1.
11. *Fort Worth Star Telegram*, May 22, 1940, p. 1; June 25, 1940, p. 1; June 26, 1940, p. 6; July 8, 1940, pp. 1, 4; July 10, 1940, pp. 1, 4; July 11, 1940, pp. 1, 6; July 20, 1940, p. 1; August 15, 1941, pp. 1, 8; Arnold, *Gamblers and Gangsters*, p. 24.
12. Arnold, *Gamblers and Gangsters*, pp. 17–18; *Fort Worth Star Telegram*, February 23, 1933, p. 1.
13. *Fort Worth Star Telegram*, September 2, 2013, p. 4B; August 10, 2014, pp. 6E–7E; February 21, 1933, pp. 1, 4; November 6, 1935, pp. 1, 4; November 19, 1935, p. 1; April 8, 2016, p. 5A; Arnold, *Gamblers and Gangsters*, pp. 84–88; Cook and Yarborough, *Prohibition in Dallas*, pp. 25–26, 37–38.
14. Arnold, *Gamblers and Gangsters*, pp. 69–70; *Fort Worth Star Telegram*, February 8, 1937, p. 1; March 19, 1935, p. 1; October 22, 1934, p. 7; October 25, 1934, p. 1; February 21, 1935, p. 18; November 2, 1936, p. 1; March 1, 1941, pp. 1–2.
15. *Fort Worth Star Telegram*, May 24, 1934, p. 10; May 25, 1934, p. 24; October 22, 1934, p. 7; December 7, 1934, p. 16; January 15, 1935, p. 11; February 21, 1935, p. 18; November 12, 1936, p. 1; March 18, 1935, p. 1; March 22, 1935, p. 1; Arnold, *Gamblers and Gangsters*, p. 17.
16. *Fort Worth Star Telegram*, August 19, 1936, pp. 1, 4; November 12, 1936, p. 1.
17. *Fort Worth Star Telegram*, June 13, 1931, p. 1; June 29, 1931, pp. 1, 7.
18. Fort Worth Chamber of Commerce, *Fort Worth* (1934), p. 7; Porterfield, *Loose Herd of Texans*; *New York Times*, April 30, 1933, p. 62; October 19, 1933, p. 26; March 30, 1934, p. 30; December 12, 1934, p. 23; *Fort Worth Star Telegram*, April 11, 2016, p. 6A; Bryant and Hess, *Top O' Hill Terrace*, p. 66.
19. *Fort Worth Star Telegram*, December 21, 1933, p. 18; July 25, 1934, p. 1; August 4, 1934, p. 1; August 7, 1941, p. 1; May 12, 1941, p. 1.
20. *Fort Worth Star Telegram*, July 19, 1932, p. 4; April 29, 1932, p. 1; October 13, 1932, p. 6.

21. *Fort Worth Star Telegram*, December 4, 1934, pp. 1, 4; December 27, 1934, p. 1; January 14, 1937, pp. 1, 4; January 30, 1937, p. 1; February 4, 1937, p. 1.
22. *Fort Worth Star Telegram*, January 14, 1937, pp. 1, 4; January 15, 1937, pp. 1, 6; January 16, 1937, pp. 1–2; January 20, 1937, p. 4; November 2, 1938, p. 1.
23. *Fort Worth Star Telegram*, June 30, 1036, p. 1; August 10, 1936, p. 2; August 12, 1936, pp. 1, 4; December 11, 2013, section BB, p. 1; Ezell, "Progressivism in Fort Worth," p. 26.
24. Clement, "Politics of Dissent," p. 64; Ezell, "Progressivism in Fort Worth," pp. 3–4; Flickwir, *Annual Report*, pp. 6, 11; *Fort Worth Star Telegram*, August 12, 1936, pp. 1, 4; December 11, 2013, section BB, p. 1.
25. *Fort Worth Star Telegram*, April 19, 1937, p. 1; September 16, 1937, p. 1; February 4, 1938, p. 1; February 5, 1938, p. 1.

Chapter Ten

1. *Fort Worth Star Telegram*, July 3, 1931, p. 8; February 25, 1990, section 1, pp. 4–5, box Fort Worth, file Ku Klux Klan, Tarrant County Archives, Fort Worth; April 26, 1935, p. 28.
2. Virginia Naylor Martin, "Challenge of the Negro in Fort Worth" (MA thesis, Southwestern Baptist Theological Seminary, 1935), pp. 4, 7, 14, 23; *Fort Worth Star Telegram*, April 8, 1931, pp. 1, 4.
3. *Fort Worth Star Telegram*, October 18, 1937, p. 1; July 15, 1939, pp. 1–2; April 10, 1940, p. 5; November 8, 1934, p. 3; September 3, 2017, p. 3D; J. H. Smith, *Negro Directory of Fort Worth, Texas, 1937–1938* (Fort Worth: Masonic, 1938), pp. 15 and 31, Briscoe Center for American History, University of Texas at Austin; "One City, Two Downtowns," Hometown by Handlebar, http://www.hometownbyhandlebar.com/?p=9419; Gayle W. Hanson, "Riley Andrew Ransom Sr. (1886–1951)," BlackPast, https://www.blackpast.org/african-american-history/ransom-riley-andrew-sr-1886-1951/.
4. Strayer, *Survey of Schools*, pp. 97–99, 103, 110, 112, 119–20.
5. *Fort Worth Star Telegram*, August 23, 1932, pp. 1, 4; May 1, 1940, pp. 1, 4; May 8, 1940, p. 15; April 10, 1940, p. 5; August 6, 1936, p. 22; Rebecca R. Sohmer, "Fort Worth's Rock Island Bottom: A Social Geography of an African-American Neighborhood" (MA thesis, Syracuse University, 1997), pp. 60–61.
6. *Fort Worth Star Telegram*, June 17, 1938, p. 29; June 18, 1938, p. 1; June 19, 1941, p. 8; June 17, 1936, p. 6; Selcer, *History of Fort Worth*, pp. 345–46.
7. *Fort Worth Mind*, February 17, 1934, p. 5; September 29, 1934, p. 1; *Fort Worth Star Telegram*, January 30, 1931, pp. 1, 6; April 27, 1932, p. 22; *New York Times*, February 2, 1931, p. 2.
8. *Fort Worth Star Telegram*, September 28, 1932, p. 8; September 30, 1932, p. 24; May 13, 1938, p. 18.
9. *Fort Worth Mind*, July 15, 1939, p. 1; January 6, 1934, p. 5; *Fort Worth Star Telegram*, November 8, 1937, p. 1; February 9, 1938, p. 7.
10. Strayer, *Survey of Schools*, p. 91; *Fort Worth Star Telegram*, August 23, 1932, pp. 1, 4; November 26, 1938, p. 10; September 7, 1938, p. 5; November 23, 1938, pp. 1, 4; *Fort Worth Press*, August 24, 1967, p. 18.
11. *Fort Worth Star Telegram*, May 13, 1939, p. 1; May 4, 1940, p. 1; Selcer, *History of Fort Worth*, pp. 333–34.
12. *Fort Worth Star Telegram*, October 24, 1931, p. 1; November 2, 1931, p. 1; January 13, 1932, p. 1; March 29, 1937, p. 1; February 17, 1939, p. 6; March 16, 1939, p. 1; March 17, 1939, p. 24.

13. *Fort Worth Star Telegram*, February 17, 1939, p. 6; August 4, 1938, pp. 1, 6; March 28, 1939, p. 11; November 9, 1939, p. 28; January 12, 1934, p. 1.
14. Joseph A. Abel, "Sunbelt Civil Rights: Race, Labor, and Politics in the Fort Worth Aircraft Industry, 1940–1980" (PhD diss., Rice University, 2011), pp. 1–2; *Fort Worth Star Telegram*, June 28, 1941, p. 8; June 30, 1941, p. 1; July 3, 1941, p. 15.
15. *Fort Worth Star Telegram*, October 3, 1935, p. 11; July 13, 1935, p. 1; March 11, 1937, p. 1; May 3, 1937, p. 1; *New York Times*, July 14, 1935, p. 3; *Fort Worth Mind*, July 15, 1939, p. 1; Young Men's Christian Association, *Fort Worth*, p. 23.
16. *Fort Worth Mind*, March 24, 1934, p. 1; *Fort Worth Star Telegram*, February 1, 1937, p. 3; July 25, 2016, pp. 1A and 13A; Selcer, *History of Fort Worth*, pp. 170–71.
17. *Fort Worth Star Telegram*, December 7, 1934, p. 8; *Fort Worth Mind*, January 13, 1934, p. 1; Strayer, *Survey of Schools*, pp. 101, 120, 312, 318; Smith, *Negro Directory*, p. 7.
18. *Fort Worth Star Telegram*, March 29, 1935, p. 11; March 20, 1935, p. 1; March 22, 1935, p. 1; July 18, 2014, p. 4B.
19. *Fort Worth Star Telegram*, July 6, 1936, p. 5; *Fort Worth Press*, August 25, 1967, p. 4; August 27, 1967, p. 14B.

Chapter Eleven

1. Jamie McIlvain, "History of Hispanic Fort Worth" (honors paper, Texas Christian University, 1993), pp. 16–18; *Fort Worth Star Telegram*, November 4, 1931, p. 1; September 15, 1939, p. 28; Strayer, *Survey of Schools*, pp. 110, 279, 283; Young Men's Christian Association, *Fort Worth*, p. 23.
2. McIlvain, "Hispanic Fort Worth," pp. 14–16; *Fort Worth Star Telegram*, March 28, 1941, p. 24.
3. *New York Times*, February 10, 1924, p. 168.
4. Musselwhite, "Texas in the 1920s," pp. 111–13; *New York Times*, July 14, 1936, p. 21; *Fort Worth Star Telegram*, June 21, 1935, p. 12. For a history of B. H. Carroll School, see *Star Telegram*, March 23, 1930, Oil, Autos, and Sports section, p. 41; May 14, 2018, p. 5A.
5. *Fort Worth Star Telegram*, January 9, 1930, p. 20; July 12, 1930, p. 1; July 29, 1930, pp. 1, 4; December 30, 1938, p. 1; January 3, 1939, p. 1; October 20, 1941, p. 1.
6. *Fort Worth Star Telegram*, June 1, 1932, p. 18; May 24, 1933, p. 1; July 27, 1931, pp. 1, 4; Keavney, "Depression Era," p. 127; Letter, John E. Mathis to C. W. Woodman, August 8, 1933, Woodman Papers, box 2, file 163-2-11, Special Collections, University of Texas at Arlington Library.
7. Barry Schiff, "Pilot Briefing," *AOPA Pilot Magazine* 59, no. 8 (August 2016): p. 38; "Notable People in Aviation History," *AOPA Pilot Magazine* 60, no. 3 (March 2017): p. 32; Knight, *Fort Worth*, pp. 170–71; *Fort Worth Star Telegram*, August 1, 1930, pp. 1, 6; June 24, 1931, p. 22; December 28, 1932, p. 5; June 29, 1933, p. 3.
8. *Fort Worth Star Telegram*, June 6, 1932, p. 10; Laurie E. Jasinski, "Fowler, Manet Harrison," Handbook of Texas Online, https://tshaonline.org/handbook/online/articles/ffo66; *New York Times*, June 19, 1938, p. D7.
9. Ruth McAdams, "Mudholes, Fairy Godmothers, and China Bells," in Sherrod, *Grace and Gumption*, p. 88; *New York Times*, August 12, 1923, p. 115.
10. *Fort Worth Star Telegram*, September 21, 2015, p. 10A; October 4, 1935, pp. 1, 8; October 5, 1935, p. 1; March 7, 1938, p. 1; October 6, 1939, pp. 1–2; June 12, 1936, pp. 1, 4; June 13, 1936, pp. 1–2; July 6, 1938, p. 1; July 11, 1938, p. 1; *New York Times*, July 29, 1933, p. 15; April 2, 1935, p. 23; May 10, 1934, p. 26; June 19, 1934, p. 1; May 23, 1936, pp. 1, 2;

June 13, 1936, p. 2; May 13, 1937, p. 27; March 7, 1938, p. 7; July 2, 1938, p. 3; July 11, 1938, pp. 1, 4; July 12, 1938, p. 18.

11. *New York Times*, November 11, 1936, p. 3; January 2, 1938, p. 12; April 15, 1939, p. 21; March 16, 1944, p. 10; June 24, 1944, p. 18; *Fort Worth Star Telegram*, September 21, 2015, p. 10A.
12. *Fort Worth Star Telegram*, June 13, 1938, p. 5; July 2, 1937, p. 1; November 17, 1938, p. 4.
13. *Fort Worth Star Telegram*, February 24, 1933, p. 4; December 27, 1934, p. 14; January 3, 1935, p. 12; April 21, 1938, p. 7; Flickwir, *Annual Report*, pp. 1, 6, 11.

Chapter Twelve

1. Horner, "Fort Worth," pp. 2–3; *New York Times*, November 12, 1933, p. 17; *Fort Worth Star Telegram*, April 4, 1934, p. 22; March 10, 1936, p. 1; October 23, 1929, p. 8; April 10, 2017, p. 6A; Fort Worth Chamber of Commerce, *Fort Worth Chamber of Commerce News* 5, no. 1 (January 1936): p. 6; Keavney, "Depression Era," p. 130; Wake, "Study in Conservative Politics," p. 40.
2. Fort Worth Chamber of Commerce, *Fort Worth Chamber of Commerce News* 5, no. 1 (January 1936): p. 6; Fort Worth Chamber of Commerce, *This Month in Fort Worth* 13, no. 3 (March 1939): p. 15; Fort Worth Chamber of Commerce, *Fort Worth: Where the West Begins* (Fort Worth: Fort Worth Chamber of Commerce, 1939), p. 5; *Monthly Business Record*, pp. 5–7.
3. *Fort Worth Star Telegram*, October 4, 1937, p. 1; May 12, 1938, Leonard's section, pp. 1–22; May 9, 1940, p. 28; Fort Worth Chamber of Commerce, *This Month in Fort Worth* 12, no. 7 (July 1938): p. 12.
4. Pate, *Livestock Legacy*, pp. 176–77; *Where the West Begins*, Fort Worth Chamber of Commerce, March 1936, file Fort Worth, Business Organizations: Chamber of Commerce, Tarrant County Archives, Fort Worth; *New York Times*, December 24, 1939, p. 43; *Fort Worth: Where the West Begins*, p. 5.
5. *New York Times*, September 13, 1939, p. 48; *Fort Worth Star Telegram*, November 17, 1941, p. 1.
6. City of Fort Worth, *Annual Budget for Fiscal Year 1938–1939* (Fort Worth: City of Fort Worth, 1938), pp. I–II; *Fort Worth Star Telegram*, April 10, 1940, p. 4; May 1, 1940, pp. 1, 4; August 20, 1940, pp. 1, 4; August 20, 1941, pp. 1, 4; January 6, 1941, p. 18; Young Men's Christian Association, *Fort Worth*, p. 32; Fort Worth Chamber of Commerce, *This Month in Fort Worth* 13, no. 3 (March 1939): p. 15.
7. *Fort Worth Star Telegram*, August 8, 1940, p. 8.
8. *Fort Worth Star Telegram*, September 30, 1940, pp. 1, 4; November 25, 1941, pp. 1, 4; August 8, 1941, p. 1; September 30, 1941, pp. 1, 4; May 16, 1940, p. 9; February 22, 1939, p. 3; March 23, 2017, p. 5A.
9. Fort Worth Chamber of Commerce, *This Month in Fort Worth* 14, no. 7 (July 1940): p. 3; Fort Worth Chamber of Commerce, *This Month in Fort Worth* 14, no. 9 (September 1940): p. 6; *New York Times*, March 19, 1941, p. 12; *Fort Worth Star Telegram*, June 7, 1940, pp. 1, 8; May 13, 1941, pp. 1, 4; September 20, 1941, p. 1.
10. *Fort Worth Star Telegram*, June 1, 1930, part 2, p. 1; April 1, 1932, p. 8; June 29, 1937, p. 13; January 11, 1939, p. 3; January 12, 1939, p. 5; January 22, 1939, p. 5; May 1, 1939, p. 2; July 16, 1940, pp. 1, 4; October 18, 2015, p. A5; Porterfield, *Loose Herd of Texans*, p. 76; *New York Times*, January 16, 1931, p. 24; July 16, 1940, p. 27.

11. *Fort Worth Star Telegram*, October 18, 2015, p. A5; May 4, 1932, p. 1; March 23, 1933, pp. 1, 4; October 18, 1933, pp. 18–19 and 28; June 29, 1937, p. 13; March 1, 1938, pp. 1, 4; "All Bidders from W. G. Clarkson, Architect," November 12, 1935, Records of the City of Fort Worth, Transportation and Public Works, Series II, PWA Projects-Buildings, Amon Carter Field, Local History Section, Fort Worth Public Library.
12. *Fort Worth Star Telegram*, June 12, 1930, p. 4; December 18, 1940, p. 2.
13. *Fort Worth Star Telegram*, October 2, 1940, pp. 1, 4; October 28, 1940, p. 1; November 27, 1940, pp. 1, 6; August 28, 1941, pp. 1, 8; October 8, 1941, pp. 1, 6; October 29, 1941, p. 8; March 27, 2017, p. 8A; Payne, *Big D*, p. 208; Paul Freeman, "Texas: Northeast Fort Worth Area," Abandoned and Little-Known Airfields, http://www.airfields-freeman.com/Tx/Airfields_Tx_FtWorth_NE.htm.
14. *Fort Worth Star Telegram*, June 7, 1940, p. 1; June 17, 1940, p. 1; J'Nell Pate, *Arsenal of Defense: Fort Worth's Military Legacy* (Denton: Texas State Historical Society, 2011), p. 67.
15. *Fort Worth Star Telegram*, January 4, 1941, pp. 1, 4; January 6, 1941, p. 1; March 3, 1941, pp. 1, 4; March 5, 1941, pp. 1–2; March 13, 1941, pp. 1, 4; April 1, 1941, p. 4; April 2, 1941, p. 6; Fort Worth Chamber of Commerce, *This Month in Fort Worth* 17, no. 2 (February 1941): pp. 4–5; Pate, *Arsenal of Defense*, pp. 72–73; Knight, *Fort Worth*, p. 212; *New York Times*, May 20, 1941, p. 15.
16. *Fort Worth Star Telegram*, March 28, 1941, p. 1; April 19, 1941, p. 1; April 21, 1941, p. 1; April 24, 1941, p. 1; September 20, 1941, p. 1; September 6, 1941, pp. 1–2; September 13, 1941, p. 1; April 28, 1941, p. 5; November 28, 1941, p. 14; October 29, 2017, p. 9B; *New York Times*, December 28, 1941, p. 21; Knight, *Fort Worth*, p. 212.
17. *Fort Worth Star Telegram*, November 17, 1941, p. 1; October 8, 1941, pp. 1, 6; *New York Times*, March 9, 1941, p. 111.
18. *Fort Worth Star Telegram*, June 19, 1940, pp. 1, 4; June 20, 1940, p. 1; December 9, 1940, pp. 1, 6.
19. *Fort Worth Star Telegram*, June 11, 1941, pp. 1, 4; May 31, 1941, p. 7; June 3, 1941, p. 9; June 28, 1941, p. 8; June 30, 1941, p. 1; July 4, 1941, p. 10; November 20, 1941, p. 1.
20. *Fort Worth Star Telegram*, May 30, 1941, p. 1; December 9, 1941, pp. 1, 11; December 6, 1941, pp. 1–2, 10.
21. *Fort Worth Star Telegram*, December 8, 1941, p. 2; December 9, 1941, pp. 1, 11; December 10, 1941, p. 1.

Conclusion

1. Young Men's Christian Association, *Fort Worth*, pp. 22–23; *New York Times*, July 13, 1940, p. 1; September 23, 1940, p. 17.
2. Robert Talbert, *Cowtown-Metropolis: A Case Study of a City's Growth and Structure (Fort Worth: Leo Potishman Foundation, Texas Christian University, 1956)*, pp. 129–32, 135.
3. *Monthly Business Record*, pp. 5–7; Talbert, *Cowtown-Metropolis*, pp. 129–32, 135; Pate, *Livestock Legacy*, pp. 186–87.
4. Edwin Caldwell, "Highlights of the Development of Manufacturing in Texas, 1900–1960," *Southwestern Historical Quarterly* 68, no. 4 (April 1965): pp. 405–12, 431; Knight, *Fort Worth*, pp. 212–13.

Bibliography

Books

Arnold, Ann. *Camp Meeting to Cathedral: Fort Worth's Historic Congregations*. Arlington: Landa, 2004.

———. *Gamblers and Gangsters: Fort Worth's Jacksboro Highway in the 1940s and 1950s*. Austin: Eakin, 1998.

Barr, Alwyn, and Robert A. Clavert, eds. *Black Leaders: Texans for Their Times*. Austin: Texas State Historical Association, 1981.

Barrow, Blanche Caldwell. *My Life with Bonnie and Clyde*. Edited by John Neal Phillips. Norman: University of Oklahoma Press, 2004.

Bryant, Vickie, and Camille Hess. *Top O' Hill Terrace*. Images of America Series. Charleston, SC: Arcadia, 2012.

Buenger, Victoria, and Walter L. Buenger. *Texas Merchant: Marvin Leonard and Fort Worth*. Kenneth E. Montague Series in Oil and Business History. College Station: Texas A&M University Press, 1998.

Bundy, William Oliver. *Life of William Madison McDonald, Ph.D.* Fort Worth: Bunker, 1925.

Cary, Reby. *How We Got Over! Second Update on a Backward Look; A History of Blacks in Fort Worth*. Fort Worth: n.p., 2006.

Cashion, Ty. *The New Frontier: A Contemporary History of Fort Worth and Tarrant County*. San Antonio: Historical Publishing Network, 2006.

Cohen, Judith Singer. *Cowtown Moderne: Art Deco Architecture of Fort Worth, Texas*. College Station: Texas A&M University Press, 1988.

Cook, Rita. *A Brief History of Fort Worth: Cowtown through the Years*. Charleston, SC: History Press, 2011.

———. *Haunted Fort Worth*. Charleston, SC: Haunted America, 2011.

Cook, Rita, and Jeffrey Yarbrough. *Prohibition in Dallas and Fort Worth: Blind Tigers, Bootleggers and Bathtub Gin*. Charleston, SC: American Palate, 2013.

Cuellar, Carlos E. *Stories from the Barrio: A History of Mexican Fort Worth*. Fort Worth: Texas Christian University Press, 2003.

Ellis, Dick. *W. I. Cook Children's Hospital: The Middle Years*. Rich Hill, MO: Bell Books, 2010.

Farman, Irvin. *The Fort Worth Club: A Centennial Story*. Fort Worth: Fort Worth Club, 1985.

Flemmons, Jerry. *Amon: The Life of Amon Carter, Sr., of Texas*. Austin: Jenkins, 1978.

Fort Worth. *Historical Pageant of Fort Worth: Diamond Jubilee, November 11-12-13-14, 1923*. Fort Worth: Marvin D. Evans, 1923.

Fort Worth National Bank and Texas Electric Service. *Population and Growth Trends of the Fort Worth Metropolitan Area, 1850–2000.* Fort Worth: Fort Worth National Bank and Texas Electric Service, 1958.

Fort Worth Newspaper Artists' Association. *Makers of Fort Worth.* Fort Worth: Fort Worth Newspaper Artists' Association, 1914.

Garrett, Julia Kathryn. *Fort Worth: A Frontier Triumph.* Fort Worth: Texas Christian University Press, 1996.

George, Juliet. *Fort Worth's Arlington Heights.* Images of America Series. Charleston, SC: Arcadia, 2010.

Hamilton, Stanley. *Machine Gun Kelly's Last Stand.* Lawrence: University Press of Kansas, 2003.

Harris Methodist Fort Worth Hospital. *The History of Harris Methodist Fort Worth Hospital.* Fort Worth: Harris Methodist Fort Worth Hospital, 2006.

Historical Committee of the Fort Worth Petroleum Club. *Oil Legends of Fort Worth.* Fort Worth: Taylor, 1993.

Jones, Jan. *Billy Rose Presents . . . Casa Mañana.* Chisholm Trail Series. Fort Worth: Texas Christian University Press, 1999.

———. *Renegades, Showmen and Angels: A Theatrical History of Fort Worth from 1873–2001.* Fort Worth: Texas Christian University Press, 2006.

Kline, Susan Allen, and the City of Fort Worth. *Fort Worth Parks.* Images of America Series. Charleston, SC: Arcadia, 2010.

Knight, Oliver. *Fort Worth: Outpost on the Trinity.* Fort Worth: Texas Christian University Press, 1990.

Liles, Debbie M. *Will Rogers Coliseum.* Images of America Series. Charleston, SC: Arcadia, 2012.

Malone, Bill C. *Country Music, U.S.A.* Austin: University of Texas Press, 1985.

McAdams, Ruth. "Mudholes, Fairy Godmothers, and China Bells." *Grace and Gumption: Stories of Fort Worth Women,* edited by Katie Sherrod. pp. 87–101. Fort Worth: Texas Christian University Press, 2007.

McBeth, Leon. *Victory through Prayer: A History of Rosen Heights Baptist Church, 1906–1966.* Fort Worth: Rosen Heights Baptist Church, 1966.

McElroy, Sherrie S. "In the Interests of the Children." *In Grace and Gumption: Stories of Fort Worth Women,* edited by Katie Sherrod, pp. 103–23. Fort Worth: Texas Christian University Press, 2007.

McGown, Quentin. *Fort Worth in Vintage Postcards.* Postcard History Series. Charleston, SC: Arcadia, 2003.

Norris, J. Frank. *Inside History of First Baptist Church, Fort Worth and Temple Baptist Church, Detroit: Life Story of Dr. J. Frank Norris.* Fort Worth: n.p., 1938.

———. *Inside the Cup: Or My 21 Years in Fort Worth.* Fort Worth: n.p., 1939.

Oliphant, Liz. *Ben E. Keith Company: The First One Hundred Years, 1906–2006.* Austin: Eakin, 2006.

Pate, J'Nell L. *Arsenal of Defense: Fort Worth's Military Legacy.* Denton: Texas State Historical Society, 2011.

———. *Hazel Vaughn Leigh and the Fort Worth Boys Club.* Fort Worth: Fort Worth Public Library, Texas Christian University Press, 2000.

———. *Livestock Legacy: The Fort Worth Stockyards, 1887–1987.* Centennial Series of the Association of Former Students, Texas A&M University. College Station: Texas A&M University Press, 1988.

———. *North of the River: A Brief History of North Fort Worth*. Chisholm Trail Series 11. Fort Worth: Texas Christian University Press, 1994.

Payne, Darwin. *Big D: Triumphs and Troubles of an American Supercity in the 20th Century*. Dallas: Three Forks, 1994.

Pope, Lean (Holston). *A Hand on My Shoulder: The Story of Lena Pope and the Home That Evolved from Her Dreams*. Fort Worth: Branch-Smith, 1966.

Porterfield, Bill. *A Loose Herd of Texans*. College Station: Texas A&M University Press, 1978.

Reynolds, Clay, and Marie-Madeleine Schein. *A Hundred Years of Heroes: A History of the Southwestern Exposition and Livestock Show*. Fort Worth: Texas Christian University Press, 1995.

Rich, Harold. *Fort Worth: Outpost, Cowtown, Boomtown*. Norman: University of Oklahoma Press, 2014.

Selcer, Richard. *Fort Worth: A Texas Original*. Fred Rider Cotton Popular History Series. Austin: Texas State Historical Association, 2004.

———. *A History of Fort Worth in Black and White: 165 Years of African-American Life*. Denton: University of North Texas Press, 2015.

Selcer, Richard, and Kevin Foster. *Written in Blood: The History of Fort Worth's Fallen Lawmen*. Denton: University of North Texas Press, 2010.

Sherrod, Katie, ed. *Grace and Gumption: Stories of Fort Worth Women*. Fort Worth: Texas Christian University Press, 2007.

Smith, J. H. *Negro Directory of Fort Worth, Texas, 1937–1938*. Fort Worth: Masonic, 1938. Briscoe Center for American History, University of Texas at Austin.

Stafford-Lowdon. *The Charter of the City of Fort Worth*. Fort Worth: Stafford-Lowdon, 1928, adopted April 14, 1925.

Stokes, David R. *The Shooting Salvationist: J. Frank Norris and the Murder Trial That Captivated America*. Hanover, NH: Steerforth, 2011.

Strayer, George D. *Report of the Survey of Schools of Fort Worth, Texas*. New York: Teachers College, Colombia University, 1931. Briscoe Center for American History, University of Texas at Austin.

Talbert, Robert H. *Cowtown-Metropolis: A Case Study of a City's Growth and Structure*. Fort Worth: Leo Potishman Foundation, Texas Christian University, 1956.

United States Postal Service. *History of the Fort Worth Post Office, 1856–1980*. N.p.: United States Postal Service, n.d.

Weiner, Hollace Ava. *Beth-El Congregation Centennial: Fort Worth, 1902–2002*. N.p.: Beth-El Congregation, 2002.

———. *Jewish Junior League: The Rise and Demise of the Fort Worth Council of Jewish Women*. College Station: Texas A&M University Press, 2008.

Williams, Joyce E. *Black Community Control: A Study of Transition in a Texas Ghetto*. New York: Praeger, 1973.

Young Men's Christian Association. *Fort Worth and Its Young Men's Christian Association*. Fort Worth: Young Men's Christian Association, 1947.

Periodicals

Caldwell, Edwin. "Highlights of the Development of Manufacturing in Texas, 1900–1960." *Southwestern Historical Quarterly* 68, no. 4 (April 1965): pp. 401–31.

Cervantez, Brian. "For the Exclusive Benefit of Fort Worth." *Southwestern Historical Quarterly* 99, no. 2 (October 2015): pp. 120–46.

Crowdell, Chester T. "Strange News from Texas." *Tom Hickey Magazine* 1, no. 7 (1925): pp. 2–9. T. A. Hickey Papers, Briscoe Center for American History, University of Texas at Austin.
"Notable People in Aviation History." *AOPA Pilot Magazine* 60, no. 3 (March 2017): p. 32.
Portz, Kevin G. "Political Turmoil in Dallas: The Electoral Whipping of the Dallas County Citizens League by the Ku Klux Klan." *Southwestern Historical Quarterly* 99, no. 2 (October 2015): pp. 148–77.
Schiff, Barry. "Pilot Briefing." *AOPA Pilot Magazine* 59, no. 8 (August 2017): p. 38.
———. "Pilot Briefing." *AOPA Pilot Magazine* 61, no. 4 (April 2018): p. 48.

Newspapers

Dallas Morning News
Fort Worth Mind
Fort Worth Press
Fort Worth Star Telegram
New York Times

Online

Cartwright, Gary. "Showdown at Waggoner Ranch." *Texas Monthly Magazine*, January 2004, 1–21. http://texasmonthly.com/articles/showdown-at-waggoner-ranch.
"Clyde Champion Barrow Fingerprint Chart, 01/22/1928- Fort Worth, Texas Police Department." Portal to Texas History https://texashistory.unt.edu/ark:/67531/metapth78876/.
Connolly, Christopher. "Meet the Man Believed to Be the First Black Millionaire in Texas." Kera News, December 19, 2016. http://keranews.org/post/meet-man-believed-be-first-black-millionaire-texas.
"Dallas." Wikipedia. https://en.wikipedia.org/wiki/Dallas.
"Fort Worth, Texas." Wikipedia. https://en.wikipedia.org/wiki/Fort_Worth,_Texas.
Freeman, Paul. "Texas: Northeast Fort Worth Area." Abandoned and Little-Known Airfields. http://www.airfields-freeman.com/Tx/Airfields_Tx_FtWorth_NE.htm.
Hanson, Gayle W. "Riley Andrew Ransom Sr. (1886–1951)." BlackPast. http://www.blackpast.org/african-american-history/ransom-riley-andrew-sr-1886-1951/.
"Houston." Wikipedia. https://en.wikipedia.org/wiki/Houston.
"One City, Two Downtowns." Hometown by Handlebar. http://www.hometownbyhandlebar.com/?p=9419.
Jasinski, Laurie E. "Fowler, Manet Harrison." Handbook of Texas Online. https://tshaonline.org/handbook/online/articles/ffo66.
Reavis, Dick J. "Fort Worth's 'Red Scare.'" *Texas Observer*, September 2, 2011. https://www.texasobserver.org/fort-worths-red-scare/.
"San Antonio." Wikipedia. https://en.wikipedia.org/wiki/San_Antonio.
Simon, Cheryl L. "Jim Hotel." Handbook of Texas Online. https://tshaonline.org/handbook/online/articles/xdj01.
Taylor, Carrie. "Texas Highways by the Number." *Houston Chronicle*, August 28, 2013. http://www.chron.com/news/houston-traffic/slideshow/Texas-highways-By-the-numbers-69108/photo-4625513.php.
"TRWD History." Tarrant Regional Water District. http://trwd-dev.azurewebsites.net/about-trwd/history/.

Unpublished Sources

History Class of Miss Clare Head. "History of White Settlement." Fort Worth, Brewer High School, 1952. Local History Section, Fort Worth Public Library.

Kellam, George. "A Guide to the George W. Armstrong Papers." Arlington: University of Texas Press, 2008. Special Collections, University of Texas at Arlington Library.

Smith, Angie. "More Than a Settlement: The Condensed History of White Settlement, Texas." Student paper, History 4970, Texas Christian University, n.d. Local History Section, Fort Worth Public Library.

Theses and Dissertations

Abel, Joseph A. "Sunbelt Civil Rights: Race, Labor, and Politics in the Fort Worth Aircraft Industry, 1940–1980." PhD dissertation, Rice University, 2011.

Cervantez, Brian. "Lone Star Booster: The Life of Amon Carter." PhD dissertation, University of North Texas, 2011.

Clement, Gail A. "Politics of Dissent: W. J. Hammond, City Councilman and Mayor, 1935–1938." MA thesis, Texas Christian University, 1967.

Doggett, Dorothy L. "Survey of Fort Worth's Negro Schools." MA thesis, Texas Christian University, 1927.

Downing, Marvin Lee. "The P. W. A. and the Effort to Secure the Fort Worth Public Library Building, 1933–1939." MA thesis, Texas Christian University, 1963.

Ezell, Marcel D. "Progressivism in Fort Worth Politics, 1935–1938." MA thesis, Texas Christian University, 1963.

Henderson, David Alvin. "Fort Worth and the Depression, 1929–1933." MA thesis, Texas Christian University, 1964.

Horner, Richard Kenneth. "Fort Worth during the Depression, September 1, 1932, to August 31, 1933." MA thesis, University of Texas at Austin, 1968.

Keavney, Mary A. "The Depression Era in Fort Worth 1929–1934." MA thesis, University of Texas at Austin, 1974.

Manwarring, Edward Henry. "A Brief History of the Union Gospel Mission." MA thesis, Southwestern Baptist Theological Seminary, 1928.

Martin, Virginia Naylor. "Challenge of the Negro in Fort Worth." MA thesis, Southwestern Baptist Theological Seminary, 1935.

McIlvain, Jamie. "History of Hispanic Fort Worth." Honors paper, Texas Christian University, 1993.

Munchus-Forde, Lady George. "History of the Negro in Fort Worth: A Syllabus for a High School Course." MA thesis, Fisk University, 1941.

Musselwhite, Lynn Ray. "Texas in the 1920s: A History of Social Change." PhD dissertation, Texas Technological University, 1975.

Olmstead, Jacob W. "From Old South to Modern West: Fort Worth's Celebration of the Texas State Centennial and the Shaping of an Urban Identity and Image." PhD dissertation, Texas Christian University, 2011.

Sandlin, Barry T. "The 1921 Butcher Workmen Strike in Fort Worth, Texas." MA thesis, University of Texas at Arlington, 1988.

Sohmer, Rebecca R. "Fort Worth's Rock Island Bottom: A Social Geography of an African-American Neighborhood." MA thesis, Syracuse University, 1997.

Wake, Eric L. "A Study in Conservative Politics: The Fort Worth City Council, 1925–1938." MA thesis, Texas Christian University, 1967.

Chamber of Commerce Publications

Fort Worth Chamber of Commerce. *Chamber of Commerce Annual Report 1940*. Fort Worth: Fort Worth Chamber of Commerce, 1940.

———. *Fort Worth*. Fort Worth: Fort Worth Chamber of Commerce, 1924.

———. *Fort Worth*. Fort Worth: Fort Worth Chamber of Commerce, 1934. Briscoe Center for American History, University of Texas at Austin.

———. *Fort Worth: The Capital City of a New Empire*. Fort Worth: Fort Worth Chamber of Commerce, 1927.

———. *Fort Worth: Where the West Begins*. Fort Worth: Fort Worth Chamber of Commerce, 1939.

———. *Fort Worth Chamber of Commerce News* 5, no. 1 (January 1932).

———. *Fort Worth Chamber of Commerce News* 9, no. 1 (January 1936).

———. *Fort Worth in Brief*. N.p.: Fort Worth Chamber of Commerce, 1925. Briscoe Center for American History, University of Texas at Austin.

———. *Industrial Fort Worth*. Fort Worth: Fort Worth Chamber of Commerce, [1940?]. Briscoe Center for American History, University of Texas at Austin.

———. *The Statistical Handbook of Fort Worth, Texas*. Fort Worth: Fort Worth Chamber of Commerce, 1930. Briscoe Center for American History, University of Texas at Austin.

———. *This Month in Fort Worth*. Vols. 12–14. Fort Worth: Fort Worth Chamber of Commerce, 1938–40.

Government Reports

Annual Report of the Police Department of the City of Fort Worth. Fort Worth: n.p., 1932. Briscoe Center for American History, University of Texas at Austin.

Annual Report of the Police Department of the City of Fort Worth. Fort Worth: n.p., 1938. Briscoe Center for American History, University of Texas at Austin.

City of Fort Worth. *Annual Budget for Fiscal Year 1938–1939*. Fort Worth: City of Fort Worth, 1938.

———. *City of Fort Worth Municipal Life: 1931–1937*. Fort Worth: Bureau of Management Research, 1937.

Fifteenth Census of the United States. Washington, DC: Government Printing Office, 1933.

Flickwir, A. H. *Annual Report of the Department of Health*. Fort Worth: n.p., 1937. Briscoe Center for American History, University of Texas at Austin.

Fourteenth Census of the United States. Washington, DC: Government Printing Office, 1922.

Sixteenth Census of the United States. Washington, DC: Government Printing Office, 1940.

Collections

Briscoe Center for American History, University of Texas at Austin. T. A. Hickey Papers. Box 3K423.

The Statistical Handbook of Fort Worth, Texas. Fort Worth: Fort Worth Chamber of Commerce, 1930.

Fort Worth Public Library Local History.
"The Depression." Oral History Project.
Federal Writers' Project. Research Data, Fort Worth and Tarrant County, Texas, 1941.
Fort Worth City Council Minutes, 1919–41.
Records of the City of Fort Worth.
Tarrant County Archives, Fort Worth.
Buildings
North Texas Traction; Post Office, 1930.
Business Organizations
Chamber of Commerce
Fort Worth
Industrial Fort Worth, 1930.
Modern Magic, 1936.
Depression, 1929–40.
Events
Diamond Jubilee, 1923.
Government
Texas Municipal Life, 1931/1937.
Hotels
Fort Worth-El Paso/Pickwick/Delaware.
Ku Klux Klan
Ruby Schmidt Collection of Bicentennial Interviews, Oral Histories of Fort Worth, Inc.
University of Texas at Arlington Library Special Collections.
Roscoe Ady Papers.
George W. Armstrong Papers.
William E. Jary Collection.
Paddock Papers.
Sam Rosen Papers, AR537.
Percy Wyly. "Memo on Robberies Using Nitroglycerin in Fort Worth and Dallas." FBI Memorandum on Dallas and Fort Worth, Texas, Bank Robberies, July 26, 1946, box GA 212.
C. W. Woodman Papers.
National Archives at Fort Worth.
Records of the National Recovery Administration Region VIII, 1934–35. Record Group 9, HM2008, E9NRF-1.

Index

Page numbers followed by *f* and *t* refer to figures and tables, respectively.